LEGAL RISKS IN THE SOFTWARE DEVELOPMENT LIFECYCLE

Legal Risks in the Software Development Lifecycle addresses the growing complexity of software development as both a technical and legal discipline. As the digital economy expands, software has become a core infrastructure asset whose lifecycle demands rigorous and enforceable contractual governance. This book analyses how legal risks arise and evolve across the Software Development Lifecycle (SDLC), providing a systematic account of the planning, delivery, and long-term maintenance of software projects.

The book takes readers through the entire SDLC, explaining each phase's technical purpose, the role and obligations of the parties involved, and the contractual documentation required to secure compliance and accountability. At every stage, it identifies the principal legal risks and demonstrates how they can be prevented through careful planning, well-defined deliverables, and tailored contractual provisions. Rather than focusing on litigation outcomes, the book emphasizes preventive strategies, providing readers with a structured roadmap to anticipate disputes before they arise. Sample clauses and checklists are included to highlight practical solutions, but the core value lies in its systematic explanation of processes, responsibilities, and risk-management mechanisms. Covering major contractual models such as Fixed-Price, Time & Material, Agile, Hybrid, and Milestone-based agreements, it highlights their advantages, limitations, and common points of dispute, while offering strategies to structure payments, allocate intellectual property rights, and manage scope changes effectively.

The book's approach is multidisciplinary. It is written for lawyers and legal advisors seeking to understand technical processes and draft precise, enforceable agreements; for project managers and clients who need to anticipate and manage contractual obligations; for software developers and vendors who want to align deliverables with contract terms and regulatory requirements; for judges, arbitrators, and mediators resolving IT-related disputes; and for students and researchers in law, technology and business, seeking a bridge between theory and practice.

Oana Gherghina is Associate Professor of Business Law at the FABIZ Faculty of Business, part of the Bucharest Academy of Economic Studies. She is also a Business Lawyer specializing in Technology and Construction Law and Managing Partner of Gherghina Law Firm.

LEGAL RISKS IN THE SOFTWARE DEVELOPMENT LIFECYCLE

OANA GHERGHINA

informa law
from Routledge

Designed cover image: Getty Images© Credit: monsitj

First published 2026
by Informa Law from Routledge
4 Park Square, Milton Park, Abingdon, Oxon OX14 4RN

and by Informa Law from Routledge
605 Third Avenue, New York, NY 10158

Informa Law from Routledge is an imprint of the Taylor & Francis Group, an informa business

British Library Cataloguing-in-Publication Data
A catalogue record for this book is available from the British Library

Library of Congress Cataloging-in-Publication Data
Names: Gherghina, Oana author
Title: Legal risks in the software development lifecycle / Oana Gherghina.
Description: Abingdon, Oxon [UK] ; New York, NY : Informa Law from Routledge, 2026. | Includes bibliographical references and index.
Identifiers: LCCN 2025043024 (print) | LCCN 2025043025 (ebook) | ISBN 9781041133971 hardback | ISBN 9781041111023 paperback | ISBN 9781003669609 ebook
Subjects: LCSH: Computer software--Law and legislation | Computer software--Development--Management
Classification: LCC K1443.C6 G44 2026 (print) | LCC K1443.C6 (ebook)
LC record available at https://lccn.loc.gov/2025043024
LC ebook record available at https://lccn.loc.gov/2025043025

ISBN: 978-1-041-13397-1 (hbk)
ISBN: 978-1-041-11102-3 (pbk)
ISBN: 978-1-003-66960-9 (ebk)

DOI: 10.4324/9781003669609

Typeset in Times New Roman
by SPi Technologies India Pvt Ltd (Straive)

CONTENTS

About the Author *xii*

Preface *xiii*

Acknowledgements *xv*

1 **Introduction** **1**
- *1.1 Overview of the Software Development Industry* *1*
- *1.2 Purpose of the Book* *1*
- *1.3 Who Should Use This Book* *3*
  - *1.3.1 Project Managers* *3*
  - *1.3.2 Lawyers and Legal Advisers* *3*
  - *1.3.3 Developers* *4*
  - *1.3.4 Clients* *4*
  - *1.3.5 Judges, Arbitrators, and Mediators* *5*
  - *1.3.6 Students and Aspiring Professionals* *5*
- *1.4 Exploring the Parallels between Construction Contracts and Software Development Agreements* *6*

2 **Software Development Lifecycle (SDLC)** **8**
- *2.1 Software Development Lifecycle (SDLC) Guidelines* *8*
- *2.2 Importance of SDLC in Software Development* *11*
- *2.3 Essential Role of SDLC in Tech Lawyers Practice* *15*
  - *2.3.1 Aligning Contractual Clauses with Project Phases* *15*
  - *2.3.2 Improved Risk Management: Anticipating Legal and Operational Pitfalls through SDLC Awareness* *16*
  - *2.3.3 Intellectual Property and Confidentiality Protections: Safeguarding Innovation Throughout the SDLC* *16*
  - *2.3.4 Clear Expectations and Communication: Structuring Collaboration through SDLC-Informed Contracts* *19*

2.3.5 *Adaptability to Development Models (Waterfall, Agile, Iterative)* 20
2.4 *Overview of Common SDLC Development Models* 21
2.4.1 *Waterfall Model* 21
2.4.2 *Agile Model* 22
2.4.3 *Iterative Model* 23
2.4.4 *Decision-Making Checklist: Choosing Between Waterfall, Agile, and Iterative Models* 25
2.5 *Relationship Between SDLC and Contractual Obligations: Sample Clauses* 27

3 **Planning and Requirement Analysis** **32**
3.1 *Importance of Planning in the SDLC* 32
3.2 *Internal Documentation Produced by the Client in the Planning Phase* 34
3.3 *Importance of Requirement Gathering and In-Depth Analysis* 35
3.4 *Cross-Departmental Involvement in Requirement Gathering* 36
3.5 *Requirement Gathering Checklist by Department* 38
3.5.1 *General Preparation — For Management and All Departments* 38
3.5.2 *Operations / Supply Chain / Logistics* 38
3.5.3 *Finance & Accounting* 39
3.5.4 *Sales & Marketing* 39
3.5.5 *IT / Technical Department* 40
3.5.6 *Legal, Compliance, & Risk Management* 40
3.5.7 *Human Resources (HR)* 41
3.5.8 *Strategy / Executive Management* 42
3.5.9 *Final Organizational Steps* 42
3.6 *Consequences of Limited Involvement During Requirement Gathering* 43
3.7 *Real Life Steps and Roles* 44
3.7.1 *Key Deliverables of the Planning and Requirement Analysis Phase* 48
3.8 *Types of Requirements and the Process of Requirement Analysis* 48
3.8.1 *Types of Requirements* 49
3.9 *Contract Guidelines* 50
3.10 *Translating Planning and Requirements into Contractual Clauses* 52
3.11 *Legal Risks of Poorly Defined Requirements* 53
3.11.1 *Common Risks and Their Manifestations* 53
3.12 *Checklist: Ensuring Comprehensive Requirement Analysis* 54

4 **Design Phase** **57**
4.1 Overview of the Design Process in SDLC *57*
4.2 Real-World Execution of the Design Phase: Roles, Best Practices, and Legal Risks *58*
4.2.1 Who Does What in Practice *58*
4.2.2 What Should Be Done (Best Practices) *62*
4.2.3 What Should Be Avoided *66*
4.2.4 Legal and Contractual Risks of Poor Design Phase Execution *70*
4.2.5 Evidence in Litigation *75*
4.3 Software Architecture and Design Documentation *76*
4.3.1 Defining High-Level Architecture *76*
4.3.2 Selecting Technology Stack and Tools *76*
4.3.3 Creating Detailed Component Designs *77*
4.3.4 Designing Data Flow and Interaction Diagrams *77*
4.3.5 User Interface (UI) and User Experience (UX) Design *77*
4.3.6 Documenting the Design *78*
4.3.7 Review and Approval Process *78*
4.4 Checklist: Key Elements of a Design Document *78*
4.5 Key Deliverables *80*
4.6 Tech Lawyer's role in Design Phase *82*
4.7 Incorporating Design Deliverables into the Contract: Sample Clauses *83*
4.7.1 Defining Design Deliverables in the Scope of Work (SoW) *84*
4.7.2 Defining Acceptance Criteria for Design Deliverables *84*
4.7.3 Quality Standards and Performance Benchmarks *85*
4.7.4 Intellectual Property and Confidentiality Clauses *85*

5 **Development Phase** **86**
5.1 Overview of the Development Process *86*
5.2 Role of the Development Team *87*
5.3 Role of the Client and Other Stakeholders *88*
5.3.1 The Client (Beneficiary) *88*
5.3.2 Project Management *88*
5.3.3 Quality Assurance (QA) and Independent Testers *89*
5.3.4 Legal and Compliance Teams *89*
5.3.5 External Consultants and Auditors *89*
5.4 Coding Standards and Best Practices *90*
5.4.1 Coding Standards *90*
5.4.2 Best Practices *91*

5.5 *Types of Code in the Development Phase* 94
5.5.1 *Proprietary Code (Custom Code)* 94
5.5.2 *Third-Party Licensed Code* 95
5.5.3 *Open-Source Code* 97
5.5.4 *AI-generated code* 98
5.5.5 *Legacy Code Reuse* 101
5.6 *Software Development Management Platforms* 103
5.6.1 *Access Rights and Stakeholder Visibility* 104
5.6.2 *Legal Risks* 104
5.6.3 *Evidentiary Value in Litigation* 104
5.7 *Ensuring Compliance with Contractual Specifications* 105
5.8 *Checklist: Development Phase Deliverables and Contractual Compliance* 106
5.9 *Legal Risks Associated with the Development Phase* 108
5.9.1 *Intellectual Property Risks* 109
5.9.2 *Licensing and Compliance Risks* 115
5.9.3 *Confidentiality and Trade Secret Risks* 119
5.9.4 *Quality and Liability Risks* 122
5.9.5 *Regulatory and Compliance Risks* 124

6 **Testing Phase** **127**
6.1 *Importance of Testing* 127
6.2 *Main Stages of Testing* 128
6.2.1 *Developer Testing* 129
6.2.2 *Client Testing* 145
6.2.3 *Final Acceptance Checklist* 151
6.2.4 *Template – Final Acceptance Certificate* 154
6.2.5 *Template – Conditional Acceptance Certificate* 155
6.2.6 *Template – Final Acceptance Rejection Notice* 157

7 **Deployment Phase** **159**
7.1 *Overview of the Deployment Phase* 159
7.2 *Stakeholders Roles in Preparing for Go-Live* 163
7.2.1 *Developer's Role and Obligations* 163
7.2.2 *Client's Role and Obligations* 167
7.2.3 *Project Manager's Role and Obligations* 173
7.2.4 *Technology Lawyer's Role and Obligations* 175
7.2.5 *Third-Party Vendors and Subcontractors' Role and Obligations* 178
7.2.6 *End-Users' Role and Obligations* 181

7.3 *Training as a Critical Component of Go-Live Readiness* 183
7.3.1 *Frequent Litigation Issues Involving Training* 185
7.4 *Deployment Strategies (Phased, Parallel, Big Bang)* 186
7.4.1 *Phased Deployment* 186
7.4.2 *Parallel Deployment* 187
7.4.3 *Big Bang Deployment* 187
7.5 *Role of Deployment in Contract Fulfilment* 188
7.6 *Managing Deployment Risks and Most Common Disputes* 189
7.6.1 *Legal Risks and Common Disputes* 189
7.6.2 *Management of Deployment Risks* 190
7.7 *Warranty Period* 192
7.7.1 *Main Obligations during Warranty Period* 192
7.7.2 *Key Provisions to Include in the Warranty Clause* 193
7.8 *Checklist: Key Considerations for Deployment Phase (Client Perspective)* 194
7.9 *Checklist: Key Considerations for Deployment Phase (Developer Perspective)* 196
7.10 *Final Acceptance* 199
7.10.1 *Definition and Role in the Contractual Lifecycle* 199
7.10.2 *Typical Preconditions for Final Acceptance* 200
7.10.3 *Obligations of the Parties During the Final Acceptance Phase* 206
7.10.4 *Legal Risks Associated with Final Acceptance* 207
7.10.5 *Evidence and Frequent Litigation Issues* 210

8 **Maintenance and Support** **212**
8.1 *Importance of Ongoing Maintenance in Software Development* 212
8.1.1 *Technical Scope of Maintenance* 214
8.2 *Legal and Contractual Significance* 216
8.2.1 *Legal Risks Arising from Poorly Defined Maintenance Obligations* 217
8.2.2 *Security Liability* 218
8.2.3 *Operational and Financial Risks* 219
8.3 *Service Level Agreements (SLAs) and Their Role* 220
8.3.1 *Definition and Overview* 220
8.3.2 *Key Components of an SLA* 221
8.3.3 *Checklist: Effective Maintenance and Support Clauses (Client Perspective)* 222
8.3.4 *Checklist: Effective Maintenance and Support Clauses (Developer Perspective)* 224

9 **Software Development Contracts** **227**
9.1 Fixed-Price Contracts *227*
9.1.1 Definition and Overview *227*
9.1.2 Advantages and Disadvantages *228*
9.1.3 Key Clauses and Considerations *229*
9.1.4 Legal Risks in Fixed-Price Contracts *231*
9.2 Time and Materials (T&M) Contracts *233*
9.2.1 Definition and Overview *233*
9.2.2 Advantages and Disadvantages *234*
9.2.3 Client's Risk *235*
9.2.4 Key Clauses and Considerations *237*
9.2.5 Legal Risks in Time and Materials Contracts *239*
9.3 Agile Contracts *240*
9.3.1 Overview of Agile Methodology *240*
9.3.2 Advantages and Disadvantages *242*
9.3.3 Key Clauses and Considerations *242*
9.3.4 Checklist: Drafting an Agile Contract *245*
9.3.5 Types of Agile Contracts (Timebox, Fixed-Scope with Flexibility) *245*
9.3.6 Aligning Agile Practices with Contract Terms *246*
9.3.7 Risk Management in Agile Contracts *248*
9.3.8 Checklist: Ensuring Agile Contract Success *249*
9.3.9 Legal Risks in Agile Contracts *251*
9.4 Milestone-Based Contracts *253*
9.4.1 Definition and Overview *253*
9.4.2 Structuring Contracts Around Milestones *253*
9.4.3 Payment Schedules and Milestones *254*
9.4.4 Ensuring Accountability Through Milestone Deliverables *254*
9.4.5 Checklist: Creating Milestone-Based Contracts *255*
9.4.6 Legal Risks in Milestone-Based Contracts *256*
9.5 Hybrid Contracts *258*
9.5.1 Definition and Overview *258*
9.5.2 Combining Different Contract Types *258*
9.5.3 Flexibility vs. Complexity in Hybrid Contracts *261*
9.5.4 Managing Risk and Uncertainty in Hybrid Contracts *262*
9.5.5 Checklist: Creating a Successful Hybrid Contract *262*
9.5.6 Legal Risks in Hybrid Contracts *263*
9.6 Licensing and SaaS (Software as a Service) Contract *265*
9.6.1 Definition and Overview *265*
9.6.2 Intellectual Property and Ownership *266*

9.6.3 Payment Structure 267
9.6.4 Service Level Agreements (SLAs) and Performance Guarantees 267
9.6.5 Data Ownership and Confidentiality 268
9.6.6 Limitations on Liability and Warranty Disclaimers 268
9.6.7 Checklist: Creating a Successful Licensing or SaaS Contract 269
9.6.8 Legal Risks in Licensing and SaaS Contracts 270
9.6.9 Selecting the Contract 272

Index 274

ABOUT THE AUTHOR

Dr. Oana Ruxandra Gherghina is a distinguished lawyer, academic, and author with over two decades of experience in business, construction, and technology law. A member of the Bucharest Bar since 2001, she is the CEO of Gherghina Law Firm, widely recognized for its expertise in complex contractual structures, dispute resolution, and cross-border legal advisory services.

She holds a Ph.D. in Law, with a doctoral thesis focused on FIDIC Construction Contracts, and is the author of several acclaimed legal works in the fields of construction and commercial law. Noting the structural and operational similarities between construction projects and software development processes, Dr. Gherghina expanded her legal practice into the tech industry—bringing a rare and interdisciplinary perspective to software contract negotiation and risk management.

Until 2024, she served as Associate Professor at the Bucharest University of Economic Studies (ASE) and Titu Maiorescu University, where she lectured in Business Law, Commercial Law, and EU Law. Following her relocation to Dubai, she now teaches at the Regional Centre for European Studies (RCES), where she also serves as President of the Scientific Committee.

Her two-volume book project, *Legal Risks in the Software Development Lifecycle* (Vol. I) and *Effective Software Development Contracts* (Vol. II), reflects her mission to demystify the legal complexity behind software development. Volume I offers a legal analysis of the SDLC phases and the risks they generate, while Volume II will guide readers through the art of drafting, negotiating, and interpreting software development contracts, complete with practical examples, model clauses, and references to relevant jurisprudence. Together, these volumes aim to bridge legal precision with technological innovation for professionals across law, tech, and business.

PREFACE

The software development process, whether it involves building a small custom application or a complex enterprise system, is becoming increasingly sophisticated and legally intricate with each passing year. As the global economy continues to digitize, software has become a critical infrastructure asset, one that must be planned, delivered, and maintained under contractual arrangements that align legal certainty with technical agility. Just as the construction industry once required a structured legal framework to manage risk and clarify obligations, the software industry now faces a similar need for contractual clarity in a rapidly evolving technological environment.

This book emerges from the recognition that software development projects, much like construction projects, follow a phased lifecycle, involve diverse stakeholders, and often become the subject of disputes due to misaligned expectations, unclear deliverables, or evolving project scopes. The software development process—whether it involves a custom application or a complex enterprise system—has evolved into a highly structured and legally intricate undertaking. As the global economy becomes increasingly digitized, software is no longer just a tool but a critical infrastructure asset that must be planned, executed, and maintained through contracts that ensure both legal certainty and technical adaptability.

Much like the construction industry before it, the software industry now requires a coherent legal framework to manage risks, define responsibilities, and provide clear remedies. Software development projects share many features with large-scale construction: they follow a phased lifecycle, involve multidisciplinary stakeholders, and frequently give rise to disputes stemming from unclear deliverables, shifting scopes, or poorly defined obligations.

Legal Risks in the Software Development Lifecycle is designed to respond to this reality. It explores the legal risks specific to each phase of the Software Development Lifecycle (SDLC), from planning and design to development, testing, deployment, and maintenance. By integrating legal analysis with practical realities, this volume offers readers the tools to identify, prevent, and manage legal vulnerabilities before they escalate into contractual breakdowns. Each chapter provides real-world examples, risk maps, case references, and actionable insights that help bridge the gap between legal theory and technical execution.

The purpose of this volume is not to address the entirety of technology law, but rather to provide lawyers, developers, project managers, and clients with a practical and phase-specific legal understanding of the development process itself. Drawing on my two decades of legal practice in construction and technology, as well as my academic experience, this book serves as both a legal primer and a risk management guide for anyone involved in software development projects.

Effective Software Development Contracts will build on this foundation. Once readers have gained a deep understanding of how each SDLC phase unfolds, and where legal risks are most likely to appear, the book will provide the contractual tools to address them.

Together, these two volumes aim to offer a comprehensive and practical legal roadmap, one that equips professionals across law and technology to navigate complexity, manage risk, and foster collaboration through clear, enforceable, and balanced agreements.

The purpose of this book is not to address every area of technology law but rather to focus on the recurring legal issues and contractual challenges that practitioners, clients, and developers most frequently encounter.

By situating software contracts within the broader context of the Software Development Lifecycle (SDLC), this work offers both the "rule" and the rationale behind it, empowering readers to draft, negotiate, and administer software agreements with confidence, foresight, and legal precision.

It is my hope that this book will serve as a bridge between legal and technical disciplines, enabling professionals on all sides of the software development table to collaborate more effectively and avoid the costly consequences of contractual ambiguity.

Oana Gherghina

ACKNOWLEDGEMENTS

I am deeply grateful to my colleagues and collaborators whose support, insight, and encouragement have played a vital role in the development of this book. I would particularly like to thank my software development clients who generously shared their practical experiences and helped shape the case studies and real-world insights presented in this work.

My sincere thanks go to the editorial team at Informa Law from Routledge, especially Guy Loft and Nicola Sharpe for their professionalism, editorial guidance, and continuous support throughout the publishing process.

I would also like to express my appreciation to my son, Vlad Gherghina, whose sharp legal mind, attention to detail, and valuable contributions to research and content refinement helped bring this manuscript to its final form. His involvement added both intellectual rigor and personal meaning to this project.

Finally, I wish to acknowledge the inspiring community of technology lawyers, project managers, and developers whose challenges and insights informed the substance of this book. Their work continues to shape the evolving intersection of law and technology.

CHAPTER 1

Introduction

1.1 Overview of the Software Development Industry

The software development industry represents a cornerstone of the contemporary digital economy, underpinning innovation, operational efficiency, and the transformation of virtually every sector. Characterized by rapid technological advancement and dynamic market demands, the industry has evolved from isolated programming efforts to highly structured, collaborative processes involving multidisciplinary teams and complex contractual frameworks.

Modern software development is no longer limited to the production of standalone applications, it encompasses the creation and continuous refinement of integrated systems, platforms, and infrastructures that support business operations, public administration, education, healthcare, finance, and countless other domains. Central to this evolution is the adoption of structured development methodologies, such as Agile, DevOps, and Waterfall, each shaping the contractual and operational dynamics between stakeholders.

Globalization and outsourcing have further contributed to the industry's complexity, with development teams often distributed across jurisdictions and governed by diverse regulatory and contractual regimes. As a result, legal considerations have become increasingly significant. Intellectual property protection, data privacy, liability for defects, change management, and dispute resolution mechanisms are now integral to software development agreements.

Against this backdrop, the software development industry emerges as both a technical and legal ecosystem, requiring a coherent integration of legal principles with project management practices to ensure project success, regulatory compliance, and equitable allocation of risks and responsibilities.

1.2 Purpose of the Book

Legal Risks in the Software Development Lifecycle is the first of a two-volume series designed to bridge the gap between legal reasoning and the operational realities of software projects. This volume goes beyond a

 DOI: 10.4324/9781003669609-1

simple focus on legal risks. It systematically examines each phase of the Software Development Lifecycle (SDLC), clarifying the role and responsibilities of each stakeholder and identifying the essential documentation that should accompany the process.

By examining legal exposure at each phase, this book helps readers understand **how and why software projects fail legally**, not just technically. The focus is on real-world risks such as unclear acceptance criteria, shifting requirements, regulatory non-compliance, maintenance disputes, and inadequate service level guarantees. Each chapter is structured to be accessible yet rigorous, helping professionals identify where contracts must preemptively allocate responsibility and reduce ambiguity.

Through clear and structured explanations, this book walks the reader through each **phase of the Software Development Lifecycle (SDLC)**, from planning to maintenance, highlighting the **specific legal risks**, technical dependencies, and stakeholder responsibilities associated with each step. Every phase is explored in depth, with practical insights on how risks arise, how they can be prevented through contractual design, and what evidence is required in case of litigation or dispute.

Instead of approaching software agreements as abstract legal constructs, this book grounds the discussion in practical project dynamics, demonstrating how legal risks materialize across the software development lifecycle. It examines the emergence of liability during requirements elicitation, design discrepancies, ambiguous acceptance criteria, incomplete testing, and deficiencies in post-deployment support. By situating these risks within real-world scenarios, the book advances a strategic framework that clarifies when, where, and why legal safeguards must be embedded into development processes, thereby linking contractual design to operational realities.

Each chapter is carefully crafted to **demystify complex legal-technical intersections**, making this book an essential foundation for tech-lawyers, project managers, clients, and developers who want to reduce risk, improve collaboration, and protect long-term project outcomes.

A comprehensive and structured understanding of each phase of the Software Development Lifecycle (SDLC), together with the legal, operational, and financial risks inherent to them, is a prerequisite for legal practitioners, developers, and clients to navigate the complexities of software contracting.

Read in conjunction with its companion volume, *Effective Software Development Contracts*, this series offers a complete analytical framework that not only elucidates the risks embedded in the software industry but also equips readers to design resilient contractual structures and to draw practical insights from real-world case studies and their resolutions. Although each book may be read independently, together they provide a broader and more coherent perspective on the intersection of law and software development, equipping readers with the comprehensive knowledge required to both understand risks and implement effective contractual safeguards.

1.3 Who Should Use This Book

1.3.1 Project Managers

This book is designed to equip project managers with a solid understanding of the legal frameworks essential for managing software development projects effectively. By covering key topics such as the Software Development Lifecycle (SDLC), various development models, intellectual property considerations, and contract types specific to the IT industry, it provides a comprehensive guide for project managers navigating the complexities of tech contracts.

The book offers insights into how legal principles intersect with project management, helping managers understand contractual obligations, identify potential risks, and ensure compliance with industry standards. With clear explanations and practical examples, this resource empowers project managers to work confidently alongside legal and development teams, enhancing their ability to oversee projects with a keen awareness of both contractual and operational requirements.

1.3.2 Lawyers and Legal Advisers

This book is designed to help a lawyer with no experience in technology gain the foundational knowledge needed to begin specializing as a tech-lawyer. By covering essential concepts like the Software Development Lifecycle (SDLC), software development models, intellectual property in tech, and contract types specific to the IT industry, this book provides a practical roadmap for lawyers looking to enter the technology field. It explains how legal principles apply uniquely to software development projects, what legal risks to anticipate, and how to structure contracts that align with industry practices.

Through clear explanations, practical examples, and structured legal analysis across all phases of the Software Development Lifecycle, **the book** equips lawyers with the foundational knowledge needed to understand the technical and legal risks specific to software projects. This grounding enables them to navigate technology-related legal matters with confidence.

Building on this base, **the companion book *Effective Software Development Contracts*** offers actionable guidance on contract structuring, complete with sample clauses, drafting strategies, and relevant jurisprudence, making the full series a comprehensive resource for those pursuing a specialization in Technology Law.

1.3.3 Developers

The book offers developers a clear and structured overview of how legal risks intersect with each phase of the Software Development Lifecycle (SDLC). By examining how legal obligations affect planning, design, coding, testing, deployment, and maintenance, the book helps developers understand the legal expectations that shape their daily work, from deliverables and quality standards to data protection and compliance requirements.

With real-world examples, simplified legal analysis, and case studies, this volume enables developers to identify legal pitfalls early and collaborate more effectively with clients, legal teams, and project managers.

The companion book *Effective Software Development Contracts* will build on this foundation by offering practical tools for understanding software development contracts, including sample clauses, drafting techniques, and key jurisprudence, helping developers engage meaningfully in contract negotiations and protect their professional interests.

1.3.4 Clients

This book is designed to help software clients, whether startups, corporations, or public institutions, gain a solid understanding of the legal risks and responsibilities embedded in each phase of the Software Development Lifecycle (SDLC). By exploring topics such as planning, requirements definition, design, development, testing, deployment, and maintenance, this volume equips clients to proactively manage risks, define expectations, and ensure legal compliance throughout the development journey.

It clarifies how contractual obligations emerge at each phase, what deliverables should be expected, and how misalignment or vague requirements can lead to disputes or project failure. With accessible language, illustrative examples, and real-life disputes, the book empowers clients to engage confidently with developers and legal advisors.

The companion book *Effective Software Development Contracts* will build on this foundation by offering clients the tools to interpret and participate in contract drafting and negotiation, with annotated model clauses, risk-allocation strategies, and relevant jurisprudence from global software disputes.

1.3.5 Judges, Arbitrators, and Mediators

This book is also designed to support judges, arbitrators, and mediators in understanding the inner workings of software development projects and the legal risks that may arise at each stage of the Software Development Lifecycle (SDLC). It explains how technical decisions intersect with contractual obligations, and highlights the types of project failures, ambiguities, and misalignments that frequently escalate into legal disputes.

By analyzing development models, risk allocation points, and operational breakdowns in accessible language, the volume equips dispute resolution professionals with the context needed to interpret evidence and contractual provisions in software-related litigation or arbitration.

The companion book will complement this foundation by offering in-depth analysis of contract structures, annotated model clauses, and relevant jurisprudence, providing a practical legal toolkit for adjudicating disputes and understanding the commercial realities behind technology contracts. Together, the two volumes serve as a comprehensive reference for resolving complex disputes in the digital era.

1.3.6 Students and Aspiring Professionals

The book is also carefully designed to support students and early-career professionals who seek to understand the intersection between law and software development. Drawing on my experience as a university lecturer, both books explain complex legal-technical concepts with clarity and pedagogical structure, making them accessible even to those without prior legal or programming background.

This book offers a step-by-step exploration of the Software Development Lifecycle (SDLC), development methodologies, and the legal risks that arise at each project phase. It helps students understand how project planning, design decisions, testing, and maintenance all carry contractual implications and legal exposure.

The companion book will build on this foundation by introducing the structure of software development contracts, key roles and responsibilities, critical clauses, and relevant jurisprudence. It includes practical tools such as annotated model clauses to help students gain not only theoretical understanding but also applied drafting skills.

Together, ***Legal Risks in the Software Development Lifecycle*** **and** ***Effective Software Development Contracts*** offer a comprehensive learning path for those looking to specialize in Technology Law or to become informed participants in software-driven projects, whether as lawyers, developers, or business stakeholders.

1.4 Exploring the Parallels between Construction Contracts and Software Development Agreements

One of the fundamental principles shared by construction and software development projects is their *division into phases or milestones*, each with specific deliverables and objectives.

In both construction and software development, defining the *project scope and detailed specifications* is paramount. In construction, the scope document outlines everything from the architectural design to material quality, dimensions, and timelines. Likewise, in software development, a clear definition of scope, detailing functionalities, design elements, performance requirements, and compatibility needs, forms the blueprint for the project.

The Software Development Lifecycle (SDLC) unfolds through a sequence of interdependent phases, like planning, requirements definition, design, development, testing, and deployment, where the integrity of each stage determines the viability of the next.

This sequential structure mirrors the logic of construction projects, where progress is measured by milestones that mark the transition between stages. In both domains, systematic testing and quality assurance at every step are indispensable to ensure conformity with specifications and to achieve the level of reliability and client satisfaction demanded in professional practice.

In both industries, successful completion of projects often relies on a wide range of stakeholders, from clients to contractors, designers, and specialist subcontractors. In construction, we have general contractors, architects, engineers, and specialized subcontractors who each bring unique expertise. Similarly, in software development, we have developers, UI/UX designers, database architects, quality assurance teams, and often third-party vendors who contribute specific functionalities like payment gateways or cloud services.

Both project types require detailed contractual frameworks to manage these parties, ensuring responsibilities are clear, deadlines are respected, and accountability is maintained. The primary contractor, whether a general contractor in construction or a lead developer in software, assumes responsibility for coordinating these players. Contracts in both fields often outline roles, specify deliverables, and establish a hierarchy for approvals to ensure smooth communication and alignment throughout the project lifecycle.

Scope changes are common challenges in both construction and software development. In construction, scope changes might involve modifications to building dimensions or materials. In software, they can include additional functionalities or design alterations. Without proper management, these changes can lead to delays, cost overruns, and disputes.

Both industries recognize the need for formal *change management processes* within contracts. Construction contracts typically require change orders, which must be documented, approved, and priced before the work proceeds. Software development contracts use similar mechanisms, often requiring "Change Requests" or "Amendments" to the Scope of Work. These change management clauses serve as vital tools for balancing flexibility and predictability, protecting both the client and the contractor from the risks associated with uncontrolled modifications.

Risk allocation is another shared area between construction and software development contracts. In both cases, the developer or contractor is responsible for ensuring that deliverables meet the agreed specifications and quality standards. However, factors beyond the contractor's control – from delays in material supply to changes in regulatory requirements – can impact project timelines and budgets. Construction contracts commonly include force majeure clauses, indemnification provisions, and limits on liability. Similarly, software development contracts cover these aspects, often including indemnity for IP infringement, limitations on liability for third-party failures, and remedies for performance-related issues.

Furthermore, both industries may involve *penalties* for delays or failure to meet specifications. In construction, liquidated damages are commonly imposed for delayed completion, and in software development, milestone payments may be withheld or penalties imposed for failure to meet performance criteria or deadlines. These provisions incentivize timely and high-quality completion and ensure accountability for both parties.

Intellectual property rights are critically important in both fields, though they manifest differently. In construction, intellectual property considerations might pertain to architectural designs, structural engineering models, or specialized construction techniques. The contract must outline ownership and usage rights, ensuring that designs can't be reused or disclosed without consent. In software development, intellectual property focuses on code, algorithms, and interfaces. Contracts specify who retains IP rights to the developed software, often stipulating that custom work produced specifically for the project is assigned to the client.

In both industries, clear IP clauses protect the client's interests while allowing the developer or contractor to retain proprietary techniques or tools that are part of their general business model. Misunderstandings in this area can lead to disputes, so it's crucial that IP rights and ownership are thoroughly addressed and agreed upon in the contract.

Both construction and software development projects embody high levels of complexity, interdependence, and risk, requiring precise coordination, communication, and planning. Understanding these similarities not only helps professionals navigate projects more effectively but also illuminates how different fields can benefit from shared approaches to achieving successful, sustainable outcomes.

CHAPTER 2

Software Development Lifecycle (SDLC)

2.1 Software Development Lifecycle (SDLC) Guidelines

The Software Development Lifecycle (SDLC) is a structured framework that outlines the sequential phases involved in the development of software applications, ranging from initial concept to final deployment and ongoing maintenance. It serves as a collaborative roadmap for developers, clients, and stakeholders, providing clarity on each phase of the process and ensuring alignment between technical execution and business objectives.

Typically, the SDLC comprises the following **key stages**:

- **Planning** (defining goals and scope)
- **Requirements analysis** (identifying what the software must do)
- **Design** (developing architecture and user interfaces)
- **Development** (writing the code)
- **Testing** (identifying and fixing defects)
- **Deployment** (making the product available to users)
- **Maintenance** (ongoing updates, bug fixes, and improvements)

Each phase builds logically upon the previous one, contributing to a coherent and traceable workflow. The SDLC is not only a technical tool but also a legal and managerial one, especially relevant in the context of software development contracts, where clarity, predictability, and risk allocation are paramount.

Understanding the SDLC enables parties to anticipate responsibilities, timelines, and deliverables at each phase, facilitating informed decision-making and communication. This structured approach reduces the likelihood of disputes and helps ensure that the final product meets the agreed specifications, budget, and timeline.

The logic of the SDLC closely parallels that of construction projects, which also rely on phased execution, milestones, and multi-stakeholder coordination. Drawing on this analogy allows legal practitioners and project managers alike to apply lessons learned from the more established field of construction law to the still-evolving domain of software contracts.

DOI: 10.4324/9781003669609-2

Understanding these stages is helpful if you're involved in a software development contract because it helps you see the big picture. You'll know what to expect at each step of the project, which makes it easier to communicate with the developers, manage your time and resources, and ensure the project stays on track.

By knowing the SDLC, you can better understand how long each stage should take, what kind of input you'll need to provide, and what the final product should look like. This clarity helps prevent misunderstandings and keeps everyone on the same page.

The SDLC also helps identify potential problems early in the process. For example, if something isn't working during the testing phase, it can be fixed before the software is fully deployed. This saves time and money in the long run.

By embedding the SDLC framework into contractual design, parties enhance transparency, reduce ambiguity, and contribute to the overall success of the project.

Table 2.1 Detailed SDLC Phases and Contractual Implications

SDLC Phase	*Detailed Description*	*Contractual Implications*
1. Planning	Initial phase where the project's purpose, scope, feasibility, constraints, cost estimates, and team structure are established. It may involve market analysis, risk assessment, and defining high-level timelines.	Defines the Statement of Work (SoW), project schedule, budget, and allocation of responsibilities. The phase establishes the legal framework and contractual baseline.
2. Requirements Analysis	In-depth discussions with stakeholders to gather, clarify, and document functional and non-functional requirements. Techniques like interviews, workshops, user stories, and use cases are commonly used.	Forms the legal foundation for Scope definition. Contracts should include clauses for Change Management, Scope Creep Control, and Approval Processes.

(*Continued*)

Table 2.1 (Continued)

SDLC Phase	*Detailed Description*	*Contractual Implications*
3. System Design	Transforming requirements into a structured system design: defining system architecture, database schemas, data flows, user interfaces, and technical specifications for developers.	Design documents should be referenced explicitly in contracts, clarifying ownership of designs, approval checkpoints, and liabilities for design flaws.
4. Development	Developers write code according to the agreed design documents. This stage also includes unit testing, integration between modules, and internal code reviews.	Requires clearly defined deliverables, coding standards, IP clauses, use of third-party code, and subcontracting terms. Timelines and penalties for delays are also set here.
5. Testing	System is tested thoroughly through various methods (functional, security, performance, regression). The goal is to ensure that the system meets the initial requirements and is defect-free.	Contract must specify test types, test plans, acceptance criteria, test data obligations, and what constitutes a failed or successful test (exit criteria).
6. Deployment	The software is deployed into the production environment. This may involve data migration, user onboarding, infrastructure provisioning, and a handover plan.	Deployment triggers key contractual events like milestone payments, client sign-off, final acceptance, and transfer of IP. Also includes service activation terms.
7. Maintenance & Support	Ongoing updates, bug fixes, performance optimization, and adaptations to changing business needs. Includes corrective, adaptive, and preventive maintenance.	Contracts must define SLA parameters (response time, uptime, issue severity levels), maintenance periods, liability for post-delivery issues, and support fees.

2.2 Importance of SDLC in Software Development

The importance of the Software Development Lifecycle (SDLC) in software development lies in its ability to structure and organize each phase of the process, from initial planning to final maintenance. By following the SDLC, all parties involved ensure that each key phase (planning, designing, coding, testing, deploying, and maintaining) is completed in a systematic way, which reduces errors, keeps the project on schedule, and aligns the final product with the client's expectations.

For example, imagine a team skips or rushes through the planning and requirements phase without a thorough understanding of what the client needs. Later in development, they might realize that certain features are missing, or that the design doesn't meet the client's goals. This oversight could lead to significant rework, delays, and added costs as the team scrambles to make changes at a much later stage. Such late-stage changes are not only costly but can also affect the quality and stability of the final product.

A concrete real-world example can be seen in banking software applications, where insufficient planning could lead to missing critical security features. If security isn't addressed in the initial phases, adding it later could be complex and prone to errors, potentially exposing sensitive financial data.

By following the SDLC from the start, the team can anticipate and incorporate these critical features, ensuring a product that is secure, reliable, and aligned with the client's needs. In short, the SDLC reduces risks, controls costs, and improves the final product's quality by making sure that each phase is thoughtfully planned and executed.

The following case study, Waste Management vs SAP, has been selected for its illustrative power in highlighting the critical importance of aligning legal, managerial, and technical perspectives within software development projects. It vividly demonstrates that every stakeholder, whether on the legal, executive, or development side, must possess a practical understanding of the SDLC. Such knowledge is essential not only to manage expectations and assess vendor claims, but also to validate functionality, ensure contractual alignment with technical deliverables, and maintain accountability across the project lifecycle. This case, therefore, serves as a cautionary example of what can go wrong when SDLC principles are neglected in strategic decision-making.

CASE BACKGROUND

In 2005, Waste Management, Inc. (WM), a Fortune 200 waste disposal and environmental services company, initiated efforts to modernize and unify its enterprise software systems. Seeking an "off-the-shelf" ERP solution to streamline operations and reduce costs, WM entered into a licensing agreement with SAP America, Inc., one of the largest providers of ERP software globally. The partnership was quickly mired in controversy.

In March 2008, WM filed a lawsuit against SAP in the U.S. District Court for the Southern District of Texas, alleging fraud, negligent misrepresentation, breach of contract, and unfair trade practices. The lawsuit claimed over **$500 million in damages**, asserting that SAP had intentionally misled WM into purchasing a non-functional and underdeveloped ERP product under the pretense that it was a sector-specific, ready-to-deploy solution.

Legal Issues and Allegations

Fraud and Misrepresentation

WM's primary allegation was that SAP knowingly and fraudulently misrepresented the maturity and market-readiness of its "Waste and Recycling" ERP solution, demonstrated mock software that was not capable of delivering promised functionality, and claimed the product was pre-configured and tested for WM's specific industry needs.

SAP allegedly manipulated pre-contractual demos to portray functionality that did not exist and deliberately concealed the fact that the software was still in development and untested in real-world environments.

Business Case Manipulation

SAP also presented a "business case" to WM projecting benefits of $106–$220 million annually, a range WM later described in its filings as part of its justification for selecting SAP's solution. The business case, although prepared by SAP for promotional purposes, was relied upon by WM without independent validation.

Waste Management's Share of Liability

While SAP bore the brunt of public scrutiny, WM was not blameless.

Inadequate Due Diligence

WM's own pleadings acknowledged that the ERP solution had been developed "specifically for Waste Management" and it relied on SAP's financial projections rather than commissioning an independent assessment.

This suggests WM overlooked basic principles of ERP procurement governance. Given its scale, WM had both the resources and obligations to validate claims independently and manage implementation risks more prudently.

Contradiction Between Stated Intent and Action

WM claimed it was looking for a mature, off-the-shelf product, yet selected a custom-developed system for which proof of concept and stability were missing. This inconsistency weakened WM's posture in the litigation and demonstrated internal strategic and project governance deficiencies.

SDLC Phases Overlooked

Requirements Gathering

SAP conducted a superficial assessment, assuming that its standard ERP features would meet Waste Management's needs. Critical details, such as complex billing processes and integration with existing systems, were overlooked.

Planning and Risk Analysis

SAP presented an optimistic timeline without accounting for potential challenges, such as data migration complexities and customization needs.

Consequences

Underestimation of Development Costs

As development progressed, SAP realized the need for additional custom features to support Waste Management's operations, leading to substantial cost increases.

Significant Delays in Project Timeline

Unforeseen technical issues, including integration challenges and system performance problems, caused the project to extend well beyond the original deadline.

Frustrated by the delays and cost overruns, Waste Management filed a lawsuit against SAP, alleging fraud and seeking damages for the failed implementation. The legal battle highlighted the severe financial and operational impacts of ERP project failures.

Resolution

In 2010, the legal dispute between Waste Management (WM) and SAP concluded through a private settlement, with SAP agreeing to a one-time, undisclosed cash payment to WM. Although the resolution involved no formal admission of liability, the consequences for SAP were profound. The company suffered significant reputational damage, a loss of credibility among enterprise clients, and internal scrutiny that culminated in the departure of several senior executives.

Beyond the immediate impact on the parties involved, the case triggered industry-wide repercussions. Organizations began placing greater emphasis on independent third-party validation, adopting stricter governance mechanisms for ERP implementation, and applying more robust legal oversight during the software procurement process.

Conclusion

At the heart of the Waste Management–SAP failure lies a fundamental disconnect between contractual promises and technical realities—one that could have been largely mitigated through a proper understanding and application of the Software Development Life Cycle (SDLC). SDLC provides a structured framework that defines each phase of a software project—from requirements gathering to deployment and maintenance. Had both parties ensured alignment between contractual obligations and the actual maturity of the product across the SDLC stages, the risks of misrepresentation, mismanagement, and, ultimately, litigation could have been substantially reduced.

Box 2.1. Case Study: *Waste Management, Inc. and USA Waste-Management, LLC vs SAP America, Inc. and SAP AG, Case no: 4:2008cv01248, U.S. District Court for the Southern District of Texas*[1]

2.3 Essential Role of SDLC in Tech Lawyers Practice

Technology lawyers are expected to understand the Software Development Lifecycle because it plays a critical role in managing the legal aspects of software development. The SDLC provides a structured framework that defines each phase of software creation, from planning to maintenance, and lawyers who understand this lifecycle can create more precise, effective contracts and mitigate legal risks specific to technology projects.

2.3.1 Aligning Contractual Clauses with Project Phases

Understanding SDLC is not just useful, it is essential for legal professionals involved in drafting, negotiating, or reviewing software development contracts. The SDLC breaks down the complex process of software creation into distinct, manageable phases and each phase involves specific activities, responsibilities, risks, and expectations.

For technology lawyers, aligning contractual clauses with these SDLC phases is critical to ensuring that legal documents reflect the real structure of the project. This alignment enables lawyers to:

- **Define precise deliverables** for each stage (e.g., a completed UI prototype after the design phase)
- **Set milestone-based payment schedules**, so that clients only release funds when tangible progress is made
- **Establish clear acceptance criteria**, ensuring that each phase is properly validated before proceeding to the next
- **Anticipate and allocate risks** (e.g., coding delays, failed tests, deployment issues) according to the natural points of failure in a development cycle
- **Coordinate timelines and dependencies**, ensuring contractual obligations reflect actual project dynamics

This approach transforms the contract from a static legal document into a ***dynamic management tool*** that promotes accountability, transparency, and trust between parties. For example, including a clause that ties payment to successful User Acceptance Testing ensures that the client only pays when the software performs according to specifications.

Moreover, when disputes arise, a contract grounded in SDLC logic provides **objective reference points** such as concrete deliverables, deadlines, and test results that courts or arbitrators can evaluate more easily.

In short, lawyers who grasp the nuances of SDLC are not just drafting contracts, they are **co-engineering the legal infrastructure** that supports the entire development process. Their legal expertise, combined with technical understanding, becomes a strategic asset for both clients and development teams.

2.3.2 Improved Risk Management: Anticipating Legal and Operational Pitfalls through SDLC Awareness

A deep understanding of the Software Development Lifecycle empowers technology lawyers to act not just as legal drafters, but as strategic risk managers. Each phase of the SDLC, **from planning to maintenance**, is associated with specific vulnerabilities, such as shifting requirements, delays in delivery, integration failures, or inadequate testing. When lawyers grasp these technical dynamics, they are better equipped to **anticipate, allocate, and mitigate risks** contractually.

For instance, during the ***planning phase***, unrealistic timelines or ambiguous scopes often lead to disputes. A lawyer familiar with the SDLC can include **well-defined scope and change control clauses**, requiring mutual consent for any material deviation.

In the ***development and testing phases***, risks include code defects or delays. The contract can preempt these issues with **detailed quality assurance protocols, acceptance testing procedures**, and **clear deadlines with associated remedies**.

In the ***deployment phase***, integration or handover failures may cause significant business disruption. A well-drafted contract would provide for **post-deployment support obligations, escalation procedures**, and **liability limits**.

By embedding these legal safeguards at the right points in the contract, mirroring the SDLC phases, the lawyer effectively builds **predictive legal structures** that minimize the likelihood of conflict and reduce exposure to costly rework, penalties, or litigation.

In contrast, a lawyer who lacks SDLC familiarity may resort to **generic or ill-timed clauses**, failing to address the realities of software development. This often leads to **vague responsibilities, unrealistic expectations**, or **unenforceable provisions**, leaving clients vulnerable to scope creep, delays, or vendor underperformance.

In short, **SDLC fluency transforms a contract into a proactive risk management instrument**, ensuring that legal protection evolves in lockstep with technical progress. For technology lawyers, this insight is not optional, it is foundational to delivering true client value in a digital economy.

2.3.3 Intellectual Property and Confidentiality Protections: Safeguarding Innovation Throughout the SDLC

Software development projects are inherently creative and collaborative endeavors, generating valuable intellectual property (IP) at nearly every phase of the SDLC. From wireframes and architecture documents in the planning stage, to source code in the development phase, and to user interfaces or proprietary algorithms in the final product, each component may raise critical legal questions regarding ownership, licensing, and confidentiality.

Lawyers who understand the SDLC can **anticipate when and how intellectual assets are created**, allowing them to draft precise clauses that delineate IP rights clearly. This includes:

- **Allocating ownership** over deliverables produced at each phase (e.g., custom code, APIs, design mock-ups), distinguishing between *foreground IP* (created during the project) and *background IP* (pre-existing tools or libraries used)
- **Structuring licensing terms** for reusable components, open-source libraries, or third-party modules integrated during development
- **Ensuring the transfer of rights** upon completion or payment, where appropriate, to avoid future disputes regarding usage or commercialization.

Equally important is the protection of **confidential and proprietary information**, which flows between the parties throughout the project. A lawyer with SDLC insight can tailor **confidentiality provisions** to the distinct needs of each phase.

During **planning and prototyping** specific clauses should protect business models, trade secrets, and technical specifications. In the **development phase**, safeguarding access credentials, architectural decisions, and internal documentation is key. Post-deployment, ensuring **non-disclosure of vulnerabilities, back-end structures**, or user data access protocols clauses should be taken into consideration.

Moreover, in an era of increasingly stringent ***data protection regulations*** (e.g. EU GDPR, UK GDPR + DPA 2018, UAE's Federal Decree-Law No. 45 of 2021 PDPL, CCPA/**CPRA** California Privacy Rights Act), embedding confidentiality and data handling clauses aligned with the development process is vital for compliance and risk reduction.

Without a solid grasp of the SDLC, legal professionals risk **drafting incomplete or misaligned IP and confidentiality clauses**, potentially leading to ambiguity over rights, exposure to infringement claims, or breaches of regulatory duties.

In conclusion, lawyers who integrate SDLC knowledge into their contract drafting can **proactively protect intellectual capital**, clarify rights and responsibilities, and reduce legal uncertainty, ultimately enabling innovation while safeguarding the interests of all parties involved.

Table 2.2 IP & Confidentiality Protections Across the SDLC – Legal Risk Matrix

SDLC Phase	*Examples of IP / Sensitive Data*	*Legal Risks*	*Recommended Clauses*
1. Planning	Business logic, technical specs, strategic goals	Misappropriation of trade secrets, unclear IP boundaries	– NDA (Mutual or Unilateral) – Clause defining *background IP*
2. Design	Wireframes, architecture, UX/UI concepts	Disputes over design ownership, lack of clarity on license rights	– IP ownership clause (design assets) – License scope for pre-existing templates
3. Development	Source code, APIs, internal documentation	Unclear code ownership, unauthorized reuse, exposure to open-source risk	– Foreground vs. background IP delineation – Open-source usage policy
4. Testing	Debug logs, user data, performance metrics	Data privacy breaches, accidental disclosure of confidential info	– Data protection clause – Internal access protocols – DPA (Data Processing Addendum)
5. Deployment	Live code, server access credentials, encryption keys	Breach of sensitive infrastructure, cyberattack vulnerabilities	– Confidentiality clause (survives termination) – Access control & liability clause
6. Maintenance	User feedback, patch code, analytics	Misuse of ongoing data, continuous IP generation without proper allocation	– - IP assignment for updates – Ongoing confidentiality & compliance obligations

2.3.4 Clear Expectations and Communication: Structuring Collaboration through SDLC-Informed Contracts

At the core of every successful software development project lies a shared understanding between client and developer. However, in practice, ***misaligned expectations***, ***vague responsibilities***, **and** ***poor communication*** are among the leading causes of project failure and legal disputes. This is where legal professionals with a solid grasp of the SDLC can make a decisive difference.

Understanding the SDLC allows lawyers to **embed communication logic and decision checkpoints directly into the contract**. Instead of relying on broad or generic language, the contract becomes a structured dialogue tool that reflects the actual flow of the project.

For example, during the ***planning phase***, the lawyer can ensure both parties agree on **requirements documentation**, delivery formats, and who holds approval authority. In the ***design and development phases***, the contract can stipulate **weekly or bi-weekly review meetings**, progress reports, and technical review sessions to foster transparency. At the ***testing and deployment stages***, the agreement can define **specific review criteria**, issue tracking systems, and communication escalation paths in case of delays or disagreements.

By integrating these ***touchpoints*** into the contractual architecture, the lawyer transforms the agreement into a **living framework for collaboration**, reducing reliance on assumptions and verbal commitments.

Moreover, clearly defining ***roles and responsibilities***, such as who provides content, who signs off on design, who handles hosting and domain access, ensures that both sides remain accountable and informed throughout the project. These clarity-enhancing clauses reduce friction, increase trust, and mitigate the risk of last-minute conflicts or scope misinterpretations.

Importantly, this structured communication is not only operational but it becomes legally enforceable. If disputes arise, courts and arbitrators can assess **contractual evidence of breakdowns in agreed-upon communication protocols** or failure to meet review deadlines.

Lawyers with a deep understanding of the SDLC are particularly well equipped to draft contracts that articulate not only the substance and timing of obligations, but also the methods of execution and the allocation of responsibilities. Such an approach fosters greater predictability and professionalism in collaboration while ensuring that agreements remain robust against legal challenges, an indispensable asset in the dynamic and high-stakes environment of contemporary technology.

2.3.5 Adaptability to Development Models (Waterfall, Agile, Iterative)

Many technology projects use specific development models within the SDLC, like Waterfall or Agile. Lawyers who understand these models can tailor contracts to fit the chosen methodology. For example, Agile projects require flexible contracts that allow for iterative changes, while Waterfall projects benefit from more structured, phase-based contracts. SDLC knowledge helps lawyers adapt contracts to suit the development model, ensuring that the agreement aligns with the project's workflow.

Technology lawyers are supposed to understand SDLC to ensure contracts are well-structured, align with project phases, and manage the unique risks of software development. This knowledge enables them to protect their clients' interests, anticipate and mitigate potential issues, and ensure smooth collaboration between clients and developers, ultimately contributing to the success of technology projects.

Before offering consulting services in the tech industry, it's crucial for lawyers to understand the SDLC. This knowledge enables lawyers to provide more accurate, relevant, and comprehensive advice on software development projects, ensuring that they address the unique legal challenges associated with each stage of the process.

A lawyer unfamiliar with the SDLC may fail to draft clauses that accurately reflect the stages and needs of a software development project. Each phase of the SDLC, like planning, design, development, testing, deployment, and maintenance, requires specific contractual protections. Without SDLC knowledge, the lawyer may overlook crucial clauses, like clear definitions for deliverables at each stage, testing and acceptance criteria, and maintenance agreements, which could lead to misunderstandings or disputes between parties.

Understanding the SDLC helps a lawyer set clear expectations for each phase, detailing specific deliverables and the scope of work. A lawyer without this knowledge might struggle to define these accurately, leading to "scope creep" where additional features or modifications are requested without extra compensation or time. This can result in increased costs, delayed timelines, and potential friction between developers and clients.

The SDLC often involves creating new intellectual property (IP) and handling sensitive data. A lawyer with technology specific knowledge can include IP rights clauses that specify ownership of the software, code, and documentation at each development phase, as well as confidentiality agreements covering each party's responsibilities during development. A lawyer who lacks this knowledge may not protect these interests adequately, risking IP conflicts or unauthorized data usage.

2.4 Overview of Common SDLC Development Models

2.4.1 Waterfall Model

The Waterfall model is a straightforward approach to software development where each step of the process flows in a single direction, like water falling down a series of steps.

In this model, the development process moves sequentially through phases: first, you plan and gather requirements, then design the software, develop (or code) it, test it, and finally, deploy and maintain it.

Each phase must be completed before moving to the next, so there's no going back to make changes once a phase is done. This makes the Waterfall model best suited for projects with clearly defined requirements and minimal need for changes during development.

Waterfall is a linear, step-by-step process where each phase (planning, designing, developing, testing, deployment) must be completed before moving to the next. It does not revisit previous phases once completed.

2.4.1.1 Risks Associated with the Waterfall Model

Rigidity. Due to its linear nature, Waterfall can be challenging to adapt when requirements change. Once a phase is finished, adjusting can be costly and time-consuming.

Late Testing. Testing occurs near the end of the process, which means that any issues or misunderstandings may not be identified until late stages, potentially resulting in significant rework if problems arise.

2.4.1.2 Benefits of the Waterfall Model

Clear Structure. Each phase has a defined beginning and end, offering a clear structure that makes it easier to track progress throughout the project lifecycle.

Predictability. Since all phases are pre-planned, the timeline and budget can be estimated with greater accuracy, which is particularly advantageous for projects with well-defined requirements.

In summary, the Waterfall model is best for projects with clear, stable requirements and a need for a predictable timeline. Its structured, sequential nature provides a straightforward path from start to finish, making progress easy to track and plan for. However, its rigidity can make adapting to new requirements challenging, so it's most effective in projects where changes are unlikely and the full scope is well-defined from the beginning.

2.4.2 Agile Model

Experts[2] state that the term "agile" refers to a broad set of software development principles. Arising due to dissatisfaction with traditional development methods, these principles form the basis for multiple software development methodologies, including Scrum, Adaptive Software Development ("ASD"), and Extreme Programming ("XP").

While these methods have differences, they all emphasize frequent delivery of working software, collaborating closely with customers, and self-organization of development teams. Unlike traditional "waterfall" development, Agile methods de-emphasize rigid project planning and the creation of comprehensive requirements and design documentation. Agile Software projects, while often more effective than waterfall implementations, can still experience delays, cost overruns, and product quality issues.

The Agile model is a flexible way of developing software where the project is broken down into smaller parts called "iterations" or "sprints." Instead of planning everything in advance, Agile focuses on delivering small pieces of the project quickly and adjusting as you go based on feedback.

In each sprint, a small, working part of the software is created, reviewed, and tested. This allows developers and clients to see progress, give feedback, and make changes before moving forward. Agile is ideal when project requirements are likely to change or evolve, as it allows the team to adapt and improve continuously until the final product meets everyone's needs.

Each sprint includes planning, developing, testing, and reviewing, allowing for quick adjustments based on client feedback. Agile emphasizes continuous improvement and collaboration between the development team and the client, enabling adjustments at any stage.

2.4.2.1 Risks Associated with the Agile Model

Scope Creep. Because Agile encourages flexibility, there's a risk of scope creep, where additional features and ideas continually get added, potentially leading to delays and increased costs.

Less Predictable Timeline. Since Agile projects adapt with each sprint, it's harder to establish a precise timeline and budget at the outset. This can be challenging if clients need a set schedule or fixed budget.

Client Dependence. Agile requires ongoing client involvement and feedback. If a client is not available for regular input, it can disrupt the flow of the project, leading to delays and misaligned deliverables.

2.4.2.2 Benefits of the Agile Model

Adaptability to Change. The iterative approach allows teams to incorporate feedback at every stage, making it ideal when project requirements are likely to evolve. This adaptability ensures that the product remains aligned with client expectations.

Client Involvement and Transparency. With Agile, clients get frequent updates and can provide feedback on each sprint. This close collaboration enhances client satisfaction and allows early corrections, preventing major issues later.

Early and Frequent Deliverables. Agile delivers functional parts of the software at each sprint, providing clients with a usable product early in the project, even if it's not fully complete. This is valuable when clients need to start using or testing the product sooner.

Risk Reduction through Testing. Each sprint includes testing, which identifies and corrects issues early in the process. Continuous testing and feedback improve the quality of the final product, reducing the likelihood of major bugs or flaws at the end.

In summary, Agile Model is best for projects where *requirements may change* and/or *client collaboration is high*. Its flexibility and iterative nature provide frequent, client-reviewed progress but may lead to scope creep or less predictable timelines. Agile excels in environments needing adaptability and rapid development but requires active client engagement to be most effective.

2.4.3 Iterative Model

The Iterative model is a way of developing software by creating the product step-by-step, through repeated cycles, called "iterations." In each iteration, a small part of the software is developed, tested, and improved. With each cycle, the software becomes closer to the final version, gradually adding new features or refining existing ones.

This model allows for adjustments and improvements to be made as feedback is gathered along the way and each iteration can add or adjust features.

Unlike starting from scratch each time, the iterative process builds on the previous version, making it a good choice when requirements aren't fully clear at the beginning and may need adjustments throughout the project.

2.4.3.1 Risks Associated with the Iterative Model

Incomplete Initial Product. Early iterations may not be fully functional or meet all requirements, which can be a concern if the client needs a working product quickly.

Potential for Rework. Since adjustments are made with each iteration, there can be more back-and-forth, which may lead to increased costs if major changes are required later.

2.4.3.2 Benefits of the Iterative Model

Early Testing and Feedback. Issues are identified and corrected throughout the process, leading to a more refined final product.

Flexibility. The iterative model enables incremental planning and development at each stage, allowing teams to adjust and improve as they gain a deeper understanding of the project's requirements. Teams can refine as they learn more about the project's needs.

The Iterative model is best for projects that benefit from gradual improvement and refinement, especially when *requirements are not fully clear from the outset*. Its cycle-based approach allows for repeated enhancements, enabling teams to test, learn, and adjust as the project evolves. While it supports flexibility and ongoing improvements, it may require more rework if significant changes arise later, making it ideal for *projects that need a balance between structure and adaptability*.

2.4.3.3 Differeces between Agile and Iterative Development Models

While often mistakenly used interchangeably, **Agile** and **Iterative** development are distinct methodologies with different philosophical foundations and operational structures.

Iterative Development is a broader software development approach that breaks the project into smaller parts (iterations). Each iteration involves a cycle of planning, designing, building, and testing, with the goal of gradually refining the product through successive versions. Feedback is typically incorporated after each cycle, but the full set of requirements is usually defined at the beginning of the project. Iterative development improves over time but retains a semi-fixed scope, often following a linear path of progressive enhancement.

Agile Development, on the other hand, is a specific **methodology rooted in the Agile Manifesto**, emphasizing **collaboration, flexibility, continuous feedback, and customer involvement**. Agile projects are iterative by nature, but they also embrace **change throughout the development cycle**, often working in short "sprints" that deliver incremental value. Unlike traditional iterative models, Agile encourages reprioritization of the backlog and adaptation of scope based on evolving needs and stakeholder input.

In essence ***all Agile models are iterative***, *but* ***not all iterative models are Agile***. **Iterative development** focuses on refinement through cycles, with less emphasis on flexibility while **Agile** prioritizes **working software, stakeholder collaboration**, and the ability to **pivot rapidly** based on user feedback and changing requirements.

Understanding this distinction is critical for contract drafting and risk allocation in software projects, as the choice of development model influences delivery timelines, cost estimation, scope management, and client expectations.

2.4.3.4 Summary Comparison

Waterfall Model is best for projects with **clear, stable requirements** where changes are unlikely. It's predictable but rigid.

Agile Model is ideal when **requirements are likely to change**, as it adapts continuously and involves clients throughout. However, it's less predictable in terms of timeline and scope.

Iterative Model is useful when a project needs **gradual improvement and refinement**, as it allows incremental progress with adjustments along the way, but it may involve more rework if requirements shift significantly.

Is important to note that each method has strengths and risks, and the best choice depends on the project's specific needs, client involvement, and likelihood of changes in requirements.

Not sure which model is best for your project? Here's an expanded **checklist** with additional questions to help in choosing between Waterfall, Agile, and Iterative Models.

2.4.4 Decision-Making Checklist: Choosing Between Waterfall, Agile, and Iterative Models

Table 2.3 Choosing Between Waterfall, Agile, and Iterative Models

Question	*Waterfall*	*Agile*	*Iterative*
Are the project scope and requirements clearly defined and unlikely to change?	☑ Yes	✖ No	⚠ Partially
Is a structured, linear approach needed, with each phase completed before moving to the next?	☑ Yes	✖ No	⚠ Partially
Is client involvement limited to reviews at specific stages rather than continuous feedback?	☑ Yes	✖ No	⚠ Partially

(*Continued*)

Table 2.3 (Continued)

Question	*Waterfall*	*Agile*	*Iterative*
Is there a strict timeline that benefits from clear deadlines set from the start?	☑ Yes	✗ No	⚠ Medium flexibility
Is a predictable budget essential, with minimal risk of scope changes?	☑ Yes	✗ No	⚠ Medium flexibility
Is the project relatively simple, with well-understood technology and minimal complexity?	☑ Yes	✗ No	⚠ Moderate complexity
Does the team prefer a structured, phase-based approach?	☑ Yes	✗ No	⚠ Moderate structure
Is thorough testing planned only at the end of the development cycle?	☑ Yes	✗ No	⚠ Regular testing with cycles
Is extensive documentation needed upfront to guide the entire development process?	☑ Yes	✗ Minimal	⚠ Flexible documentation
Does the project require a high level of initial planning with a focus on defined objectives?	☑ Yes	✗ No	⚠ Flexible planning
Are all project requirements clear from the outset, minimizing the need for revisions?	☑ Yes	✗ No	⚠ May need revision
Is rapid delivery of functional parts of the project important?	✗ No	☑ Yes	⚠ Limited rapid delivery
Does the project benefit from regular improvements and refinements based on user feedback?	✗ No	☑ Yes	☑ Yes
Does the team have experience in working with adaptable, iterative processes?	✗ No	☑ Yes	☑ Yes

(Continued)

Table 2.3 (Continued)

Question	*Waterfall*	*Agile*	*Iterative*
Are compliance and regulatory requirements high, requiring fixed deliverables?	☑ Yes	⚠ Medium	⚠ Medium
Will the project require regular updates or changes after the initial release?	✖ No	☑ Yes	☑ Yes
Does the client expect to see incremental results at various stages of the project?	✖ No	☑ Yes	☑ Yes
Is there a need to assess and refine the project's progress at regular intervals?	✖ No	☑ Yes	☑ Yes
Will the project benefit from flexible, adaptable project management that allows for changing priorities?	✖ No	☑ Yes	☑ Yes

Legend:

- ☑ Yes: Suitable for this model.
- ✖ No: Not ideal for this model.
- ⚠ Partially: Model can accommodate this requirement with some flexibility.

These additional questions provide a more nuanced perspective, helping clients and developers decide on the best development model by assessing specific needs in project management, client involvement, flexibility, and ongoing support.

2.5 Relationship Between SDLC and Contractual Obligations: Sample Clauses

The SDLC is fundamental to understanding and structuring the contractual obligations that govern software projects. Each phase of the SDLC, like planning, design, development, testing, deployment, and maintenance, carries specific obligations and deliverables that influence how contracts are drafted, interpreted, and enforced.

In the ***planning phase***, for instance, contracts should stipulate detailed requirements to define the project's scope. This phase is where the client must clearly outline their expectations for the software, providing a comprehensive vision of the desired functionality, performance, and any specific operational needs.

This phase establishes the foundation of a software project, defining its scope, objectives, and initial requirements. Contracts often include specific clauses for this phase to ensure that the developer conducts thorough requirement gathering and creates a Scope of Work (SoW) document. The developer, in turn, should conduct an in-depth analysis, to ensure the client's expectations are feasible and accurately translated into technical requirements. If a developer bypasses this phase or fails to conduct a thorough analysis, it may constitute a breach, particularly when scope and deliverables are explicitly defined in the contract. Clear documentation of planning obligations helps clarify each party's responsibilities, reducing ambiguities that could lead to misunderstandings or claims of incomplete work.

Sample contract clause:

> The Developer shall undertake a thorough and comprehensive requirements analysis within a period of [specified timeline], during which the Developer shall engage in consultative sessions with the Client to accurately identify and document the Client's needs, expectations, and functional specifications for the software project.
>
> The Developer shall deliver a Requirements Analysis Report ("the Report") detailing functional, non-functional, and technical specifications, along with any identified constraints or dependencies critical to project execution. This Report is subject to the Client's review and written approval.
>
> Failure by the Developer to perform the requirements analysis as outlined herein, or to deliver the Report within the stipulated timeline, shall constitute a material breach of contract. The Developer acknowledges that this requirements analysis phase is fundamental to the project's success, and any deviation from the terms of this clause shall invoke the remedies stipulated herein, without prejudice to any other rights or remedies available to the Client under this Agreement or applicable law.

The ***design and development phases*** further illustrate the SDLC's impact on contractual terms. Contracts generally specify design deliverables, coding standards, and timelines that align with these stages. A contract might include clauses requiring the developer to produce design prototypes or adhere to best practices in coding. If the developer fails to meet these standards, the client could claim non-compliance or seek remedies, depending on the contractual language. Similarly, adherence to agreed coding practices or architecture standards can influence the final product's quality, with the contract holding the developer accountable for maintaining these standards.

Sample contract clause:

> The Developer shall document and apply consistent coding practices, including modular design, appropriate code documentation, version control, and error handling protocols. The Developer shall ensure that code is structured for readability, reusability, and efficient debugging.

> The Developer must follow secure coding practices that mitigate vulnerabilities, particularly regarding data handling, authentication, and access control, in alignment with the latest security guidelines. All code shall be subject to peer review and automated quality checks, including but not limited to static analysis, to ensure adherence to security and quality standards. Each module or feature developed shall include comprehensive documentation detailing its functionality, dependencies, and integration requirements.
>
> Documentation shall be provided in a format accessible to future developers and sufficiently detailed to enable easy understanding and maintenance.
>
> The Developer agrees to conduct regular code reviews at specified milestones or upon request, involving both the Client and third-party auditors if necessary. Any issues identified in the review shall be promptly addressed in compliance with the agreed standards, with documentation of all resolutions provided to the Client.

Testing and deployment highlight additional contractual obligations closely tied to the SDLC. Contracts often include testing milestones, requiring the developer to conduct unit, integration, and user acceptance tests to ensure the software meets performance and functional requirements. Failure to achieve these milestones, or to document testing results as outlined in the contract, may entitle the client to reject the deliverable or seek penalties. The deployment phase might carry provisions for final acceptance, warranties, and support, ensuring that the software operates as expected post-launch (Go-Live). In cases where deployment obligations are inadequately defined, disputes can arise regarding post-deployment support and defect resolution.

Sample contract clause:

> The Developer is required to conduct comprehensive testing at each specified milestone, including but not limited to unit tests, integration tests, system tests, and User Acceptance Testing (UAT).
>
> Each testing phase shall verify that the software meets the functional, performance, and security requirements set forth in the Scope of Work and other project documentation. Testing results must be documented in a Testing Report and submitted to the Client within [specified timeframe] following each milestone.
>
> The Developer shall compile detailed testing results, including issues identified and steps taken to resolve them, in a Testing Report. This report must be submitted for Client review within [specified number of days] of each testing phase. Failure to provide accurate and complete documentation may result in a delay in acceptance or withholding of milestone payments.

Maintenance, often governed by a Service Level Agreement (SLA) or specific contract clauses, addresses the obligations tied to ongoing software support. The maintenance phase may require the developer to perform corrective, adaptive, or preventive updates, with timelines and performance standards explicitly outlined in the contract. When such maintenance provisions are neglected, clients may claim breach of contract or seek specific performance, especially if contractual terms set clear expectations for post-deployment support.

Each phase of the SDLC, therefore, directly informs contractual obligations, structuring a project's legal framework from inception to completion. A robust understanding of this relationship allows legal professionals and adjudicators to interpret agreements accurately, align deliverables with industry practices, and address disputes by assessing compliance with both the SDLC and the contractual language. This alignment not only ensures that both parties' interests are safeguarded but also provides clarity and consistency in software contract enforcement.

For legal professionals, a deep understanding of these contractual dependencies helps in interpreting and enforcing software agreements, providing a clearer path for dispute resolution when conflicts arise.

As a conclusion to this chapter, the Software Development Lifecycle (SDLC) emerges as more than just a technical process, it is a legal and strategic framework essential to structuring software development contracts. By understanding each phase of the SDLC, legal professionals can draft agreements that anticipate challenges, allocate responsibilities, and foster effective collaboration. This knowledge not only reduces project risks but also adds tangible value to clients by ensuring that the legal structure evolves in step with technical execution. In tech-driven environments, SDLC fluency is no longer optional… it is a core legal competency.

Notes

1 Waste Management Inc. v. SAP America Inc., U.S. District Court for the Southern District of Texas, Case No. 4:08-cv-01248. See case summary at Justia, https://dockets.justia.com/docket/texas/txsdce/4:2008cv01248/572804.
2 Tom Ashley, *When Agile Development Goes Wrong: Common Pitfalls in Agile Software Implementations*, https://www.disputesoft.com/when-agile-development-goes-wrong-common-pitfalls-in-agile-software-implementations/#f02b36e9-f3c1-43b4-9909-130d7bc4cb1f.

Bibliography

Waste Management Inc. v. SAP America Inc., U.S. District Court for the Southern District of Texas, Case No. 4:08-cv-01248. See case summary at Justia, https://dockets.justia.com/docket/texas/txsdce/4:2008cv01248/572804

Supply Chain Digest, *SAP and Waste Management in Legal Battle over $500 Million Failed ERP Project*, archived court filing PDF available at https://www.scdigest.com/assets/reps/Waste_Mngt_SAP_Lawsuit.pdf.

Chris Kanaracus, "SAP, Waste Management Settle Lawsuit," *Computerworld*, May 3, 2010, https://www.computerworld.com/article/1555077/sap-waste-management-settle-lawsuit.html.

Pemeco Consulting, *SAP v. Waste Management: A $500M ERP Implementation Fiasco*, https://pemeco.com/sap-v-waste-management-a-500m-erp-implementation-fiasco/.
Panorama Consulting, *ERP Failures: What We Can Learn from the Waste Management SAP Lawsuit*, https://www.panorama-consulting.com/waste-management-erp-failure/

CHAPTER 3

Planning and Requirement Analysis

The **Planning and Requirement Analysis** phase is a foundational stage in the Software Development Lifecycle (SDLC) that sets the direction for the entire project. The main goal of this phase is to identify and document the project's objectives, scope, and requirements. By doing so, it ensures that all stakeholders share a common understanding of what the software is intended to achieve, minimizing the risk of scope creep, delays, or misunderstandings.

The Planning and Requirement Analysis phase is a collaborative effort in which each party plays a critical role. By holding detailed requirement gathering sessions, defining the project scope, assessing risks, and formalizing a Scope of Work document, this phase ensures that all stakeholders share a common understanding of the project's objectives.

3.1 Importance of Planning in the SDLC

The planning phase is providing a structured foundation on which the entire SDLC is built. In this phase, both the client and developer engage in a collaborative process to define the project's objectives, scope, resources, timelines, and potential risks. Proper planning minimizes uncertainties, aligns expectations, and establishes clear pathways for each subsequent SDLC phase.

One of the primary benefits of a robust planning phase is risk reduction. By thoroughly analysing requirements, identifying technical challenges, and evaluating resource availability early on, teams can mitigate unforeseen issues that might arise later in the development process. For instance, projects with well-defined objectives and comprehensive timelines experience fewer delays and budget overruns, as each stakeholder has a clear understanding of their responsibilities and the project's deliverables.

In the Planning phase of a software project, several foundational elements are established to set the *strategic direction*. This phase defines the initial project vision and the overarching business objectives that the software is expected to support. It also involves identifying the key stakeholders and clearly assigning their roles and responsibilities within the project.

A preliminary outline of the project scope is developed at this stage, clarifying what will be included and what is explicitly excluded. Alongside

DOI: 10.4324/9781003669609-3

scope definition, high-level estimates for the project timeline and budget are discussed to ensure feasibility from both a financial and operational perspective.

Strategic risks are also identified early, allowing the team to anticipate potential barriers and consider mitigation strategies. An important outcome of this phase is the establishment of a governance structure that outlines how decisions will be made and escalated throughout the project lifecycle. During this phase, each stakeholder contributes to shaping the foundation of the project.

Client executives play a crucial role in articulating the business needs, operational constraints, and long-term goals that the software must support. The client/project sponsor confirms the available budget, the project's strategic value, and the internal approval processes required.

The project manager designs the collaboration framework, sets up the communication channels, and establishes a timeline structure that aligns with the project's complexity and internal workflows.

The legal advisor becomes involved early to assess the appropriate contractual structure, to raise preliminary regulatory concerns, and to prepare for the legal formalization of project expectations. Meanwhile, the developer or technical lead evaluates the high-level technical feasibility of the project, identifies integration challenges, and suggests an appropriate technology stack that aligns with both current and anticipated requirements.

In real-world software projects, the Planning and Requirement Gathering phases are closely connected but serve distinct purposes. Understanding their differences is critical to structuring the project correctly and avoiding misalignment, scope creep, or missed objectives.

The Planning phase focuses on **setting the foundation and direction** of the project before technical details are explored. This is where the **project vision**, **business goals**, **high-level scope**, **resource allocation**, and **collaboration model** are defined. The emphasis is on aligning all stakeholders around *why* the project is being built, *what* it should generally achieve, and *how* the teams will work together.

Moreover, effective planning results in a Scope of Work (SoW) document that serves as a definitive guide for the project. The SoW outlines deliverables, milestones, and evaluation criteria that ensure the project remains on track. It clarifies what is within the project's boundaries and what is not, reducing ambiguities and setting realistic client expectations.

In conclusion, the planning phase is a critical step in the SDLC that ensures alignment, reduces risks, and establishes the legal and operational framework for project success. Proper planning not only streamlines the development process but also protects both the client and the developer by setting clear, actionable, and measurable goals from the outset.

3.2 Internal Documentation Produced by the Client in the Planning Phase

In the **planning phase** of a software development project, the client organization, whether a private company, a public institution, or a consortium, plays a decisive role.

Before a development contract is even drafted, the client must articulate its internal vision, objectives, and constraints in a structured way. This is done through a series of **internal planning documents**, which serve both as managerial tools and as legal reference points in later contractual negotiations.

The most common internal documents are:

1. **Business Case**
   - Defines the *strategic rationale* for the project: why the software is needed, what business objectives it supports, and how it aligns with corporate strategy.
   - Includes cost–benefit analysis, risk assessment, and preliminary budget allocation.
   - From a legal perspective, the Business Case is often referenced to demonstrate that the investment decision was formally validated by management.
2. **Project Charter**
   - Officially authorizes the project within the client's organization.
   - Names the project sponsor, project manager, and steering committee.
   - Establishes governance rules (decision-making authority, reporting lines).
   - While primarily managerial, it has legal implications by identifying accountable persons within the client's structure.
3. **Initial Requirements Brief (High-Level Requirements Document)**
   - Summarizes functional needs and desired outcomes without going into detailed specifications.
   - Acts as a bridge between business stakeholders and technical consultants.
   - Later becomes the foundation of the Statement of Work (SoW) or Annexes to the software contract.
4. **Budget and Funding Approval Note**
   - Formal internal approval of financial resources.
   - In regulated industries (e.g., banking, telecom, public sector), this document is required to show compliance with internal control procedures and sometimes with external regulators.

5. **Risk Register (Preliminary Version)**
   - Identifies potential project risks (technical, operational, legal, regulatory).
   - While often high-level, it can highlight issues such as data protection (GDPR compliance), intellectual property concerns, or cybersecurity threats.
6. **Stakeholder Register**
   - A structured list of internal and external stakeholders, their roles, and their interests.
   - Helps clarify who must be consulted, informed, or involved in decision-making.
   - Minimizes legal risks arising from omitted consultations (e.g., ignoring compliance departments).
7. **Preliminary Project Plan / Roadmap**
   - Outlines major milestones, estimated timelines, and dependency on external factors (procurement, integration with legacy systems).
   - Though not legally binding, it sets expectations that later may influence contractual deadlines.

Observation for lawyers and project managers:

While these documents are internal to the client, they are **not legally enforceable against the developer** unless incorporated into the contract. However, they become highly relevant in disputes if they demonstrate the client's initial expectations, risk awareness, or internal approvals. Courts and arbitral tribunals often look at these planning materials to interpret the parties' true intent.

3.3 Importance of Requirement Gathering and In-Depth Analysis

The Requirement Gathering and In-Depth Analysis phase is a crucial part of the Software Development Lifecycle (SDLC) where the project's specific needs and technical requirements are meticulously documented. In this phase, the client and developer engage in detailed discussions to thoroughly understand the functional, non-functional, and technical aspects required for the project. This phase provides a precise and structured foundation, translating the project's initial vision into actionable, measurable specifications that guide the development process.

A key benefit of this phase is achieving clarity and alignment on project requirements. By engaging in a comprehensive analysis, the team ensures that all stakeholders share a unified understanding of the project's objectives and deliverables. Detailed requirements gathering helps uncover potential complexities, dependencies, or constraints, enabling the team to anticipate and address these early, rather than facing costly adjustments or delays later in development. For example, understanding a requirement for real-time data processing might highlight the need for specific technological infrastructure or integration with third-party systems, which would impact project timelines and costs.

This phase also establishes a framework for accountability and expectation management. When requirements are precisely defined, it becomes easier to set clear contractual obligations. Each functional and non-functional requirement is documented, categorized, and assigned specific performance criteria or standards that the final product must meet.

For instance, if an ERP system for a food distributor requires automated inventory tracking with low-stock alerts, this requirement is documented in detail, ensuring that the development team understands exactly how the feature should function and can plan accordingly. This specificity not only guides development but also helps avoid scope creep by setting firm boundaries on what the project *will* and *will not* include.

Another outcome of this phase is the creation of a **Requirement Specification Document**, which serves as a definitive reference for the development team and client throughout the project. This document lists each requirement, categorized by functionality, performance, security, usability, and other criteria, creating a comprehensive blueprint.

The Requirement Specification Document clarifies expectations and offers a concrete basis for verifying that each deliverable aligns with the client's needs. When requirements are well-documented, the development team can create a roadmap that reflects project priorities and aligns resource allocation with critical milestones.

Furthermore, an in-depth analysis of requirements ensures that risks are minimized and managed proactively. By analysing requirements in detail, the team can identify dependencies, challenges, or regulatory considerations, allowing these to be addressed in advance.

For example, if a system must comply with data protection regulations, this requirement is noted early, so the team can design appropriate security features. Identifying such requirements beforehand mitigates the risk of non-compliance and reduces the need for costly changes at later stages.

3.4 Cross-Departmental Involvement in Requirement Gathering

In large organizations the success of the *Requirement Gathering* phase depends not only on documenting current workflows, but also on envisioning how the new software can support future growth and strategic objectives. It is therefore critical that all relevant departments, such as Operations, Finance, Sales, HR, Compliance, Logistics, and IT are actively involved from the earliest stages of this process. Their collective input ensures that the system is not merely a digital replica of existing processes, but a scalable, forward-looking solution that aligns with the company's medium and long-term goals.

Each department brings a unique perspective regarding operational pain points, regulatory obligations, user needs, and untapped opportunities for automation or optimization. For instance, the Finance team may highlight the need for real-time budget tracking and integration with external accounting systems, while the Sales department may anticipate future CRM functionalities or predictive analytics to support expansion into new markets. If these future needs are not articulated and integrated early, the resulting software may require costly post-deployment changes or, worse, become obsolete before it delivers full ROI.

It is essential that departments go beyond merely describing how processes are currently executed. Instead, they should reflect critically on how these processes *should* evolve and what functionalities would support their future needs.

This forward-thinking mindset enables the development team to co-design innovative features that support business transformation, rather than perpetuate legacy inefficiencies. For example, a logistics department planning to adopt AI-driven route optimization or real-time fleet tracking should communicate these ambitions during requirement workshops, even if such features are not yet in use.

In this context, the collaboration between internal stakeholders and the development team becomes a strategic exercise. Developers must not only listen and document but also *challenge assumptions*, *propose modern alternatives*, and *guide* departments toward best practices informed by industry standards and technological advances. This process results in enriched discussions, smarter designs, and a software architecture that anticipates the company's evolution.

Moreover, meticulous *documentation* is essential. All insights, proposed improvements, and desired functionalities must be captured in a structured manner. This includes detailed process flows, user scenarios, data structures, and performance expectations. These documents serve as a reference throughout the SDLC and form the basis of legal agreements that define deliverables, accountability, and change management procedures.

Involving all departments and adopting a visionary approach during the Requirement Gathering phase transforms the development process from a reactive, technical task into a strategic, business-enabling initiative. By aligning software capabilities with future organizational objectives and ensuring robust documentation, the company sets the stage for long-term operational efficiency, competitive advantage, and successful digital transformation.

In conclusion, the Requirement Gathering and In-Depth Analysis phase is an essential step in the SDLC that transforms the project's initial vision into clear, measurable requirements. This phase reduces the risk of misunderstandings, improves alignment among stakeholders, and provides the legal and operational clarity necessary for a successful project.

3.5 Requirement Gathering Checklist by Department

3.5.1 General Preparation — For Management and All Departments

Before any technical workshop, organize a cross-departmental prep session to answer:

- What are the strategic goals of the company for the next 3–5 years?
- What role should the software play in supporting those goals?
- What manual tasks currently cause the most inefficiencies?
- What features are absolutely critical for launch (MVP)?
- Are there pain points in cross-department communication or data sharing?
- Are you trying to reduce operational costs, improve customer service, increase speed, or ensure compliance?
- Do you expect the software to scale (users, branches, countries)?
- What budget, timeline, and internal resources are allocated?

3.5.2 Operations / Supply Chain / Logistics

Purpose: Optimize internal workflows, resource tracking, inventory, and vendor coordination.

Key Questions

- What are your current workflows from request to delivery? (Draw process maps.)
- Which steps are manual? Can they be digitized or automated?
- How is inventory tracked? Do you need real-time stock updates?
- Are perishable items involved? Would IoT integration (e.g., temperature sensors) be useful?
- How do you track equipment, materials, deliveries, or maintenance?
- Do you currently integrate with suppliers or logistics companies? How?
- Are there bottlenecks, e.g., delays in approvals, receiving, or dispatching?

Action Steps

- Document current workflows step-by-step.
- Identify pain points or delays.
- Prioritize automation opportunities.
- Suggest KPI dashboards needed for operations management.

3.5.3 Finance & Accounting

Purpose: Ensure accurate reporting, compliance, cost tracking, and cash flow visibility.

Key Questions

- What accounting system is used (if any)? Does it meet your needs?
- How do you manage:
  - Invoicing (manual, recurring)?
  - Expense approvals?
  - Vendor payments?
  - Bank reconciliation?
- What reports are created monthly/quarterly?
- Do you need support for multiple currencies or tax jurisdictions?
- What audit or compliance standards must be met (IFRS, SOX, VAT reporting)?
- Are there ERP modules or integrations required (e.g., with tax portals)?

Action Steps

- Provide sample reports you generate regularly.
- List all financial workflows (AP, AR, payroll, etc.).
- Identify manual steps that can be automated.
- Define permission levels for financial data access.

3.5.4 Sales & Marketing

Purpose: Improve client tracking, pipeline visibility, and campaign performance.

Key Questions

- How do you track leads, clients, or sales activities?
- Is there a CRM in use? If not, what functionalities would be helpful?
- How do you qualify leads or assign them to reps?

- What reporting do you need (e.g., revenue by region/product)?
- Do you need email/SMS/WhatsApp integration for campaigns?
- Do you segment customers by profile, behavior, or product use?
- Do you track marketing ROI or channel performance?

Action Steps

- Map the customer journey (from lead to conversion to renewal).
- Define sales funnel stages.
- List integrations (e.g., Google Ads, Meta).
- Describe your ideal dashboards and alerts.

3.5.5 IT / Technical Department

Purpose: Ensure technical feasibility, security, performance, and infrastructure alignment.

Key Questions

- What platforms are currently used (cloud/on-premise)?
- Are there systems to integrate with (ERP, CRM, custom apps)?
- What are the preferred programming languages, frameworks, or environments?
- What security protocols and access control mechanisms are needed?
- Do you need SSO (Single Sign-On) or MFA (Multi-Factor Authentication)?
- What are the uptime, performance, and latency expectations?
- What data backup, disaster recovery, and logging systems are in place or needed?

Action Steps

- List all integrations (APIs, webhooks, data exchange formats).
- Define hosting preference (e.g., AWS, Azure, local).
- Outline user access hierarchy and permissions logic.
- Identify constraints (legacy systems, outdated tech).

3.5.6 Legal, Compliance, & Risk Management

Purpose: Ensure regulatory compliance and protect data and IP.

Key Questions

- What local, international, or industry-specific regulations apply (e.g., GDPR, HIPAA, ISO)?
- Are user consents or audit trails needed?
- How is data classified (e.g., public, internal, confidential)?
- Are there license or copyright implications (e.g., client logos, data sets)?
- Are there sector-specific compliance forms or workflows?
- What access controls and data retention policies must be implemented?
- Do you need embedded legal workflows (e.g., approval chains for NDAs)?

Action Steps

- List all compliance requirements.
- Propose features that reduce legal risk (e.g., digital signatures, logs).
- Indicate jurisdictional variations if the business operates across borders.
- Define escalation processes for risk or policy violations.

3.5.7 Human Resources (HR)

Purpose: Automate employee management, ensure legal compliance, and improve experience.

Key Questions

- How are employee records maintained?
- Do you need modules for:
  - Onboarding?
  - Performance reviews?
  - Leave & absence tracking?
  - Payroll?
- What legal obligations do you have (contracts, GDPR, visa documentation)?
- How do employees currently access policies or submit requests?
- What roles or access levels exist in HR systems?
- Would self-service HR portals help reduce manual work?

Action Steps

- Map the employee lifecycle and all HR touchpoints.
- List compliance requirements (contracts, retention periods).
- Suggest employee dashboards or manager views.
- Prioritize automation of repetitive processes (e.g., vacation requests).

3.5.8 Strategy / Executive Management

Purpose: Define vision, ensure alignment, and establish metrics for long-term success.

Key Questions

- What are your top five business goals?
- What decisions are difficult today due to lack of data?
- What reports or real-time indicators would help you manage better?
- Do you need a global or multi-branch view?
- Are you planning expansion (new branches, markets, languages)?
- What future features/products should be considered even if not implemented now?

Action Steps

- Define strategic KPIs.
- Specify cross-department metrics needed.
- Share growth plans that should influence the system design.
- List reports needed for board/investor oversight.

3.5.9 Final Organizational Steps

1. *Internal Workshops*: Schedule dedicated time per department.
2. *Appoint a Central Project Coordinator*: To collect and unify requirements.
3. *Create a Requirements Register*: Grouped by category (functional, non-functional, compliance, integrations).
4. *Prioritize Requirements*:
    - Must-Have
    - Should-Have
    - Nice-to-Have

3.6 Consequences of Limited Involvement During Requirement Gathering

One of the most underestimated risks in the early stages of software development is the *passive or superficial involvement of internal departments* during the Requirement Gathering phase. When employees fail to fully understand the importance of this phase, or are not engaged at all, the consequences can significantly impact the success, usability, and cost-efficiency of the final product.

The main consequences of poor involvement are:

Critical Functionalities Overlooked. If employees only describe what they do today rather than what they actually *need*, essential features may be excluded from the scope. This results in software that fails to meet business objectives, forcing costly changes post-development.

Costly Change Requests and Delays. Requirements that emerge late, after design or development has begun, are significantly more expensive to implement. This often leads to scope creep, budget overruns, and timeline extensions.

User Resistance and Low Adoption. When users are not involved in defining their future tools, they are less likely to embrace them. This can lead to internal resistance, underutilization of the system, or workarounds that compromise data integrity and process control.

Incomplete Legal and Regulatory Compliance. Departments like Finance, HR, or Legal may unintentionally omit compliance-related requirements if no one is tasked with analyzing them thoroughly. This can result in software that fails audits or exposes the organization to penalties.

Fragmented Vision and Contradictory Requirements. Without clear ownership, different stakeholders may present inconsistent or even conflicting requests, causing confusion, rework, and architectural misalignment.

To avoid these issues, it is strongly recommended that **each department assigns a dedicated representative**, referred to as a *Requirements Coordinator*, who will take ownership of their team's contributions during the Planning and Requirement Gathering phase.

The Departmental Coordinator is responsible for leading internal workshops to identify team needs and challenges; translating business processes into structured requirements; maintaining direct communication with the Project Manager and developers; ensuring that departmental needs are accurately documented in official project materials; anticipating future functionality aligned with the department's goals; incorporating legal and compliance-related requirements; and managing feedback and sign-off throughout the documentation and prototyping stages.

The ideal coordinator is a mid to senior-level team member with a deep understanding of internal workflows; the ability to think both operationally and strategically; strong communication skills for liaising with internal and external stakeholders; and solid familiarity with compliance obligations, KPI frameworks, and reporting requirements relevant to their department

3.7 Real Life Steps and Roles

In the Planning and Requirement Analysis phase, each party involved (Client, Project Manager, Developer, and Legal Advisor) engages in a structured, collaborative process to define the project's scope, requirements, and deliverables. This phase involves multiple meetings and documentation efforts, with each party bringing their expertise to ensure a clear understanding of the project objectives and responsibilities. The primary goal is to create a solid foundation for the project, reducing the risk of misunderstandings or conflicts as development progresses.

1. **Initial Kick-Off Meeting**

The Planning phase typically begins with a **kick-off meeting** where all parties (Client representatives, the Project Manager, lead Developer(s), and, if applicable, the Legal Advisor) gather to discuss the project's objectives at a high level. This initial meeting provides a space for each stakeholder to voice their expectations, and it establishes a collaborative framework for the project.

The *Client* presents their overall vision for the software, including business goals and high-level functional requirements. For instance, in the case of developing an ERP solution for a food distributor, the Client would outline core needs, such as real-time inventory tracking, order processing, and warehouse management.

The *Project Manager* facilitates the discussion, ensuring that all relevant topics are covered and taking notes on key points and action items. They set the agenda for the meeting and outline the steps of the Planning phase.

The *Developer* listens to the Client's requirements and asks clarifying questions, especially on technical aspects that may affect feasibility, such as the need for integration with existing systems or data processing requirements.

The *Legal Advisor* identifies any preliminary legal or regulatory issues, such as data protection and intellectual property concerns, and ensures that initial requirements can be incorporated into contract clauses later.

This meeting serves as a starting point, ensuring that everyone has a shared understanding of the project's purpose and that all parties are aligned on the initial objectives.

2. **Requirement Gathering Workshops**

Following the kick-off, the parties typically engage in more detailed **requirement gathering sessions or workshops**. These meetings are often split by functionality, focusing on specific areas of the software to ensure all requirements are covered comprehensively.

During these sessions, the *Client* provides in-depth information about their workflows, specific needs, and expectations for each aspect of the software. For example, in an ERP project for a leasing company, the Client may explain how they currently manage lease agreements, process customer applications, and calculate interest rates for different types of leases.

They may detail specific needs, such as the ability to automate complex interest calculations based on factors like credit score, lease duration, and payment frequency. The Client might also describe their requirements for generating mandatory financial reports, such as balance sheets and profit and loss statements, that must be submitted periodically to regulatory authorities. Additionally, they could highlight the importance of tracking asset depreciation schedules and integrating with tax and compliance systems to ensure accurate, timely reporting.

The *Project Manager* leads the sessions, using structured questions or requirements templates to ensure that all functional and non-functional requirements are captured. They document these requirements in a format that will later serve as the basis for the project's Scope of Work (SoW).

The *Developer* participates in these workshops not only to gather requirements but to gain a practical, in-depth understanding of the Client's business model and operational needs. This hands-on insight allows the Developer to assess the technical feasibility of each requirement, ensuring that proposed solutions align with the Client's goals and business processes. The Developer's team is expected to have qualified personnel who possess both technical expertise and a thorough understanding of the Client's industry.

For instance, if the Client requests real-time tracking of perishable goods in their inventory, the Developer would consider how the ERP system could integrate with IoT sensors to monitor stock conditions. The Developer's role goes beyond simply implementing the request; they would also evaluate the Client's existing workflow and suggest modernized approaches that maximize the ERP system's capabilities.

The Developer's team must therefore have personnel capable of understanding the Client's business dynamics and identifying areas for improvement. This means going beyond technical knowledge, they must understand the business model, client management practices, regulatory obligations, and specific operational challenges. By aligning their technical solutions with the business realities, the Developer's team can make informed suggestions on automation, data management, and reporting features that may further enhance the ERP's effectiveness.

In these workshops, the Developer is encouraged to suggest innovative ways to streamline processes, automate manual tasks, or enhance reporting capabilities, based on the ERP system's potential. For instance, if the Client's business requires extensive regulatory reporting, the Developer might propose adding real-time analytics and automated reporting features to reduce manual work and improve accuracy. By offering such modernization opportunities, the Developer adds value to the project, ensuring the ERP solution is not only tailored to current needs but is also adaptable to future growth and changing requirements.

Thus, the workshops are designed as a collaborative effort where the Client outlines their needs, while the Developer leverages their expertise to propose technical improvements and modernization strategies. This proactive approach, grounded in a deep understanding of the Client's industry and business model, helps to ensure that the ERP system aligns closely with business objectives and provides maximum operational efficiency.

The *Legal Advisor* may participate in some sessions to ensure that requirements align with legal and regulatory needs. For example, they may advise on compliance with food safety regulations, which the ERP may need to support through tracking and reporting functionalities.

These sessions ensure that the Client's business needs are accurately translated into technical specifications, setting clear expectations for the development phase.

3. **Defining the Scope of the Project**

Once the requirements are gathered, the Project Manager, Client, and Developer collaborate to define the **scope and boundaries** of the project. This includes determining which features and functionalities are essential and which may be considered optional or deferred to later phases.

The *Client* identifies core functionalities that are critical for the software's success and those that may be desirable but are not essential. For example, tracking inventory in real-time and managing orders may be non-negotiable, whereas a customer analytics feature might be an optional addition.

The *Project Manager* consolidates this information into the Scope of Work document. They ensure that each requirement is clearly defined, with specific deliverables and milestones that are realistic and achievable within the given timeline.

The *Developer* reviews the scope to ensure technical feasibility and to anticipate any challenges. If a requested feature is technically complex or likely to affect the timeline, the Developer raises these concerns so that adjustments can be made.

The *Legal Advisor* reviews the scope from a contractual standpoint, ensuring that deliverables, timelines, and responsibilities are clearly defined and that any potential risks are addressed through clauses or conditions.

This step is crucial in managing expectations and preventing scope creep, as the final Scope of Work document will serve as a reference for the entire project.

4. **Risk Assessment and Timeline Development**

After defining the project scope, the team engages in a **risk assessment and timeline development** exercise. This is essential for identifying any potential obstacles, setting realistic deadlines, and ensuring that all stakeholders understand the project's timeline.

The *Client* provides insight into any operational constraints that may impact the project timeline, such as peak business periods during which new systems cannot be implemented. For example, a food distributor may have higher demand during holiday seasons, necessitating specific go-live dates.

The *Project Manager* leads the risk assessment, identifying technical, financial, and operational risks. They also outline a realistic timeline, setting specific milestones for each SDLC phase and allocating time for client reviews and approvals.

The *Developer* provides feedback on technical risks, such as potential challenges with integration or data migration, and suggests mitigation strategies. If custom features are complex, they estimate the time required and recommend additional resources if necessary.

The *Legal Advisor* ensures that risk mitigation strategies are reflected in the contract, such as including clauses for penalties on missed deadlines or specifying conditions for extending timelines in case of unforeseen delays. This collaborative assessment helps set a practical timeline and prepares all parties for potential challenges, ensuring that there are mechanisms in place to address delays or issues.

5. **Creating the Scope of Work (SoW) Document**

The planning phase culminates in the creation of the **Scope of Work (SoW)** document, a formalized summary of all project requirements, deliverables, and agreed terms.

The *Client* reviews the SoW document to confirm that it accurately reflects their needs and expectations, including functional requirements, timeline, and milestone deliverables. They provide final approval, which will serve as the basis for all future work.

The *Project Manager* compiles all gathered information into the SoW, ensuring that it is clear, comprehensive, and easily understandable. They verify that each requirement is measurable and has an associated deliverable.

The *Developer* reviews the SoW to confirm that all technical specifications align with the team's capabilities. They also check that integration points, security requirements, and other technical details are accurately captured.

The *Legal Advisor* ensures that the SoW aligns with the contract, adding clauses that link deliverables to payment milestones, setting conditions for approval, and defining remedies for potential breaches. They ensure that both parties' rights and responsibilities are clearly outlined to reduce future disputes.

The finalized SoW becomes the primary reference document throughout the project, ensuring accountability and providing a benchmark for assessing progress and compliance.

3.7.1 Key Deliverables of the Planning and Requirement Analysis Phase

1. **Requirements Document**: A comprehensive document capturing all client needs, technical specifications, and workflows.
2. **Scope of Work (SoW)**: The SoW outlines the project's boundaries, deliverables, and milestones. It may specify, for example, that the ERP will include modules for inventory, logistics, and sales, while excluding customizations unrelated to distribution processes.
3. **Initial Project Timeline**: A timeline identifying milestones for each development phase, including design, coding, testing, and deployment, along with key review points for client feedback.

3.8 Types of Requirements and the Process of Requirement Analysis

Understanding the taxonomy and lifecycle of requirements is essential for both legal clarity and technical feasibility. Requirements form the backbone of all contractual deliverables, and their proper categorization and management can dramatically reduce project risk and ensure alignment between business objectives and system capabilities.

The requirement process is not only a technical effort but a legally meaningful stage in the software development lifecycle, with far-reaching contractual implications. It unfolds through several interconnected activities that, together, define the foundation upon which delivery obligations are built.

The effectiveness of this process depends significantly on the involvement of key actors. Contracts should explicitly identify these stakeholders, define their roles, and establish their obligation to participate throughout the lifecycle of requirement development. The use of requirement management platforms, version control systems, and standardized documentation protocols enables accurate monitoring of changes. Legal frameworks should support these mechanisms through clauses that manage how requirement modifications affect scope, budget, and deadlines.

A further layer of importance is added by the quality assurance and continuous improvement components of the requirement process. Techniques such as internal audits, review cycles, and the use of key performance indicators (KPIs) help ensure that requirements are complete, unambiguous, and aligned with both technical feasibility and business need. These mechanisms justify contractual inclusion of testable acceptance criteria and structured validation checkpoints, which are critical to preventing disputes and ensuring delivery success.

3.8.1 Types of Requirements[1]

Customer Requirements reflect the expectations of the client in terms of mission goals, system constraints, and environmental context. They define high-level needs and often form the foundation of the Statement of Work (SoW). These are typically expressed in terms of measures of effectiveness and suitability of the system.

Functional Requirements describe what the system must do, detailing the inputs, outputs, and behavior. These are actionable and measurable and often relate to specific user workflows or business logic. In contractual terms, they define the core obligations of the developer.

Performance Requirements relate to the degree or quality with which functions are executed. They include response times, data processing speeds, system availability, and throughput. These requirements are critical when drafting service level agreements (SLAs) or acceptance criteria.

Design Requirements prescribe how the system will be built, covering software architecture, maintainability, sustainability, modularity, and upgradeability. These requirements are usually relevant when ownership, licensing, or intellectual property rights are negotiated.

Derived Requirements emerge from high-level business or system goals and are further decomposed during functional analysis. For instance, a high-level requirement for remote accessibility might generate specific design needs for cloud integration, encryption, and session management.

System and Software Requirements distinguish between what is required of the full system (hardware, software, interfaces) and what is expected specifically from the software component. This distinction becomes crucial in contracts involving third-party hardware providers or multi-vendor system integrators.

3.9 Contract Guidelines

In the Planning and Requirement Gathering phase, it is typically impossible for a developer to propose a fully accurate fixed price, as the scope of the project has not yet been precisely defined. From a practical standpoint, this is one of the most legally sensitive and operationally fragile moments in the software development lifecycle. Business stakeholders often have high-level objectives in mind, but lack detailed clarity on the underlying technical processes, interdependencies, and potential constraints. Conversely, developers need to understand the business logic, workflows, and expectations in granular detail before they can commit to specific functionalities, delivery deadlines, or associated costs.

From a contractual perspective, this uncertainty makes it highly risky to adopt a classic fixed-price structure too early. Committing to a fixed total price before completing the requirement analysis can expose both parties to significant legal and financial risks. For the developer, there is a high likelihood of absorbing unanticipated effort due to vague or evolving requirements, leading to scope creep, resource strain, and budget erosion. For the client, there is a risk of dispute if the delivered product fails to match business expectations that were never formally captured or agreed upon. In worst-case scenarios, this disconnect can escalate into contract termination, liability claims, or even litigation.

To mitigate these risks, experienced practitioners use adaptive and phased contracting methods during the early stages of the project. One of the most common approaches is the **Time and Materials (T&M) model**, where the developer is compensated based on actual time spent and costs incurred. This model is particularly well-suited for the Planning and Requirement Gathering phase, where the workload is exploratory, collaborative, and may shift depending on the information uncovered. T&M allows both parties to remain flexible, while still progressing meaningfully. For example, in a real-world ERP implementation for a multi-branch logistics company, the initial Planning phase revealed a previously undocumented need for fleet monitoring, which required integration with third-party IoT systems, something that would have been missed entirely under a rushed fixed-price scope.

Once requirements have been clearly analyzed and documented, typically through workshops, stakeholder interviews, and a formal Requirements Specification Document, both parties are better positioned to reassess the scope and move toward more structured pricing for the design, development, and testing phases.

Another contractual model used in practice is the **Milestone-Based Agreement**, in which the contract is structured in successive phases with defined deliverables, such as completion of the Scope of Work, production of wireframes, or finalization of API requirements. Each milestone may have its own pricing and acceptance criteria. This approach ensures progressive commitment, facilitates mutual control over the project direction, and introduces natural review points that reduce legal exposure. In enterprise settings, this model is often used when multiple vendors or subcontractors are involved, allowing the client to align payment with value delivered at each step.

In certain cases, clients may request a **Fixed Price contract from the outset**, either due to procurement policies or internal budgeting constraints. While such contracts are not inherently problematic, they must include **clear clauses that allow for price renegotiation or scope revision** after the requirement analysis is complete. These may be labelled as "price adjustment clauses," "change request mechanisms," or "conditional scope clauses." Without such protections, a developer could be forced to deliver beyond what was initially estimated, or the client could end up with a rigid deliverable that no longer aligns with their operational reality.

From a legal standpoint, this phase also raises questions about **ownership of deliverables** created during requirement analysis (e.g., flowcharts, mock-ups, SoW drafts); **confidentiality of business information** exchanged during workshops; and **liability boundaries** for advice or recommendations given at a pre-contractual stage. Legal counsel should ensure that these aspects are covered in preliminary agreements, such as a T&M Statement of Work, a Letter of Engagement, or a Pre-Contractual Framework Agreement before deeper collaboration begins.

In summary, the Planning and Requirement Gathering phase is not just a technical or managerial step, it is a legally critical stage where uncertainty must be openly acknowledged and managed through adaptive contracting and clear mutual expectations. The ability to structure this phase with appropriate legal safeguards, pricing models, and decision checkpoints often determines whether a project will evolve into a successful, scalable solution or become a costly and contentious experience for both sides.

3.10 Translating Planning and Requirements into Contractual Clauses

After the Planning phase, lawyers also play a crucial role in translating Planning and Requirements into Contractual Clauses, by crafting key contractual terms to ensure that all project details are clearly defined and legally binding.

This step involves reviewing the Scope of Work, milestones, and specifications gathered during Planning, then embedding them into precise contractual clauses. Lawyers transform these elements into enforceable obligations, covering aspects like deliverables, timelines, quality standards, and change management. By doing so, they help establish a structured framework that aligns the client's expectations with the developer's commitments, laying the legal foundation for a successful project execution.

The **Scope of Work (SoW) clause** establishes the project's objectives, core functionalities, and any inclusions or exclusions, helping to prevent scope creep. Sharing the opinion of other authors,[2] it is critical that the SoW clearly describe all services and deliverables the customer expects to receive. Without that clarity, the customer may not receive what they expect, cost overruns may result, and delivery schedules may be missed. Remarkably, even though SOWs are keys to the success of the project, they are frequently written at the last minute, seldom given the time they deserve to perfect, and generally fail to provide the level of detail necessary to clearly diene the services and deliverables to be provided.

The **Deliverables and Milestones clause** specifies major deliverables and sets deadlines for each milestone, promoting structured progress and accountability for timely delivery.

To ensure that the software meets specific criteria, a **Functional and Technical Specifications clause** outlines the required features and technical standards, providing the development team with clear guidelines.

For quality assurance, the **Quality and Performance Standards clause** defines expectations for performance, security, and usability. The **Timeline and Penalty clause** further reinforces these expectations by setting a project timeline and establishing penalties for missed deadlines, encouraging adherence to the agreed schedule.

To address any changes, a **Change Management clause** outlines how alterations to the project's scope will be handled, including documentation, cost adjustments, and potential impacts on timelines. To ensure deliverables meet the client's needs, an **Acceptance Testing clause** specifies the process for testing, reviewing, and approving the project's outcomes.

The **Intellectual Property and Confidentiality clause** defines ownership rights for the software and includes terms to protect any confidential information exchanged during the project. Lastly, the **Warranties and Support clause** offers a warranty period during which the developer will correct issues at no extra cost and outlines any post-deployment support.

Together, these clauses, rooted in the planning and requirements phase, establish a comprehensive framework for responsibilities, quality standards, and expectations, setting the foundation for a successful project.

3.11 Legal Risks of Poorly Defined Requirements

Poorly defined or undocumented requirements represent one of the most common and costly sources of project failure. Their absence or inadequacy often results in misunderstandings between parties, budget overruns, delivery delays, and even litigation. From a legal standpoint, such gaps create ambiguity in contractual obligations, while from an operational perspective, they hinder effective project execution.

3.11.1 Common Risks and Their Manifestations

Misalignment Between Business Needs and Technical Delivery

When the functional expectations of the client are not translated accurately into technical specifications, the resulting product may meet technical parameters while failing to deliver business value.

Example Case: On October 1, 2013, the U.S. government launched HealthCare.gov, the federal insurance marketplace mandated by the Affordable Care Act. Within hours of launch, the platform experienced severe performance failures. Only **six users succeeded** in enrolling on day one due to bottlenecks and incomplete logic, revealing a fundamental misalignment between stakeholder expectations and technical implementation. Initial estimates[3] (~$94 million) ballooned to nearly **$840 million** due to rework, contractor changes, and emergency remediation work after the launch failed. Federal oversight entities criticized the client, U.S. Health and Human Services, for ignoring repeated warnings, failing to conduct proper planning, and lacking contractual change-control mechanisms. One of the root causes of the failure was the lack of clear business requirements aligned with user experience needs.

Disagreements About Scope or Functionality

Unclear definitions of scope often lead to conflicting interpretations about what is included in the deliverable.

Regulatory Non-Compliance Due to Missed Constraints

Failing to integrate legal or regulatory requirements in the initial documentation can result in costly retrofits or regulatory sanctions.

Uncontrolled Requirement Changes (Scope Creep)

Scope creep occurs when requirements continue to evolve after development has begun, usually without corresponding adjustments in cost or timelines.

3.12 Checklist: Ensuring Comprehensive Requirement Analysis

This checklist helps ensure that the Requirement Analysis phase captures all necessary details.

1. Preliminary Understanding and Scope Definition
   - Has the project scope been clearly defined and documented?
   - Are high-level goals and objectives established?
   - Has the Client's business model and key workflows been fully understood?
   - Are the project boundaries clear, specifying what is in-scope and out-of-scope?
2. Functional Requirements
   - Have all core functionalities been identified and described (e.g., inventory tracking, customer management, reporting)?
   - Are the requirements documented in clear, actionable terms?
   - Have specific scenarios or use cases been created to illustrate each major functionality?
   - Have automation and optimization opportunities been explored and documented?
3. Non-Functional Requirements
   - Has performance been specified (e.g., response times, data processing speed)?
   - Are security requirements detailed, including user access control and data protection?
   - Has usability been considered, ensuring the interface aligns with the Client's needs?
   - Have reliability and uptime expectations been defined?
4. Technical Requirements
   - Are platform specifications, such as the required operating system, database, and cloud infrastructure, documented?
   - Have integration requirements been specified, detailing any systems or tools with which the ERP must connect?
   - Has scalability been discussed, allowing for future growth or added functionalities?
   - Have the data storage and backup needs been addressed?

5. Compliance and Regulatory Needs
   - Are all industry-specific compliance requirements documented?
   - Have any necessary standards or certifications been identified?
   - Are privacy regulations, such as GDPR or industry-specific data handling rules, included?
6. User Roles and Access Control
   - Have all user roles and permissions been identified?
   - Are access control requirements specified for each role?
   - Is there a clear definition of user authorization levels and restrictions?
7. Reporting and Analytics
   - Are reporting requirements detailed, specifying what data and insights are needed?
   - Have analytics features been considered, such as data visualization or KPI tracking?
   - Are regulatory reporting needs identified, including automated report generation where applicable?
8. Client Review and Feedback
   - Has the Client reviewed and approved the initial requirement documentation?
   - Are feedback sessions scheduled to ensure requirements remain aligned with business needs?
   - Is there a clear process for addressing changes or updates to requirements?
9. Documentation and Sign-Off
   - Is the Requirement Specification Document (RSD) comprehensive, covering all functional, non-functional, and technical requirements?
   - Has the Client formally approved the RSD?
   - Are all stakeholders aligned on the project's requirements and expectations?
10. Risk Assessment and Mitigation
    - Are potential risks related to each requirement identified and documented?
    - Have mitigation strategies been proposed for high-risk areas?
    - Has the project timeline been adjusted to address complex or high-risk requirements?

In conclusion, the Planning and Requirement Gathering phase lays the strategic and operational foundation for any successful software project.

It transforms a business vision into a clearly defined roadmap by aligning all stakeholders, identifying risks, and translating complex needs into actionable, contractual obligations. When conducted rigorously and collaboratively across departments and with legal oversight, this phase minimizes misunderstandings, prevents scope creep, and enables the drafting of legally sound, adaptable contracts. In practice, it is not just a preliminary step, but a critical safeguard that determines whether the project delivers real value or fails to meet expectations.

Notes

1 Gunawardhana, L. (2019) Process of Requirement Analysis Link to Software Development. *Journal of Software Engineering and Applications*, **12**, 406–422. doi: 10.4236/jsea.2019.1210025.

2 Overly, M.R. and Karlyn, M.A. (2013) *A Guide to IT Contracting*, CRC Press, p. 57.

3 https://time.com/3060276/obamacare-affordable-care-act-cost.

Bibliography

Gunawardhana, L. (2019) Process of Requirement Analysis Link to Software Development. *Journal of Software Engineering and Applications*, **12**, 406–422. doi: 10.4236/jsea.2019.1210025

Overly, M.R. and Karlyn, M.A. (2013) *A Guide to IT Contracting*, CRC Press, p. 57.

CHAPTER 4

Design Phase

The Design phase in the Software Development Lifecycle (SDLC) is a crucial moment in any software project. It is the stage where the initial ideas, business goals, and user expectations (gathered during the Planning and Requirements phases) are translated into clear, structured plans that guide how the software will actually be built.

In other words, it is the phase where the "*what*" becomes the "*how*." Up to this point, the project has focused on identifying what the software needs to do. Now, the attention shifts to figuring out how to do it, how the system will be organized, what technologies will be used, how the user will interact with it, and how different parts of the software will communicate.

This phase is not just a technical step. It is the architectural foundation of the entire project, much like the blueprint for a building. A well-designed software system reduces the risk of errors, delays, and costly changes during development. It ensures that all parties involved share the same understanding of how the final product will function and what should be delivered.

In this chapter, we will break down the design phase in practical terms: what happens during it, who is involved, what documents are created, and how legal and contractual aspects are integrated into the process.

4.1 Overview of the Design Process in SDLC

The Design phase bridges the gap between the client's vision and the technical requirements, setting the foundation for a coherent and functional product. In this phase, developers create a *blueprint* that outlines how the software will function, what its architecture will be, and how individual components will interact. This blueprint, often referred to as the *Software Architecture*, serves as the structural framework for the entire project, guiding the development team in implementing features that meet the specified requirements.

The design phase also involves creating detailed diagrams and models, which visually represent the software's data flow, component interactions, and overall structure. These models help developers and stakeholders visualize how the system will operate and identify any potential inefficiencies or conflicts before actual development begins.

 DOI: 10.4324/9781003669609-4

During this phase, developers and stakeholders work closely to define the technical specifications, including database design, user interface layouts, and system integrations.

Each component is mapped out to ensure it fits within the project's scope and complies with any regulatory, security, or performance standards set during the planning phase. For example, in designing an ERP system, specific modules for inventory management, customer data, and order processing would be developed with detailed attention to how they communicate and exchange data. This approach ensures that each module not only fulfils its individual function but also operates seamlessly within the larger system.

The design phase typically concludes with a comprehensive *design document*, which includes the software's architecture, interface specifications, and technical guidelines. This document provides a reference for the development team, guiding the coding and implementation phases that follow. By carefully structuring the software's design and addressing potential issues early, this phase reduces the risk of costly changes and enhances the likelihood of delivering a product that aligns with the client's expectations and business needs.

4.2 Real-World Execution of the Design Phase: Roles, Best Practices, and Legal Risks

In real-world software projects, the design phase is a highly collaborative, yet often underestimated stage. It serves as the bridge between abstract requirements and tangible software architecture. When managed properly, it prevents many of the costly problems that emerge during development and post-delivery. Here's how this phase typically unfolds in practice:

4.2.1 Who Does What in Practice

Software Architects / Lead Developers analyze requirements and define the high-level system architecture. They choose architectural patterns and make key decisions on scalability, integration, and resilience.

For instance, imagine a logistics company that wants to develop a platform to manage real-time orders, inventory, and deliveries across multiple warehouses located in different cities. After analysing the requirements, the software architect understands that the system needs to support hundreds of users accessing the platform simultaneously, respond in real time to new orders and stock changes, and integrate with third-party services such as supplier APIs and delivery tracking tools.

Based on these needs, the architect decides to adopt a **microservices architecture**, which allows different parts of the system, such as order management, inventory control, and user authentication, to function independently while still communicating with each other efficiently. This architectural pattern supports scalability, because each service can be deployed and scaled separately depending on usage. Through these decisions, the architect transforms abstract business goals into a structured, scalable, and robust system architecture that will guide the rest of the design and development process.

Senior Developers / Technical Leads break down the architecture into detailed components, defining how each module functions and interacts with others.

Once the high-level architecture is defined, the technical lead or senior developer begins breaking it down into specific components or modules, each with a clearly defined function and responsibility. Continuing with the logistics platform example, the overall system may be divided into modules such as **Order Management, Inventory Tracking, User Authentication**, and **Delivery Scheduling**.

For each of these modules, the developer specifies what it does and how it interacts with the rest of the system. For instance, the **Order Management** module handles the creation, updating, and tracking of customer orders. It must communicate with the **Inventory Tracking** module to check product availability before an order is confirmed. Similarly, once an order is ready for dispatch, it sends the relevant data to the **Delivery Scheduling** module, which assigns the order to a delivery route and notifies the appropriate courier.

Each interaction is carefully mapped out. For example, when a user places an order through the platform, the system triggers a request to the Inventory module to verify stock. If the stock is available, the Order module proceeds to create the order, while also updating the inventory count and initiating a delivery task. These flows are documented using component diagrams or flowcharts, making it clear how data moves between modules and what each module is responsible for.

By decomposing the architecture in this way, the development team creates a blueprint that ensures modularity, simplifies future updates, and helps prevent errors caused by unclear or overlapping responsibilities between system components.

UI/UX Designers translate requirements into wireframes and interactive prototypes, ensuring that the design is user-friendly, accessible, and aligned with the product's goals.

UI/UX designers take the functional requirements and transform them into wireframes and interactive prototypes that show what the user will see and how they will interact with the system. Their goal is to ensure that the application is intuitive, visually appealing, and easy to use, while also supporting the business objectives.

For example, in the logistics platform, one of the key requirements is that warehouse staff must be able to quickly check stock levels and update quantities as shipments arrive. Based on this, the UX designer creates a streamlined interface that allows users to scan product codes and update stock with just a few taps, reducing the number of clicks and visual clutter. Meanwhile, the UI designer develops a clean layout with color-coded alerts for low inventory, ensuring that the most important information is easy to spot even in a fast-paced environment.The designers also produce a clickable prototype, a simplified version of the interface that simulates user interactions. This prototype is used to gather feedback from stakeholders before development begins, helping to refine usability and prevent costly redesigns later. In doing so, UI/UX designers translate technical and business requirements into a visual and interactive form that makes the software functional and user-centric from day one.

Project Managers ensure that timelines, scope, and team coordination are respected. They also facilitate stakeholder alignment and validation checkpoints.

They play a central role in ensuring that the design phase runs smoothly and remains aligned with the project's overall goals. They are responsible for managing timelines, monitoring scope, coordinating communication between team members, and ensuring that everyone stays on track. But more importantly, they act as the link between the technical team and the business stakeholders.

In the case of the logistics platform, the project manager begins by creating a detailed timeline for the design phase, including deadlines for architecture approval, UI/UX prototypes, and documentation. As developers and designers work on their respective deliverables, the project manager organizes regular check-in meetings to track progress, identify blockers, and reassign resources if necessary.

At the same time, The project manager organizes validation sessions with stakeholders, such as presenting a prototype of the user interface to the warehouse operations team or reviewing proposed data flows with the client's IT department. These sessions ensure that the design corresponds to real business requirements and help prevent misalignment that could otherwise result in delays or costly revisions.

By maintaining structure, clarity, and alignment across all parties involved, the project manager keeps the design process efficient, collaborative, and focused on delivering a solution that meets both technical standards and business objectives.

Tech Lawyers / Legal Consultants review deliverables to ensure contractual consistency, verify IP and data protection compliance, and update relevant clauses (e.g., deliverables, milestones, acceptance criteria, change requests).

Tech lawyers or legal consultants play a vital role during the design phase by ensuring that the technical deliverables are consistent with the contractual framework and that all legal and regulatory obligations are met. Although they are not involved in coding or design decisions, their work ensures that what is being designed can be legally enforced, protected, and delivered without exposing the parties to risk.

For example, in the logistics platform project, once the Software Architecture Document and UI/UX prototypes are finalized, the tech lawyer reviews them against the Scope of Work outlined in the contract. If the original contract described a basic inventory module, but the design now includes advanced real-time tracking and integration with external carriers, the lawyer updates the deliverables section to reflect this enhanced functionality and ensures that it is tied to a corresponding payment milestone.

At the same time, the lawyer assesses whether any third-party libraries or APIs introduced in the system design raise intellectual property concerns and verifies that appropriate licensing terms are in place. If the platform is expected to handle personal data—such as customer addresses or delivery preferences—the lawyer checks that the system design includes the necessary security measures and aligns with applicable data protection laws, such as GDPR.

Additionally, if design decisions introduce scope changes, the lawyer updates the change management and acceptance criteria clauses to reflect how these additions will be evaluated, delivered, and billed.

By carefully reviewing and aligning the design deliverables with contractual and legal standards, the tech lawyer ensures that the foundation of the project is not only technically sound but also legally robust.

Clients / Product Owners approve architecture and design proposals, provide feedback on functionality, and validate UI/UX flows.

They play an essential role in the design phase by validating that the proposed solutions align with their business needs, operational goals, and user expectations. While they may not be involved in technical details, their input ensures that the software being designed truly reflects what the organization needs to function efficiently.

In the logistics platform example, after the development team proposes the high-level system architecture, the client reviews it to ensure it supports their operational workflows, such as real-time inventory visibility across warehouses and automated order dispatching. If the architecture includes third-party integrations or automation features, the client confirms whether those align with their internal systems and logistics strategy.

Similarly, when the UI/UX team presents wireframes and interactive prototypes, the client or product owner evaluates them from a business and usability perspective. For example, the warehouse manager might request that stock level alerts be made more prominent on the dashboard or that the order processing screen be optimized for mobile devices, since staff use tablets on the warehouse floor.

Through this feedback and approval process, clients validate that the technical design supports real-world scenarios. Their early involvement prevents costly misalignments later in development and ensures that the final product delivers true business value.

4.2.2 What Should Be Done (Best Practices)

4.2.2.1 Document Everything

Architecture diagrams, data flows, component specs, and interface designs must be formally documented.

A critical best practice during the design phase is to *document* every architectural, technical, and design decision in a formal and structured manner. This includes system architecture diagrams, component specifications, data flow maps, and UI/UX designs. Documentation transforms informal discussions and conceptual ideas into tangible references that align the entire team and reduce the risk of miscommunication.

In a real-world logistics software project, for instance, the software architect creates a set of architecture diagrams that illustrate how the system is divided into modules such as inventory management, order processing, user authentication, and delivery tracking. These diagrams show not only the structure of each component but also how they interact, what data is exchanged, how requests flow, and where potential failure points may exist.

Meanwhile, the development team documents component-level specifications, describing the exact responsibilities of each module. For example, the inventory module's specification might include its input and output data formats, update frequency, interaction protocols with other services, and business rules for low-stock alerts.

The data flow diagrams provide a visual representation of how information moves through the system, from the moment a customer places an order to how it is processed, allocated to a warehouse, and handed off to the delivery team. These diagrams clarify interdependencies and highlight areas where security, synchronization, or scalability must be addressed.

UI/UX designers, on the other hand, contribute wireframes and interactive prototypes, accompanied by annotations that explain user paths, expected behaviors, and accessibility considerations. This ensures that front-end developers implement interfaces that match both the user journey and the system logic behind it.

Without this documentation, misunderstandings can easily arise between developers, clients, testers, and legal teams. Key details may be lost, deliverables may fall short of expectations, and it becomes nearly impossible to enforce the contract in the event of a dispute. Comprehensive, structured documentation is therefore not just a technical necessity, it is a legal safeguard and a foundation for accountability throughout the project.

4.2.2.2 Validate Early

Each deliverable should be reviewed and validated by both technical and business stakeholders before proceeding.

A common cause of failure in software projects is delayed validation, when stakeholders only review deliverables at the end of development, after significant time and resources have already been invested. To prevent this, each major design deliverable should be reviewed and validated as early as possible by both technical stakeholders (e.g., developers, architects, security experts) and business stakeholders (e.g., clients, product owners, operational managers). Early validation ensures that the design remains aligned with both the technical constraints and the business goals, while still allowing time to adjust course if necessary.

For example, in the logistics platform scenario, once the high-level system architecture is drafted, the software architect organizes a technical review session with senior developers to assess feasibility, scalability, and maintainability. In parallel, a meeting is scheduled with the client's operations manager to validate whether the proposed module structure (such as the division between inventory, orders, and deliveries) accurately reflects how their workflows function in the real world.

Similarly, when the UI/UX team produces the first set of wireframes, these are shared in an interactive prototype with key users from the client side, such as warehouse staff or dispatch supervisors. Their feedback might reveal that some interface elements are unintuitive or that key functions are buried under too many clicks. This feedback, gathered early, allows the design to be adjusted before any code is written, avoiding expensive rework later in the process.

Early validation also provides a critical opportunity for legal review. For instance, if a proposed feature involves processing personal data in a way not covered in the original contract or data protection framework, the legal team can raise compliance concerns and recommend contractual updates before development proceeds.

By validating early, teams reduce ambiguity, uncover hidden assumptions, and strengthen the alignment between what is being built and what the client truly needs. It is a proactive approach that protects time, budget, and trust.

4.2.2.3 Align with Contract

Design deliverables must match the Scope of Work and contractual expectations, including functionalities, deadlines, and performance benchmarks.

Every design deliverable produced during this phase must be explicitly aligned with the contractual obligations outlined in the Scope of Work (SoW). This means that all functionalities, deadlines, technical specifications, and performance benchmarks defined in the contract must be reflected, without deviation, in the architectural plans, component designs, data flows, and interface prototypes.

In real-world projects, it's common for technical teams to explore innovative solutions or propose enhancements during the design process. However, if these additions exceed what was originally agreed, they risk generating scope creep, cost overruns, or delivery delays unless they are contractually recognized.

For example, if the contract specifies a logistics platform that must process 5,000 concurrent users and include basic order and delivery modules, but the design team introduces a real-time geolocation dashboard or predictive analytics, these features, however useful, go beyond the contract's scope.

To manage this, the project manager and legal consultant must ensure that each design document is mapped back to the contract. If any proposed design element is not covered, the client must formally approve a change request, and the contract must be updated to reflect the revised deliverables, timelines, or budget. This alignment guarantees that both parties share the same expectations and that no element of the design becomes a future point of dispute.

By consistently aligning the design with contractual expectations, the project maintains legal integrity, controls risks, and ensures that the development phase can proceed based on a mutually agreed and enforceable foundation.

4.2.2.4 Security and Privacy by Design

Ensure compliance with applicable regulations (e.g., GDPR) from the start, especially when handling sensitive or personal data.

Integrating security and privacy considerations from the earliest stages of design is not only a best practice, it is a legal necessity in most jurisdictions.

The principle of *Security and Privacy by Design* means that system architecture, data flows, storage protocols, and user interactions must be developed with built-in mechanisms to protect data confidentiality, integrity, and availability. This is especially critical when the software handles sensitive or personal data, such as user profiles, financial information, health records, or geolocation data.

For example, in the logistics platform scenario, if the system stores delivery addresses, customer contact details, or real-time courier locations, it must comply with regulations such as the General Data Protection Regulation (GDPR). This involves ensuring that personal data is collected only when necessary, stored securely (e.g., using encryption and access control), and processed with clear, documented legal grounds. It also requires that users are informed about how their data is used and have the ability to request deletion or correction.

From a design perspective, this translates into concrete technical decisions: anonymizing certain datasets, implementing role-based access control, encrypting data both in transit and at rest, and logging access to personal information. It also affects the user interface, for example, by requiring explicit user consent or offering privacy settings within the platform.

Failing to embed these principles in the design phase can expose both the client and developer to significant legal risks, including regulatory penalties, reputational damage, and liability for data breaches. By proactively integrating security and privacy into the software architecture and documenting these measures clearly, the development team creates a system that not only functions well but also protects users and complies with legal standards from day one.

4.2.2.5 Maintain Traceability

Link each design decision to a corresponding requirement to avoid functionality gaps.

One of the most overlooked but essential practices in the design phase is maintaining clear traceability between each design decision and its corresponding requirement. Traceability ensures that every element in the design, whether it's a software module, a data flow, or a user interface, directly responds to a documented need identified during the requirements phase. Without this connection, there is a significant risk of functionality gaps, redundant features, or misaligned priorities.

For example, in the logistics platform, the requirement analysis might state that "warehouse managers must receive real-time alerts when stock levels fall below a critical threshold." To maintain traceability, the design team must link this requirement to a specific component in the architecture (perhaps a stock monitoring module) that includes logic for threshold detection, integration with the inventory database, and a user interface element that triggers an alert notification.

This traceability should be documented formally, often in the form of a **Requirements Traceability Matrix (RTM)**, which maps each requirement to its corresponding design elements, test cases, and future code modules. This matrix allows the team to verify, at any point in the project, that all requirements are being addressed, and that nothing has been omitted, misinterpreted, or added without justification.

From a legal perspective, traceability also supports contract enforcement. If the contract is challenged (e.g., the client claims that a promised functionality is missing), traceability documents provide evidence of how each requirement was interpreted, designed, and implemented. It becomes a tool for quality assurance, legal protection, and project transparency.

By maintaining traceability throughout the design phase, the team ensures that the software remains aligned with business needs, reduces the risk of rework, and provides a clear audit trail that supports accountability and trust.

4.2.3 What Should Be Avoided

4.2.3.1 Skipping Review Rounds

Approving architecture without sufficient review leads to misalignment and downstream rework.

One of the most frequent and costly mistakes in the design phase is rushing to approve the system architecture or component specifications without conducting thorough review rounds. Design documents are often seen as "internal" deliverables that don't require the same level of scrutiny as client-facing outputs. This mindset can lead to serious consequences: unvalidated assumptions, overlooked constraints, and architectural flaws that only surface later, when correcting them becomes exponentially more expensive and time-consuming.

For instance, imagine a logistics platform where the architecture is approved after a single internal meeting, without involving operations staff or legal advisors. Weeks into development, the team discovers that the inventory module, as designed, does not support multiple warehouse locations, a core business need. This misalignment was not caught earlier because the architecture was never reviewed by the operational side of the client's team. As a result, the development team must refactor major parts of the system, delay delivery, and potentially renegotiate milestones and budget.

To prevent this, structured review rounds should be built into the design schedule and involve both technical experts and business stakeholders. These reviews should cover not just whether the design "works" technically, but whether it meets regulatory obligations, aligns with business workflows, and accurately reflects what was agreed in the contract. Ideally, each round results in documented feedback, tracked changes, and formal sign-offs from key roles, including project managers, client representatives, and legal consultants.

Skipping review rounds doesn't just create technical risk, it undermines transparency, stakeholder trust, and legal defensibility. In complex projects, oversight at this stage can cascade into disputes, rework, and failure to meet contractual obligations. A well-reviewed design, on the other hand, sets the stage for predictable execution and durable client satisfaction.

4.2.3.2 Ambiguity in Deliverables

Vague or undocumented decisions open the door to disputes over what was "promised" or "expected."

Ambiguity in design deliverables is a silent but dangerous risk in any software development project. When decisions are vague, undocumented, or based on verbal understandings rather than written specifications, the result is often confusion over what was actually promised versus what is ultimately delivered. This lack of clarity can lead to serious disagreements between the client and the developer, especially when the functionality, performance, or quality of the final product comes under scrutiny.

For example, suppose a logistics platform project includes a verbal agreement that the system will support "real-time inventory updates." The phrase sounds clear but is never defined in technical terms or documented in the design specification. The development team interprets it to mean updates every five minutes, using batch synchronization, while the client expects instant, event-driven updates reflected in the user interface within seconds. Once the software is delivered, the client is dissatisfied, claiming that the promised functionality is missing. The developer, on the other hand, insists that they built exactly what was discussed. Without clear documentation, neither party can conclusively prove their position, and the disagreement may escalate into a formal dispute.

To avoid this situation, every design deliverable must be explicitly defined, documented, and linked to a measurable requirement or standard. If a feature is discussed during a meeting, it must be captured in the design documentation, described with enough detail to remove ambiguity, and validated by both technical and legal stakeholders.

Terms like "fast," "user-friendly," or "real-time" must be translated into specific, testable criteria. For example, instead of stating that the system should be "fast," the contract should specify: "The system shall process and display search results within 2 seconds in 95% of cases under normal server load conditions."

Similarly, instead of describing the interface as "user-friendly," a precise requirement would be: "The application shall allow a new user with no prior training to complete the registration and profile setup process within 5 minutes."

Finally, the vague term "real-time" can be translated into a concrete obligation: "The system shall update the dashboard with new transaction data within 1 second of entry into the database." Such formulations provide objective benchmarks that can be tested, audited, and enforced, thereby reducing ambiguity and potential disputes.

Ambiguity not only threatens project outcomes; it undermines contractual enforceability. Courts and arbitrators rely on written records to interpret obligations, and undocumented intentions rarely hold legal weight. Eliminating vagueness in the design phase is therefore both a technical discipline and a legal safeguard that protects relationships, timelines, and the integrity of the final product.

4.2.3.3 Disregarding Legal Input

Leaving legal analysis until the end of the design phase often results in non-compliance or unclear IP ownership.

One of the most critical yet frequently neglected errors in the design phase is *postponing legal involvement* until after key architectural and functional decisions have already been made. While design is often perceived as a purely technical or creative process, it has significant legal implications, from intellectual property (IP) allocation and licensing risks to regulatory compliance and contractual enforceability. Ignoring legal input at this stage creates blind spots that can result in costly rework, liability exposure, or even the invalidation of the entire software agreement.

Consider a scenario in which a software development team designs a logistics platform that integrates several third-party libraries to speed up development. These libraries are selected for their performance benefits, but no legal review is conducted during the design phase. Only later does the legal team discover that one of the libraries is licensed under the GNU General Public License (GPL), which imposes obligations that conflict with the client's intention to retain proprietary rights over the entire platform. At this point, replacing the library would require substantial redesign, additional costs, and delays, not to mention the legal risk already introduced.

Similarly, if the system is designed to process personal data across multiple jurisdictions but legal counsel is not involved early, the architecture may violate data protection regulations like GDPR or fail to include necessary safeguards, such as data minimization, encryption, or user consent mechanisms. Fixing these omissions retroactively is significantly more difficult, as it often requires reengineering the system's core logic or integrations.

Legal counsel should be integrated into the design process, not as an afterthought, but as an active participant. Their input is crucial when defining IP rights, structuring data flows involving sensitive information, clarifying confidentiality obligations, and ensuring that design deliverables align with the terms of the contract.

Disregarding legal input does not just introduce technical risk, it undermines the legal viability of the entire project. By involving lawyers early and consistently during the design phase, teams ensure that the software is not only functional and scalable, but also compliant, enforceable, and secure from a contractual and regulatory standpoint.

4.2.3.4 Overloading a Single Role

Assigning both architectural and legal responsibilities to a single actor creates gaps and conflicts of interest.

In complex software projects, specialization is key. When distinct responsibilities, such as system architecture and legal oversight, are assigned to a single individual or role, the project becomes vulnerable to oversight gaps, cognitive overload, and even conflicts of interest. While efficiency or budget constraints may tempt teams to consolidate roles, doing so in the design phase often leads to decisions that are either technically sound but legally flawed, or contractually correct but misaligned with the system's actual capabilities.

Take, for example, a situation in which a senior developer is also tasked with handling the legal aspects of the design, like reviewing intellectual property clauses, checking for licensing conflicts, drafting acceptance criteria, and ensuring GDPR compliance.

While the developer may be highly competent from a technical standpoint, they are unlikely to have the legal training needed to identify complex contractual nuances or regulatory implications. As a result, design choices may expose the client to hidden legal risks, or the contract may describe functionalities that the system's architecture does not actually support.

This blending of roles also compromises objectivity. The person making design decisions may avoid flagging legal risks that reflect poorly on those same decisions. For instance, an architect who chooses to use an open-source component might downplay its licensing implications if they are also responsible for legal review (consciously or not). The absence of a second pair of eyes creates blind spots that can later escalate into contractual disputes, non-compliance issues, or liability claims.

A best-practice approach is to ensure a clear separation of duties: architects focus on the structure, performance, and integration of the system, while legal experts assess the contractual and regulatory consequences of those choices. These roles must collaborate closely, but remain distinct, so that each brings a focused, specialized perspective to the design table.

Overloading a single role with both legal and architectural responsibility undermines the integrity of the design phase. By distributing responsibilities appropriately, teams gain both technical precision and legal resilience, ensuring that the software is not only well-built, but also contractually and ethically defensible.

4.2.4 Legal and Contractual Risks of Poor Design Phase Execution

4.2.4.1 Scope Creep and Disputes

Without clear design documentation, clients may claim that features were promised implicitly. This leads to disputes over additional costs or delays.

One of the most prevalent legal risks associated with a deficient design phase is scope creep, understood as the progressive and undocumented expansion of project requirements beyond the scope originally agreed by the parties. Scope creep typically arises when new features, functions, or modifications are introduced without formal approval or contractual amendment, thereby increasing costs, delaying timelines, and exposing both parties to disputes regarding responsibility and payment.

This typically arises when the design documentation lacks clarity, precision, or formal validation, leaving room for misinterpretation. Without a solid, traceable link between what was contractually promised and what was technically designed, clients may later assert that certain features or functionalities were "implicitly understood" or "discussed informally," even if they were never part of the official scope.

Consider a real-world scenario involving the development of a SaaS platform for a retail chain. The client initially contracted for a solution that would allow store managers to generate sales reports and monitor inventory. However, the design documentation failed to explicitly state the reporting limitations, such as the fact that reports would only cover in-store data, not online sales. The client, assuming that "sales reports" included omnichannel data, requested additional integrations mid-development to pull e-commerce figures from a separate system.

Because the deliverables were vaguely described, and because there was no signed design document clarifying this scope boundary, the client insisted that the online sales dashboard had been part of the original agreement. The developer, on the other hand, viewed this as a new requirement requiring additional budget and time. With no objective reference point, the disagreement escalated, delaying delivery, freezing milestone payments, and requiring legal mediation to resolve the dispute.

This type of conflict can be avoided by ensuring that all features and functionalities are clearly documented during the design phase and explicitly tied to the contractual Scope of Work (SoW). Detailed architecture diagrams, functional specifications, and acceptance criteria should form part of the contract annexes or be referenced in the main agreement. Any feature not documented and approved should be treated as a potential change request, subject to new terms.

Scope creep is not just a project management issue; it is a legal risk. By documenting the design comprehensively and ensuring mutual understanding of what is *in scope* and *out of scope*, both parties are protected from disputes that can damage relationships, delay delivery, and result in financial loss.

4.2.4.2 Unenforceable Deliverables

If the design is not incorporated into the contract, the client may struggle to hold the developer accountable for missing or defective features.

Even the most carefully crafted software designs are legally meaningless if they are not properly incorporated into the contract. When design documents, such as architecture diagrams, data flow charts, or UI/UX prototypes, remain informal or external to the contractual framework, the client loses a critical enforcement mechanism. In the absence of binding language, there is no legal obligation for the developer to deliver exactly what was designed, which can lead to significant disputes over missing, partial, or defective functionalities.

Take for example a case involving a fintech startup that contracted a software firm to develop a mobile banking application. During the design phase, the UI/UX team created detailed wireframes for multi-language support and biometric login features. These features were reviewed and approved internally but were never attached to the contract or referenced in the Scope of Work. The developer delivered a functional app, but without biometric login or translation options. When the client raised objections, the developer pointed to the contract (which made no mention of these features) and argued that the deliverables had been fulfilled as specified.

Despite the existence of design documents, the client had no legal basis to claim breach of contract, as the unincorporated deliverables were considered non-binding. The client faced the difficult choice of either paying additional costs to include the missing features or pursuing a legal dispute with limited chances of success.

This situation highlights a core legal principle: **only what is expressly included in the contract can be enforced**. To avoid such outcomes, the final design documents must be either annexed to the contract or explicitly referenced in key clauses, including those relating to scope, milestones, payment conditions, and acceptance criteria. Where appropriate, the contract should also include a sign-off procedure confirming mutual approval of the design before development begins.

Unenforceable deliverables create a dangerous grey zone where expectations are high but legal obligations are unclear. Incorporating the design into the contract transforms it from an internal planning tool into a legally binding standard, one that protects the client's interests and holds the developer accountable throughout the build process.

4.2.4.3 Intellectual Property Conflicts

Failure to clearly define ownership of architectural decisions or UI designs can result in IP disputes, especially when third-party libraries or reused code are involved.

Intellectual property (IP) issues often emerge during the design phase, particularly when ownership of architectural decisions, technical components, or UI/UX designs is not clearly defined. If the contract fails to specify who owns what, or under what conditions reused code, third-party libraries, or design templates are incorporated, both parties risk becoming entangled in costly disputes over rights, licenses, and usage restrictions. A common scenario arises when developers use pre-existing code or open-source libraries to accelerate delivery, but do not disclose this during the design phase.

For example, in a project involving the development of a customized e-commerce platform, the developer relied on an open-source front-end framework and integrated a proprietary third-party payment module licensed under restrictive terms. The client, assuming full ownership of the software, later attempted to reuse the front-end and payment code in a new platform targeting a different market. Upon doing so, the client received a legal notice from the payment module provider, alleging unauthorized redistribution of licensed code. At the same time, the developer claimed they retained partial ownership over the architecture and front-end components based on their internal development practices.

The root of the conflict lay in the fact that IP rights over the system architecture and UI design had never been contractually clarified, nor had the integration of third-party software been disclosed or addressed. The contract simply stated that the "software solution" would be delivered, without distinguishing between custom code, reused components, or licensed tools.

To prevent such disputes, the contract must clearly state:

- Who owns the custom-developed elements of the design (architecture, components, diagrams, interfaces)
- What third-party components are being used, under what licenses, and whether the client has the right to reuse, modify, or distribute them
- Whether the developer retains any rights over generic frameworks, proprietary methods, or modular templates used across multiple projects

Without this clarity, the client may find themselves unable to freely use the software they believe they own, while the developer may risk legal liability for unauthorized use of protected libraries or unlicensed design assets.

IP conflicts are not theoretical risks, they are real, recurring problems that often begin with ambiguous ownership in the design phase. By addressing these issues early, through both design documentation and precise contractual language, parties can secure their rights, reduce exposure, and avoid disputes that could undermine the entire value of the software being developed.

4.2.4.4 Regulatory Non-Compliance

Ignoring data flow implications can lead to violations of data protection laws (e.g., GDPR, HIPAA), exposing both parties to significant fines.

A critical yet often underestimated legal risk during the design phase is regulatory non-compliance, particularly in relation to data protection laws such as the General Data Protection Regulation (GDPR) in the EU or the Health Insurance Portability and Accountability Act (HIPAA) in the U.S. When system designers overlook how personal or sensitive data moves through the platform, is stored, accessed, or shared, they can unintentionally create software that violates legal standards, placing both the client and developer at risk of fines, lawsuits, and reputational harm.

Consider a real-world example involving a health-tech startup that commissioned a platform for managing patient appointments, prescriptions, and medical records. During the design phase, the team focused on functionality and user experience but failed to map the flow of sensitive health data through the system. Data was stored unencrypted on local servers, audit trails were missing, and there was no consent mechanism embedded in the interface for processing patient information. The design documents made no mention of data retention periods, access control policies, or secure data transmission protocols.

After deployment, a routine audit by a regulatory body uncovered multiple violations of HIPAA rules. The platform was found non-compliant, and both the startup and the software vendor were subjected to investigations and financial penalties. The root cause was not malicious intent or poor development, but a design phase that had failed to account for regulatory obligations from the outset.

To avoid this, compliance must be embedded at the architectural level. **"Privacy by design"** and "**security by default**" are not just best practices, but legal requirements in many jurisdictions. During the design phase, the team should conduct a Data Protection Impact Assessment (DPIA); define how data flows between components; and ensure that encryption, access controls, consent tracking, and auditability are built into the technical design. The legal team must review these measures and ensure they are also reflected in the contract, especially in clauses relating to liability, breach notification, and data controller/processor responsibilities.

Regulatory non-compliance is not merely a technical flaw, it is a legal failure that can have severe financial and reputational consequences. By addressing data protection from the design phase onward, teams ensure not only functional reliability but also legal defensibility, user trust, and long-term platform sustainability.

4.2.4.5 Misalignment with Acceptance Criteria

Vague or undocumented acceptance standards based on poorly defined design documents can delay delivery or block payment milestones.

A critical yet often underestimated legal risk in the design phase is misalignment with acceptance criteria. This occurs when the standards used to determine whether the delivered software meets contractual expectations are either ambiguous, incomplete, or missing altogether. Without clear acceptance metrics, disagreements easily arise between client and developer: the client may argue that the product fails to satisfy requirements, while the developer may insist that delivery obligations have been met.

Consider a real-world example involving a financial services company that commissioned a customer relationship management (CRM) platform. The design documents contained general references to "user-friendly dashboards" and "fast reporting," but no measurable acceptance criteria. After several months of development, the vendor delivered a system that functioned technically but required users to navigate multiple layers of menus to access basic reports. The client rejected the delivery, claiming it was not "user-friendly," while the developer insisted it was functional and complete. With no objective acceptance criteria to resolve the dispute, the project stalled, triggering delayed payments, arbitration proceedings, and reputational damage for both sides.

To avoid such risks, acceptance criteria must be drafted with precision during the design phase and incorporated into the contract. Criteria should be measurable, testable, and directly linked to the requirements specification. For example, instead of stating that the system should be "fast," the acceptance standard should specify that "95% of reports must generate in under three seconds under normal server load." Likewise, "user-friendly" can be translated into quantifiable terms such as "a new user with no prior training must be able to complete the onboarding process in under five minutes."

The legal team plays a crucial role by ensuring that acceptance procedures are clearly defined, including who conducts the testing, what documentation is required, how defects are classified, and within what timeframe issues must be remedied. These provisions should be mirrored in contractual clauses governing delivery, payment milestones, and dispute resolution mechanisms.

Misalignment with acceptance criteria is not simply a technical inconvenience; it is a contractual vulnerability. By embedding precise, testable acceptance standards into both design documentation and the contract, parties ensure not only smoother project delivery but also legal certainty, enforceability, and reduced risk of costly disputes.

4.2.5 Evidence in Litigation

In litigation or contractual disputes, the following evidence can be critical to proving whether the Design Phase was executed in compliance with the contract and industry standards:

Version-Controlled Design Documents: Repository-stored and time-stamped architecture diagrams, component specifications, data flow diagrams, and UI/UX prototypes showing when and by whom they were created or updated.

Requirements Traceability Matrix (RTM): A documented mapping between contractual requirements and design elements, demonstrating that each requirement was addressed in the design.

Change Request Records: Signed change orders or amendments documenting any modifications to the design scope, along with cost and timeline impacts.

Stakeholder Review Minutes: Meeting records, sign-off sheets, or email confirmations showing that design deliverables were reviewed and approved by both technical and business stakeholders.

Compliance and Security Design Reports: Documentation of privacy-by-design measures, security architecture, and regulatory compliance assessments (e.g., GDPR Data Protection Impact Assessment).

IP Disclosure Logs: Records of all third-party libraries, APIs, or templates included in the design, with corresponding license terms and ownership confirmations.

Annotated Prototypes and Mockups: Prototypes with embedded annotations showing intended functionality, navigation flows, and accessibility considerations.

These evidentiary materials strengthen contractual enforcement, help resolve disputes faster, and serve as proof that the design phase met both technical and legal obligations.

4.3 Software Architecture and Design Documentation

Software Architecture and Design Documentation is a structured, collaborative process where the development team, often led by software architects and senior developers, creates a comprehensive blueprint that guides the entire project.

This phase translates high-level requirements into detailed plans and specifications that ensure all components of the software are well-integrated, scalable, and aligned with the client's goals. In real-world settings, this phase involves several critical steps, roles, and checkpoints to ensure accuracy and quality. Here's a closer look at how it works:

4.3.1 Defining High-Level Architecture

The process begins with defining the high-level architecture, often led by the **Software Architect** or **Lead Developer**. At this stage, the architect outlines the software's overarching structure, deciding on architectural patterns such as microservices, layered architecture, or event-driven design based on the system's requirements and future scalability needs.

The architect's goal is to create a framework that supports the software's core functionalities, performance expectations, and integration needs. For instance, if the system must handle a high volume of transactions in real-time, the architect may choose a distributed, scalable architecture.

Timing: This step typically occurs right after the requirement analysis phase and before any detailed design work begins.

4.3.2 Selecting Technology Stack and Tools

Once the high-level architecture is established, the architect, in consultation with senior developers and sometimes with client input, selects the **technology stack**. This includes choosing programming languages, databases, frameworks, and tools that best align with the project's requirements.

Decisions at this stage impact development speed, maintenance, and scalability. For example, choosing a cloud-based database might be ideal if the software requires remote access and high availability.

Timing: This phase is parallel with defining the high-level architecture, as technology choices often influence architectural decisions.

4.3.3 Creating Detailed Component Designs

Following the architectural setup, **Senior Developers** or **Technical Leads** break down the high-level architecture into individual components or modules. Each component, such as a user management system, data processing module, or external API integration, is mapped out in detail.

This step involves specifying how each component will function, interact with others, and fit within the overall system. For example, if the software includes a payment processing feature, the component design will detail how payment data is handled securely and integrates with other parts of the application.

Timing: This step follows the technology selection and precedes interface design, as component functionality influences user interface requirements.

4.3.4 Designing Data Flow and Interaction Diagrams

With the components defined, the **Development Team** collaborates to create **data flow diagrams** and **interaction diagrams**. Data flow diagrams map how data will move through the system, while interaction diagrams illustrate how different components communicate.

This visual representation helps to clarify how the full system will function, preventing potential integration issues and ensuring that each component is well-connected.

For example, a data flow diagram for an inventory management system might show how stock data moves from purchase orders to warehouse updates in real-time.

Timing: This occurs after component designs are in place, ensuring that interactions are planned once each module's role is clear.

4.3.5 User Interface (UI) and User Experience (UX) Design

If the project includes a front-end component, **UI/UX Designers** work on designing the user interface. The UI/UX team collaborates with developers to create wireframes and prototypes that map out the user journey, ensuring the software is intuitive and meets user needs.

This step is especially important in applications where user interaction is critical, such as e-commerce platforms or CRM systems. For example, designers will create a mock-up of the interface for a dashboard, allowing users to navigate and access key functions seamlessly.

Timing: This step happens after component and interaction designs, as the UI needs to reflect the underlying structure and data flows.

4.3.6 Documenting the Design

Once designs are complete, **Technical Writers** or **Senior Developers** compile all design-related documents into a comprehensive **Design Document**. This document includes architectural decisions, component designs, data flow and interaction diagrams, and UI/UX designs.

This document serves as a reference for the entire development team, providing clarity on the intended structure and behaviour of the software. It is also shared with stakeholders for approval, ensuring alignment on the planned design.

Timing: This is the final step of the design phase, completed before development begins to serve as a clear blueprint for implementation.

4.3.7 Review and Approval Process

Finally, the Design Document goes through a review process involving **stakeholders**, **project managers**, and **lead developers**. This review ensures that the design aligns with client expectations, technical requirements, and any regulatory constraints.

Once approved, the Design Document is signed off, marking the official end of the design phase and signalling that development can proceed.

Timing: This step occurs immediately after documentation, acting as a final quality check before the project moves into development.

4.4 Checklist: Key Elements of a Design Document

This checklist outlines the essential components of a comprehensive design document, ensuring that all necessary details are covered and ready for the development phase.

1. **Software Architecture Overview**
    - Is the chosen architectural pattern (e.g., microservices, layered architecture) clearly defined?
    - Are the main components and their relationships documented?

- Does the document explain why this architecture was selected for this project's requirements?

2. **Technology Stack**
    - Are all chosen programming languages, frameworks, and tools listed?
    - Is there an explanation of why each technology was selected?
    - Are platform and compatibility requirements specified?
3. **Component Design Specifications**
    - Are all major components or modules defined with clear purposes and functions?
    - Are dependencies and interactions between components detailed?
    - Does each component have documented constraints, such as performance or storage limitations?
4. **Data Flow Diagrams (DFD)**
    - Is there a high-level DFD showing how data flows through the entire system?
    - Are component-level DFDs included for critical data processes?
    - Are sources, processing points, and data destinations clearly marked?
5. **Interaction Diagrams**
    - Are sequence diagrams or communication diagrams included to illustrate component interactions?
    - Do the diagrams cover key workflows or processes?
    - Is it clear how components will interact during system operation?
6. **User Interface (UI) and User Experience (UX) Design**
    - Are wireframes or mockups for key screens included?
    - Does the document describe the user journey and navigation flow?
    - Are any specific usability or accessibility standards addressed?
7. **Database Design and Data Storage Requirements**
    - Is the database schema or structure outlined, with tables, fields, and relationships?
    - Are data storage requirements, including expected data volume and scalability, documented?
    - Are any data protection or backup protocols specified?
8. **Security and Compliance Requirements**
    - Are security measures for data handling, access control, and user authentication outlined?
    - Does the document address compliance requirements (e.g., GDPR, HIPAA) as applicable?

- Are specific encryption or data protection methods detailed?

9. **Performance Standards and Non-Functional Requirements**
   - Are performance benchmarks, such as response times and processing speeds, specified?
   - Are reliability and availability requirements documented?
   - Are system scalability and future growth considerations included?
10. **Integration Points and External Dependencies**
    - Are all third-party integrations or APIs that the system will connect with listed?
    - Is there a description of each integration's role and function within the system?
    - Are any specific compatibility or data format requirements detailed?
11. **Testing and Quality Assurance Plan**
    - Is there a preliminary plan for how each component will be tested?
    - Are acceptance criteria for testing phases clearly defined?
    - Are guidelines for quality assurance and bug tracking outlined?
12. **Documentation and Maintenance Plan**
    - Is a plan for ongoing documentation during development specified?
    - Are instructions for system maintenance and support included?
    - Are any guidelines for future updates or enhancements addressed?
13. **Approval and Sign-Off Section**
    - Is there a section for stakeholders to review and approve the design document?
    - Does the sign-off page include spaces for relevant parties to sign and date?
    - Are any conditions for approval or revisions before development begins specified?

4.5 Key Deliverables

In the design phase of the Software Development Lifecycle (SDLC), several key documents are created to provide a detailed blueprint for the development process. These documents ensure that all aspects of the system's architecture, functionality, and user experience are well-defined and aligned with the project's objectives.

The primary documents include:

Software Architecture Document (SAD). This document provides a high-level overview of the system's architecture, including the architectural patterns (e.g., microservices, layered architecture) and main components. It explains how the components interact, the rationale for architectural decisions, and the technology stack chosen for the project. The SAD serves as the foundational framework for development, guiding technical decisions and ensuring scalability, reliability, and maintainability.

Component Design Document. This document breaks down the system into specific modules or components, detailing each one's purpose, functionality, and interactions with other components. Each module's structure, dependencies, and constraints are documented to ensure consistency throughout development. For example, in an ERP system, separate sections may cover components for inventory management, customer tracking, and financial reporting.

Data Flow Diagram (DFD). The DFD visually represents how data moves through the system, showing how information is transferred between different components and identifying any data dependencies. This diagram is essential for understanding how the system processes, stores, and retrieves data, ensuring that data handling is efficient and secure.

Interaction Diagrams (e.g., Sequence Diagrams, Communication Diagrams). These diagrams depict interactions between system components and how they communicate to achieve specific functionalities. Sequence diagrams, for instance, outline the order of operations for complex processes, while communication diagrams focus on how components exchange information. These diagrams help clarify workflows and prevent integration issues by showing exactly how different parts of the system should interact.

User Interface (UI) and User Experience (UX) Design Prototypes. If the system has a front-end component, UI/UX prototypes and wireframes are developed to outline the visual and interactive aspects of the software. These designs ensure that the user journey is intuitive, and they provide developers with clear guidelines for implementing the front-end features. Prototypes may include mock-ups of key screens, navigation flows, and interactive elements to give stakeholders a clear sense of the end product.

Technical Specifications Document. This document provides a detailed outline of the technical requirements, including platform compatibility, database structures, security protocols, and performance benchmarks. It translates high-level requirements into specific technical details, guiding developers on which technologies and methods to use for various system components.

Design Document (Comprehensive Design Specification). The Design Document compiles all design-related information, including architecture, component specifications, data flows, interaction diagrams, UI/UX designs, and technical requirements. This comprehensive document serves as the final blueprint and primary reference for the development team, ensuring consistency and alignment with the project's goals.

Review and Approval Sign-Off Document. After the Design Document and associated diagrams are reviewed by stakeholders, a sign-off document is created to formally approve the design. This document marks the transition from design to development, indicating that all parties agree on the design specifications and are ready to move forward.

These documents collectively ensure that the development team has a clear, detailed plan for building the software. By thoroughly documenting the system's architecture, component interactions, data flows, and UI/UX designs, these key documents reduce ambiguity and align the development process with the client's expectations and requirements.

4.6 Tech Lawyer's role in Design Phase

In the **design phase** of a project, lawyers play a critical role in ensuring that all technical and architectural decisions are properly documented from a contractual perspective and that they comply with legal and regulatory requirements. While they are not directly involved in technical activities, lawyers help secure the interests of both parties by defining, clarifying, and protecting contractual obligations and rights. Here are some key responsibilities lawyers typically handle during this phase.

Lawyers ensure that the design documents (such as the Software Architecture Document, Component Design Document, and Data Flow Diagrams) align with the Scope of Work (SoW) and other contractual terms. They verify that the deliverables match the client's expectations as stated in the contract, minimizing potential disputes later.

Based on the detailed design, lawyers may update or refine deliverable and milestone clauses to reflect any specific technical details or features defined in this phase. This includes setting clear criteria for what constitutes an "acceptable" deliverable, based on the finalized design specifications.

As specific components and modules of the software are outlined in the design phase, lawyers assess any potential intellectual property (IP) issues. They ensure that ownership of custom code, third-party integrations, and proprietary designs is clearly defined in the contract, and they add clauses if new IP concerns arise based on design decisions.

Lawyers review design decisions to ensure that the software complies with data protection laws (such as GDPR or other regulatory rules applicable in the contractual jurisdiction) and industry security standards. If the software handles sensitive data, lawyers may work with the design team to confirm that the system architecture supports necessary security measures and that these are documented in the contract.

With detailed designs now in place, lawyers may add or update confidentiality clauses, especially if sensitive or proprietary information is involved. They work to ensure that any data flows, storage protocols, and access controls comply with confidentiality obligations in the contract.

Lawyers translate design details into precise acceptance criteria, specifying how each deliverable will be tested and approved. This includes defining standards for functionality, performance, and security to confirm that the final product aligns with the client's requirements as per the design documentation.

The design phase often highlights potential changes in scope or requirements. Lawyers work on establishing or refining change management clauses, which outline how modifications to the design or additional requests will be handled, including the process for approving changes and adjusting costs or timelines.

In summary, during the design phase, lawyers ensure that the design aligns contractually and legally with the client's expectations and regulatory standards. Their work provides a structured legal framework that supports smooth development and protects both the client and developer through well-defined contractual obligations and safeguards.

4.7 Incorporating Design Deliverables into the Contract: Sample Clauses

Incorporating design deliverables into the contract is a crucial step in ensuring that the agreed-upon design specifications become legally enforceable obligations for the developer.

By formalizing these design elements within the contract, both the client and developer gain clarity on project expectations, deliverables, and quality standards, reducing the risk of misunderstandings or disputes as the project progresses. This process involves translating the detailed design documentation into specific contractual clauses that outline the responsibilities of each party, define key deliverables, establish acceptance criteria, and address quality standards.

4.7.1 Defining Design Deliverables in the Scope of Work (SoW)

One of the primary areas for incorporating design deliverables into the contract is the **Scope of Work (SoW)**. This section of the contract should specify each design deliverable clearly, based on the documentation developed during the design phase. Examples of design deliverables might include architecture diagrams, data flow diagrams, UI/UX prototypes, or component specifications.

Sample contract clause:

> The Developer agrees to prepare and deliver, within [specify number] business days from the start date of this Agreement, a Software Architecture Document, Data Flow Diagrams, and UI/UX Wireframes in strict accordance with the specifications set forth in the Requirement Specification Document. The Software Architecture Document shall define the system's structural framework, including all key components, inter-component dependencies, and integration points with external systems, ensuring compliance with scalability and reliability standards. The Data Flow Diagrams shall accurately depict data flow, processing pathways, and adherence to security protocols. The UI/UX Wireframes shall reflect the layout and functional elements of the user interface, consistent with usability and accessibility standards as specified by the Client. If the Developer fails to deliver any of the above-designated deliverables within the specified timeline or fails to meet the quality and functionality standards outlined herein, such failure shall constitute a material breach of this Agreement. In the event of such breach, the Client reserves the right to (a) impose a penalty of [specify penalty, e.g., a daily fee of X for each day of delay], (b) withhold any outstanding payments until satisfactory completion, (c) request immediate corrective actions at the Developer's expense, or (d) terminate this Agreement with cause and seek damages for any losses incurred as a result of the Developer's non-compliance.

4.7.2 Defining Acceptance Criteria for Design Deliverables

Incorporating **acceptance criteria** for design deliverables within the contract is essential to establish the standards and specifications each deliverable must meet. Acceptance criteria define the benchmarks for quality and functionality that the design elements must satisfy to be deemed acceptable by the client. For instance, if the design includes a UI/UX prototype, the contract might specify that the prototype should reflect the navigational flow outlined in the initial requirement analysis and must align with accessibility standards.

Sample contract clause:

> All design deliverables shall be subject to acceptance testing by the Client, who shall verify that each deliverable aligns with the specifications detailed in the Requirement Specification Document. Any deliverable not meeting these standards shall be returned to the Developer for revision within 7 business days.

By defining these criteria, the contract provides a clear process for assessing each design component and ensures that any necessary revisions are completed without additional cost or delay.

4.7.3 Quality Standards and Performance Benchmarks

Quality standards and performance benchmarks derived from the design documentation should be formally included in the contract. These standards ensure that the developer produces deliverables that meet the client's technical and operational requirements. Quality standards might cover aspects like system scalability, response times, or adherence to specific regulatory requirements, depending on the project's nature. For example, a performance benchmark clause for a software architecture document might require the system to support a specified number of concurrent users or transactions.

Sample contract clause:

> The design deliverables must support a scalable architecture capable of handling up to 10,000 concurrent users. Failure to meet this standard may result in additional design revisions at the Developer's expense.

4.7.4 Intellectual Property and Confidentiality Clauses

Design deliverables often contain proprietary or sensitive information, making **intellectual property and confidentiality clauses** essential. The contract should clearly define who owns the rights to each design component and specify how the information within these deliverables may be used or disclosed. Typically, the client retains ownership of custom-developed design materials, while the developer may retain the rights to general design frameworks or methodologies unless otherwise specified.

Sample contract clause:

> All custom design materials developed specifically for this project, including architecture diagrams and data flow models, shall be the exclusive property of the Client. The Developer shall not use or share these materials outside the scope of this project without prior written consent.

This clause protects the client's ownership rights over the design deliverables and restricts the developer's use of the project-specific materials.

As a conclusion of the entire chapter, the design phase in a real-world SDLC involves defining the architecture, selecting technologies, designing components, visualizing data flows, and creating a comprehensive Design Document. This document guides the development phase, and the structured review ensures alignment with the client's goals and the project's technical demands. Each team member, from architects to designers and technical writers, plays a vital role in transforming initial ideas into a robust, detailed plan for building the software.

CHAPTER 5

Development Phase

5.1 Overview of the Development Process

The Development Phase is the stage where the project's design is transformed into actual, working code. In real-life scenarios, this phase begins once the design documents are approved, and the development team can start building the software according to the specifications. The development team, often composed of software engineers, frontend and backend developers, and technical leads, is responsible for coding each component of the software. They work closely with the design and requirement specifications to ensure that every feature, function, and integration point aligns with what was agreed upon in the earlier phases.

In the early stages of development, developers usually begin by setting up the foundational structure or architecture of the software. Backend developers focus on server-side functionality, including database setup, server configurations, and any core functions that operate behind the scenes. Meanwhile, frontend developers work on the user interface, creating the visual components that users interact with. Each developer typically specializes in specific parts of the software, with responsibilities clearly divided among the team members.

Throughout this phase, the development team follows coding standards and best practices to maintain code quality and readability. They also frequently test individual units of code, known as unit testing, to ensure that each component works as expected. This testing is usually done by the developers themselves to catch any issues early in the process before they become larger problems. As coding progresses, developers also check in with technical leads or project managers to update on their progress, discuss any technical challenges, and ensure they remain aligned with the project's goals.

Once major components are completed, the code undergoes regular reviews, where other developers or quality assurance (QA) specialists check it for adherence to standards, functionality, and security. These code reviews help catch potential issues and ensure that all parts of the software are compatible and operate smoothly when integrated. During this time, QA specialists may also perform integration testing, where individual modules are combined and tested as a group to verify that they work together correctly.

DOI: 10.4324/9781003669609-5

The Development Phase is dynamic, involving constant collaboration among team members and regular testing to refine the code and confirm that it meets the project requirements. By the end of this phase, the software should be functional and ready for the final stages of testing and deployment, where it will be rigorously checked to ensure it meets all contractual specifications and is prepared for launch.

5.2 Role of the Development Team

The role of the Development Team is central to the success of any software project, as they are responsible for transforming design plans and requirements into functional, high-quality software. In a typical project, the development team is composed of various specialized roles, including frontend and backend developers, software engineers, quality assurance (QA) testers, and often a technical lead who coordinates the team's efforts.

Each team member has specific responsibilities that contribute to the overall functionality and usability of the software:

Frontend developers focus on building the user interface (UI), implementing the visual components that users interact with, such as forms, buttons, and navigation menus. They work closely with UI/UX designers to ensure that the software is not only visually appealing, but also intuitive and accessible.

Backend developers, on the other hand, handle the "behind-the-scenes" functionality, such as setting up the server, managing the database, and creating the logic that powers features like user authentication or data processing. They ensure that the application is fast, secure, and able to manage user data effectively.

The **technical lead** oversees these efforts, acting as a bridge between the development team and project management. They ensure that coding standards are maintained, deadlines are met, and that each team member understands their role and responsibilities. The technical lead also assists with complex technical decisions, such as selecting frameworks, optimizing performance, or resolving integration challenges between frontend and backend components.

Quality assurance (QA) testers play an equally important role within the development team. They are responsible for ensuring that each part of the software meets the required standards and functions as intended. QA testers conduct various tests, such as unit testing, integration testing, and user acceptance testing, to identify bugs, performance issues, or any other flaws in the software. By finding and reporting issues early, QA testers help the development team maintain a high standard of quality throughout the project.

Throughout the development phase, collaboration and communication are key. The development team works closely with project managers, designers, and sometimes directly with the client to ensure that the software aligns with the initial vision and requirements. Each member of the team contributes their unique expertise to the project, making the final product both technically sound and user-friendly. The development team's coordinated effort, guided by clear roles and responsibilities, is essential to delivering a successful software solution that meets the client's needs and contractual expectations.

5.3 Role of the Client and Other Stakeholders

While the development team is primarily responsible for coding and implementing the system, the **client organization** and several **external stakeholders** play equally important roles in ensuring that the software produced aligns with contractual obligations and business needs. The development phase is therefore not a purely technical exercise but a **collaborative process** requiring active involvement from multiple actors.

5.3.1 The Client (Beneficiary)

***Providing Feedback and Validation*:** The client's representatives (often product owners or business analysts) must review partial deliverables, prototypes, and sprint results. Timely feedback reduces the risk of scope creep and late-stage disputes.

***Clarifying Business Needs*:** Even after the design phase, ambiguities may arise. The client has the duty to clarify workflows, regulatory requirements, or integration needs with existing systems.

***Ensuring Regulatory Oversight*:** In regulated industries (banking, healthcare, telecom), the client often involves internal compliance officers to check that the code respects applicable regulations (GDPR, HIPAA, PCI DSS).

***Contractual Relevance*:** If the client fails to provide feedback or clarifications within the deadlines specified in the contract, they may bear responsibility for delays or additional costs.

5.3.2 Project Management

***Bridging Technical and Legal Requirements*:** Project managers (either from the client's side or jointly agreed in the contract) monitor progress against both the project plan and the contractual milestones.

***Change Management*:** They oversee change requests, ensuring that any scope modifications are documented, approved, and aligned with budget and timeline adjustments.

***Risk Management*:** Project managers maintain a live risk register, escalating issues to legal or executive levels when necessary.

5.3.3 Quality Assurance (QA) and Independent Testers

***Internal QA Team*:** Conducts functional and performance testing to confirm compliance with contractual acceptance criteria.

***Independent Verification and Validation*:** In large or critical projects, an external QA provider may be contracted by the client to independently verify the quality of the deliverables. This adds a layer of assurance and legal protection.

5.3.4 Legal and Compliance Teams

***Contract Compliance Checks*:** Lawyers and compliance officers review whether deliverables meet contractual obligations, licensing terms, and regulatory standards.

***IP Protection*:** Legal advisors verify that third-party or open-source components are correctly licensed and that ownership of custom code is secured for the client.

***Documentation Review*:** They ensure that deliverables such as user manuals, technical documentation, and test reports are produced in the format required by the contract.

5.3.5 External Consultants and Auditors

***Specialized Consultants*:** Cybersecurity experts, data protection officers, or industry-specific auditors may be engaged to validate aspects of the software.

***Audit Trail*:** External reports can serve as legally relevant evidence of due diligence in case of disputes.

The Development Phase is not only about writing code but about **governance and accountability**. Misalignment between these actors (e.g., a client that delays feedback, a project manager who overlooks scope changes, or legal teams that ignore open-source license conflicts) can generate disputes, cost overruns, or even regulatory sanctions. Clearly defining each role in the contract and project documentation is therefore essential.

5.4 Coding Standards and Best Practices

Coding Standards and Best Practices are essential guidelines that developers follow to ensure that the software is written in a clear, consistent, and maintainable way. In real-life development, coding standards act as a shared language among developers, making it easier for everyone on the team to understand, review, and modify code efficiently. By adhering to these standards, the development team ensures that the software is not only functional but also well-structured and easy to update or scale in the future.

5.4.1 Coding Standards

Coding standards can be compared to internal policies or legal norms: they are common rules that every developer on a team must follow to avoid inconsistency, confusion, and errors. Just as legal drafting benefits from uniform terminology and structure, software development benefits from consistent coding practices. Coding standards typically cover a range of areas, including naming conventions, file organization, indentation, and error-handling protocols.

Naming Conventions are rules about *how things are named in the code*, for example, variables, functions, or classes. In practice, this means agreeing whether a customer name is written as client_name (using lowercase with underscores) or ClientName (using capital letters for each word). If every developer invented their own style, the code would become unreadable, just as a contract would be confusing if each clause used different definitions for the same term.

***Legal Risk*:** Inconsistent naming can make it difficult to identify whether contractual deliverables have been implemented. For example, if the contract requires a module named "CustomerData," but in the codebase developers refer to it as cData or clientinfo, the client may struggle to prove whether the obligation was fulfilled. In disputes, this ambiguity may hinder expert inspections, delay acceptance, or even shift liability for defects.

File Organization refers to how the project's files are structured and stored. For instance, keeping all legal documents in separate folders, like "Contracts," "Court Filings," or "Correspondence" makes it easier for lawyers to find the right document quickly. In the same way, developers place source code, test files, and configuration files in well-structured folders. A clear structure avoids mistakes, saves time, and helps new team members understand the project.

***Legal Risk*:** Poor file organization can make it impossible to demonstrate compliance with the Scope of Work or to identify deliverables.

For example, if test scripts required under the contract are scattered across different folders without labeling, the developer may not be able to prove that contractual testing obligations were met. Regulators or auditors (e.g., in banking or healthcare) may also penalize the client if required documentation cannot be produced in a structured, verifiable form.

Indentation and Formatting is the spacing and alignment of code lines so that the structure of the program is visually clear. It works much like formatting in legal writing: imagine a contract where sub-clauses are never indented and paragraphs run together. The meaning might still be there but finding it would be tedious. Proper indentation in code ensures that developers can see the logical structure immediately.

Legal Risk: Poor formatting can conceal defects or create misunderstandings when the code is reviewed in an audit or litigation. For example, a misplaced indentation in Python can change the execution logic of an entire function without being obvious to a reviewer. If this leads to a data breach or service outage, the client may argue that the developer failed to exercise due professional diligence, exposing them to damages or breach-of-contract claims.

Error-Handling Protocols is the practice of anticipating problems in the software and managing them gracefully. For example, if a user enters the wrong password, the system should not "crash" but should display a polite message: "Incorrect password, please try again." In legal terms, this is like including fallback clauses or remedies in a contract: you anticipate breaches and specify what should happen if something goes wrong.

Legal Risk: Inadequate error-handling can create direct liability. For instance, if an online banking application fails to handle a network error properly and instead corrupts transaction data, both the developer and the client may face significant financial and regulatory consequences. Courts may treat the absence of proper error-handling as negligence, especially if the contract required the software to meet specific reliability or availability standards.

Coding standards are not about "style" or "aesthetics" alone. They are safeguards that ensure the code is readable, maintainable, and legally defensible when it comes to questions of quality, liability, or compliance.

5.4.2 Best Practices

Best practices go beyond formatting rules; they are techniques that improve the software's **performance**, **security**, and **robustness**. They can be compared to professional standards in law or finance: not strictly mandatory by statute but widely recognized as benchmarks of quality and due diligence.

Modular Code. Developers are encouraged to write **modular code**, meaning they break down large, complex functions into smaller, reusable components. This makes the system easier to test, debug, and modify without destabilizing the entire application. In legal terms, this is like structuring a contract into clear clauses. If one clause is amended, the whole agreement does not collapse.

***Legal Risk*:** If the code is not modular, any small change may create widespread defects. For example, a poorly structured banking application might require rewriting the entire payment module just to add a new transaction type. This increases costs, delays delivery, and may expose the developer to liability for failing to provide "maintainable code," especially if maintainability was a contractual requirement.

Secure Coding Practices. Best practices also require developers to anticipate security risks. This includes sanitizing inputs, encrypting sensitive data, and avoiding outdated libraries. In essence, it is the "compliance by design" of the software world.

***Legal Risk*:** Failure to follow secure coding practices can create direct liability. For instance, if a healthcare application does not properly encrypt patient data and suffers a breach, both the developer and the client may face penalties under GDPR or HIPAA. Courts may treat insecure coding as negligence, even if the contract does not explicitly list every security measure.

Error-Handling Strategies. Beyond coding standards, best practices emphasize **anticipating errors** and ensuring the software responds predictably. For example, if a server becomes overloaded, the system should queue requests instead of crashing entirely. This is comparable to having contingency clauses in contracts, foreseeing problems and specifying remedies.

***Legal Risk*:** Inadequate error-handling can trigger breach-of-contract claims when downtime or data loss occurs. Imagine an e-commerce platform that fails to manage payment gateway errors properly: instead of rejecting failed transactions, it processes duplicates, leading to financial losses for customers. The client may then claim damages against the developer for failure to meet contractual service levels.

Documentation of Best Practices. Another crucial best practice is documenting code logic and architecture decisions. Just as lawyers annotate contracts for future reference, developers are expected to leave comments and explanations.

This ensures that other team members, or even new developers hired later, can understand and maintain the system. In practice, developers write short explanations directly inside the code to clarify how certain parts work. These are called **comments**. They do not affect how the software runs, but they help other developers (or auditors) understand the logic.

Without Commenting is like a lawyer reading a contract with no headings, no definitions, and no explanatory notes. The clauses may be valid but interpreting them would take hours.

With Commenting it is as if each clause had a short annotation explaining its purpose, making the document much easier to use.

Here is a simple code example:

```
python
# Function to calculate the total price of an
order including tax
def calculate_total (price, tax_rate):
# price: base amount of the product
# tax_rate: percentage of tax (e.g., 0.19 for 19%)
total = price + (price * tax_rate)# apply tax
return total
```

Explanation:

The first comment explains what the function does overall (*calculate the total price including tax*).

The second block of comments documents what each parameter means (*price* and *tax_rate*).

The inline comment (`# apply tax`) clarifies what the specific line of code is doing.

The key point is that Comments in code are not "decoration"; they are evidence of maintainability. Many IT contracts explicitly require delivery of "documented source code" to ensure the client can later maintain or transfer the system without excessive cost.

Legal Risk: If comments and documentation are missing, future developers may not understand how the software works. For example, if a government client receives undocumented code for a public health system, new contractors may need months to interpret it. This could delay urgent updates and expose the developer to claims for failure to deliver maintainable software as required by contract. Lack of documentation can be grounds for dispute. If the developer delivers functioning software but without adequate documentation, the client may argue that the deliverable is incomplete under the contract. For example, public procurement contracts often require "user manuals and technical documentation" as part of the scope; omission may justify withholding payment or claiming penalties.

Best practices are not "nice to have" technical habits. They are **quality safeguards** that determine whether the software will be maintainable, secure, and legally defensible. Ignoring them exposes both parties to hidden risks, from regulatory sanctions to disputes over incomplete or defective deliverables.

In practice, coding standards and best practices are enforced through regular code reviews, where team members check each other's work for consistency and quality. These reviews help ensure that everyone follows the agreed-upon standards, and they provide an opportunity to learn from each other's work and improve collectively. By adhering to coding standards and best practices, the development team builds software that is more reliable, maintainable, and scalable, ultimately supporting the long-term success of the project.

5.5 Types of Code in the Development Phase

Not all software code is created equally, nor does it originate from a single source. In the development phase, teams typically combine several categories of code to build a functional system: *custom code* written specifically for the client; *third-party licensed components*; *open-source libraries*; and, increasingly, *AI-generated snippets*. While these elements may appear indistinguishable once integrated into the final product, their **legal DNA** is fundamentally different.

Each category carries unique implications for **ownership, licensing, and liability**. Proprietary code can usually be assigned to the client; third-party code is bound by contractual license terms; open-source code is subject to community-driven licenses that may impose unexpected obligations; and AI-generated code exists in a grey area of copyright and accountability.

For lawyers and project managers, understanding these distinctions is critical. A line of code may look like any other, but the rights and risks it carries can determine whether the client truly owns the software, whether additional license fees are due, or whether the project may be exposed to litigation or regulatory penalties. This section examines each type of code, explaining both its technical role and the legal risks it introduces.

5.5.1 Proprietary Code (Custom Code)

Proprietary code is software written specifically for the client by the developer's team. This is the "bespoke" part of the project, similar to a lawyer drafting a contract uniquely for a client's needs. The client often expects to own this code once the project is complete.

***Legal Risk*:** If the contract does not clearly state who owns the intellectual property, disputes may arise. For example, a developer may argue that they retain copyright and only grant the client a license to use the software. This could prevent the client from modifying, sublicensing, or reselling the software in the future.

***Real-World Examples*:** In the case of a **custom ERP system for a manufacturing company**, the client expected to receive full ownership of the source code. However, because the contract only mentioned "delivery of the software," the developer later claimed they had only licensed it. When the client attempted to hire a new IT provider to extend the system, the original developer blocked access, forcing the client into costly negotiations.

In a **public procurement project**, a government agency commissioned a custom tax-reporting system. The contract explicitly transferred ownership of the source code to the state, ensuring that the system could be maintained by any future contractor. This avoided vendor lock-in and reduced long-term costs.

***Industry Practice in Custom Projects*:** In business-to-business (B2B) **custom software contracts**, it is common for clients to negotiate **assignment of IP rights** over the proprietary code, so that they become the legal owner. The developer may retain rights only to pre-existing tools, frameworks, or libraries.

Alternatively, some contracts use a **license-back model**, where the client owns the code but grants the developer a license to reuse non-confidential components in future projects. This balances the client's control with the developer's ability to capitalize on their expertise.

Large organizations often include **audit rights** or **escrow arrangements**, requiring the source code to be deposited with a trusted third party. This protects the client in case the developer goes bankrupt or refuses to cooperate.

***Key Insight*:** In custom-made projects, proprietary code is the core deliverable. Unless the contract explicitly secures the client's rights, they may face vendor lock-in, inflated maintenance costs, or even lose practical control over the software that was built for them.

5.5.2 Third-Party Licensed Code

Third-party licensed code includes libraries, frameworks, or APIs provided by external vendors, such as Oracle drivers, Microsoft components, or payment gateways. Using these tools accelerates development, much like lawyers relying on official templates, databases, or commentary volumes instead of drafting everything from scratch. They save time, reduce errors, and bring in proven, high-quality functionality.

***Legal Risk*:** These components are governed by license agreements that can restrict how they are used. For example, if a developer integrates a commercial library licensed "per server," but the client deploys it across ten servers without purchasing additional licenses, the client could face infringement claims and unexpected costs. In extreme cases, the vendor may suspend access, terminate the license, or demand retroactive fees, disrupting the client's operations.

Real-World Examples:

Oracle Database Licenses: Many companies have faced multimillion-dollar claims because their IT systems were deployed on more servers or virtual machines than allowed by the Oracle license. Even if the developers set up the system correctly, the client's expansion of infrastructure without additional licenses triggered violations.

Payment Gateways (e.g., Stripe, PayPal APIs): Integration is straightforward, but the use of these APIs is subject to strict terms. If developers circumvent usage restrictions (e.g., storing card data locally instead of using the gateway's secure storage), the client risks PCI DSS non-compliance and potential liability in case of a data breach.

Microsoft Components: Enterprise licenses often require per-seat or per-device subscriptions. If developers deploy Microsoft libraries in an internal system without counting end-users properly, the client may later face license audits and substantial retroactive fees.

Industry Practice in Custom Projects:

License Responsibility Clauses: Contracts usually allocate responsibility for licenses explicitly. Either (a) the developer is required to procure all necessary third-party licenses and pass the cost transparently to the client, or (b) the client is responsible for purchasing licenses directly, while the developer simply integrates them.

Compliance Warranties: Sophisticated clients negotiate warranties obliging the developer to use only properly licensed third-party components and to indemnify the client against any claims arising from misuse.

Audit Preparedness: Large enterprises often require that license usage be documented and periodically audited, ensuring that the client can demonstrate compliance to vendors or regulators.

Open vs. Commercial Choice: In many custom projects, the contract obliges the developer to prefer open-source solutions unless there is a strong justification for commercial software, thereby reducing ongoing license risks and costs.

Key Insight: Third-party licensed code speeds up delivery but comes with hidden legal exposure. The central contractual question is: Who bears responsibility for ensuring that all licenses are properly obtained, maintained, and renewed? Without clear allocation, disputes with software vendors can quickly escalate into expensive compliance failures.

5.5.3 Open-Source Code

Open-source code consists of components made available under open-source licenses such as MIT, Apache, or GPL.

These libraries and frameworks are widely used because they are free, reliable, and supported by large developer communities. In practice, almost every modern software project includes open-source components, whether for basic functionality (e.g., handling dates, encrypting data) or complex frameworks (e.g., React, Angular, TensorFlow).

Legal Risk: Not all open-source licenses are equally flexible. **Permissive licenses** such as MIT or Apache allow a company to use the code freely, even in commercial software, provided that the original copyright notice is preserved. However, these licenses also state that the software is provided "as is," which means the original authors cannot be held liable for errors or security flaws.

By contrast, **copyleft licenses** such as the GNU General Public License (GPL) are stricter. If GPL code is combined with a company's proprietary program and that program is given to third parties, the company must also give those recipients the full source code of the combined program under GPL. The obligation is not to publish the code to the entire world, but to share it with everyone who receives the software.

Open source code introduces specific *legal risks* that differ depending on the license type:

5.5.3.1 Permissive Licenses (MIT, Apache, BSD)

Risk profile: Minimal. The license permits broad use, including in commercial projects. The main conditions are to preserve copyright notices and accept the code "as is," without warranties.

Legal risk: The client cannot sue the original authors for defects or damages, as liability is expressly disclaimed.

5.5.3.2 Copyleft Licenses (GPL—General Public License)

Risk profile: Significant. If GPL code is combined with a proprietary program and that program is **distributed**, the distributor must provide the **entire combined source code** under GPL.

Legal risk: A company that unknowingly incorporates GPL code into a proprietary system may be forced to release its own confidential code to its customers, effectively losing exclusivity over its intellectual property. Suppose a developer adds a GPL library into custom accounting software built for a client. If the client later distributes that software to its subsidiaries, it must also provide them with the source code of the whole application, not just the GPL part. This could expose the client's confidential business logic. If the same library were under the MIT license, no such disclosure would be required.

5.3.3.3 Network Use Licenses (AGPL—Affero GPL)

***Risk profile*:** High for online services. Unlike GPL, the AGPL extends the duty of disclosure even where software is not "distributed" but merely made accessible over a network.

***Legal risk*:** A SaaS provider using AGPL components could be legally obliged to disclose its full source code to every user accessing the system over the internet.

Industry Practice in Custom Projects

Open Source Policies: Many enterprises adopt internal "open source usage policies" requiring developers to document every open-source component and its license before integration.

Due Diligence and SBOMs: Contracts often require the developer to deliver a **Software Bill of Materials (SBOM)** listing all open-source and third-party components, ensuring full transparency.

Substitution Clauses: Some clients insist that if a restrictive license (like GPL) is discovered, the developer must replace it with a permissive alternative at no additional cost.

Indemnities: Sophisticated clients negotiate indemnity clauses obliging the developer to protect the client from claims arising from non-compliance with open-source licenses.

***Key Insight*:** Open source is indispensable in modern software, but it comes with hidden obligations. The contract must balance the benefits of free, community-driven code with safeguards against license traps that can compromise the client's intellectual property strategy.

5.5.4 AI-generated code

AI-generated code refers to software code produced with the help of artificial intelligence tools, such as GitHub Copilot or ChatGPT. Instead of writing every line manually, developers can ask these systems to generate functional snippets of code, which can significantly speed up the development process.

Legal Risk: The legal status of AI-generated code is still unsettled. Unlike traditional software, where authorship and ownership are easier to identify, AI tools raise complex questions:

Copyright Infringement Risk: AI systems are trained on vast amounts of publicly available code, some of which may be protected by copyright. If the AI reproduces a fragment from this training data, the output could inadvertently copy copyrighted material.

Example: If GitHub Copilot generates a substantial piece of code that comes directly from a licensed repository (e.g., under GPL), and the developer includes it in a client's proprietary system, the client may unknowingly deploy infringing code. This could expose the client to claims of license violation or copyright infringement.

Unclear Ownership: Traditional copyright law assumes a human author. If a piece of code is created entirely by an AI tool, it is uncertain whether the copyright belongs to the developer who used the tool, the client who commissioned the work, the company providing the AI service, or potentially no one at all.

Example: If a dispute arises between a client and a developer over exclusive ownership of AI-generated code, courts may struggle to determine whether the code qualifies as a protectable "work" and, if so, who owns it.

Liability and Due Diligence: If AI-generated code contains errors, security flaws, or license conflicts, responsibility for damages will still fall on the developer and, ultimately, the client. Courts are unlikely to accept "the AI produced it" as a defense.

Example: A financial institution integrates AI-generated code into its trading platform. If the code fails and causes losses, the institution may be liable to its customers, regardless of the fact that the faulty logic originated from an AI tool.

5.5.4.1 Industry Practice in Custom Projects

Disclosure Requirements: Some clients now require developers to disclose whether AI tools were used in coding, to ensure traceability.

Sample clause—AI Tool Disclosure:

1. The Developer shall disclose in writing to the Client whether any artificial intelligence ("AI") tools, automated code generation systems, or machine learning models have been used in the creation, modification,

or review of the Software. Such disclosure shall be made (i) at the commencement of the Services, and (ii) upon delivery of each major milestone or deliverable.

2. The disclosure shall identify, with reasonable specificity:
   a. the AI tool(s) used,
   b. the scope and nature of the contribution generated by such tools (e.g., code snippets, documentation, testing outputs), and
   c. any applicable license terms or usage restrictions associated with the AI tool.
3. Failure by the Developer to disclose the use of AI tools as required under this Clause shall constitute a material breach of this Agreement, entitling the Client to (i) withhold acceptance of the deliverables, (ii) suspend payment, or (iii) terminate the Agreement for cause.
4. The Developer shall remain fully responsible and liable for all deliverables produced with or without the use of AI tools, including compliance with intellectual property rights, confidentiality obligations, data protection laws, and quality standards under this Agreement.

Warranty Clauses: Sophisticated contracts may include warranties that the developer will not insert infringing or unlicensed AI-generated code.

Sample warranty clause—AI-generated code warranty:

1. **Warranty of Non-Infringement**: The Developer represents and warrants that no portion of the Software delivered under this Agreement contains code, materials, or content generated by artificial intelligence ("AI") tools or systems that infringes, misappropriates, or otherwise violates any intellectual property rights of third parties.
2. **Warranty of Proper Licensing**: The Developer further represents and warrants that any AI-generated code, if used, has been lawfully generated, acquired, and incorporated in compliance with all applicable license terms, usage restrictions, and open-source obligations, and that the Client's use of the Software shall not require the Client to obtain additional licenses or pay third-party royalties beyond those expressly disclosed in writing and accepted by the Client.
3. **Liability and Indemnification**: The Developer acknowledges that it shall remain fully liable for all deliverables, regardless of whether AI tools were used, and agrees to indemnify, defend, and hold harmless the Client from and against any and all claims, damages, losses, or expenses (including reasonable attorneys' fees) arising out of or relating to any breach of the warranties set forth in this Clause.

Audit Rights: Clients sometimes reserve the right to audit the codebase to detect AI outputs that could present IP risks.

Sample contract clause—AI audit rights:

1. **Right to Audit**: The Client shall have the right, upon providing not less than ten (10) business days' written notice, to audit the Software, including the source code, related documentation, and development records, for the limited purpose of verifying whether artificial intelligence ("AI")

tools were used in the development of the Software and whether such use complies with the warranties, representations, and disclosure obligations set forth in this Agreement.

2. **Scope of Audit**: The audit shall be conducted (i) during normal business hours, (ii) in a manner that does not unreasonably disrupt the Developer's business operations, and (iii) subject to reasonable confidentiality, data protection, and security safeguards to protect the Developer's proprietary information and trade secrets.
3. **Third-Party Auditors**: The Client may appoint an independent third-party auditor, mutually agreed upon by both Parties, to perform the audit. The auditor shall be bound by strict confidentiality obligations and shall disclose to the Client only those findings relevant to verifying compliance with this Agreement, without unnecessarily revealing the Developer's proprietary information.
4. **Costs**: Audits shall be at the Client's expense, unless the audit reveals a material breach of this Agreement (including undisclosed or improperly licensed AI-generated code), in which case the Developer shall reimburse the Client for all reasonable audit costs incurred.
5. **Consequences of Non-Compliance**: If the audit identifies AI-generated outputs that present intellectual property risks, violate applicable license terms, or breach the Developer's warranties, the Developer shall promptly (i) remediate such non-compliance at its sole cost and expense, and (ii) indemnify the Client against any resulting losses, damages, or third-party claims in accordance with this Agreement.

***Key Insight*:** AI-generated code may accelerate development, but it creates legal uncertainty around **authorship, ownership, and liability**. Until legislation or case law provides clarity, contracts should address AI explicitly, requiring disclosure, allocating ownership, and ensuring that the developer remains responsible for compliance and quality.

5.5.5 Legacy Code Reuse

Legacy code refers to software components that were originally written for a different project and later reused by developers in a new project. This practice is common in the industry. Developers often rely on proven code snippets, modules, or even entire subsystems they wrote in earlier jobs to save time and reduce errors. While efficient, *legacy code reuse raises significant legal concerns* because the rights to that code may still belong to a previous client or employer, not the developer who reused it.

***Legal Risk*:** If legacy code is inserted into a new project without proper authorization, the new client may unknowingly receive software that is partially owned by a third party. This can trigger intellectual property disputes, claims of breach of contract, or even litigation for copyright infringement. Unlike open-source or licensed code, where terms are at least documented, legacy code often has no clear licensing framework, making ownership disputes harder to resolve.

5.5.5.1 Real-World Examples

Employee Mobility: A developer who worked at a fintech company writes an algorithm for fraud detection. Later, after joining a new employer, the developer reuses parts of that algorithm in a new system. The original employer may claim ownership and sue both the developer and the new company for misappropriation of intellectual property.

Consulting Projects: In consulting environments, it is common for developers to reuse templates, libraries, or utilities created in prior engagements. Without explicit permission, this reuse can breach non-disclosure or IP assignment clauses, exposing the consulting firm and the client to liability.

Litigation Cases: Courts have seen disputes where companies discovered that their software contained modules traced back to another vendor's proprietary system, raising claims of infringement and breach of exclusivity.

5.5.5.2 Industry Practice in Custom Projects

A. **IP Warranties**: Contracts often include warranties from the developer stating that all code delivered is either original, properly licensed, or lawfully reused.

   Sample contract clause for Intellectual Property warranty:

   > The Developer represents and warrants that all code, materials, and deliverables provided under this Agreement are either (i) the original work of the Developer, (ii) properly licensed from third parties with full disclosure of applicable license terms, or (iii) lawfully reused in a manner that does not infringe any intellectual property rights. The Developer further warrants that the Client's use of the deliverables will not result in any violation of third-party intellectual property rights.

B. **Disclosure Obligations**: Sophisticated clients require developers to disclose any reused code and its provenance, allowing assessment of IP risks before acceptance.

   Sample contract clause for disclosure of reused code:

   > The Developer shall promptly disclose in writing to the Client any portion of the Software that incorporates reused code, including open-source components, third-party libraries, or code previously developed for other projects. Such disclosure shall specify the provenance of the reused code, the applicable license terms, and any associated obligations or restrictions. The Client's acceptance of the deliverables shall be subject to its prior review and approval of such disclosures, and the Developer warrants that no reused code shall be included without the Client's written consent.

C. **Carve-outs for Tools and Utilities**: Some contracts allow developers to reuse generic tools or libraries they created in the past (e.g., logging functions, database connectors) provided they grant the client a perpetual license, while excluding client-specific legacy code.
D. **Indemnity Clauses**: To protect the client, contracts frequently include indemnities obliging the developer to bear the cost of defending against third-party claims related to reused code.

Key Insight: Legacy code reuse may save time and resources, but it also imports hidden legal baggage. Unless carefully documented and authorized, it can expose the client to disputes with third parties who retain ownership rights. The safest approach is to require **full disclosure of reused components** and clear contractual allocation of intellectual property rights.

As a conclusion, different types of code may look the same on the surface, but their **legal DNA** is very different. Proprietary code is usually subject to ownership clauses, third-party licensed code to contractual restrictions, open-source code to public licenses, and AI-generated code to legal uncertainty. Each type must be explicitly addressed in contracts to avoid hidden liabilities.

5.6 Software Development Management Platforms

Jira and **Azure DevOps** are among the most frequently used platforms for managing software development projects. They provide teams with tools for task planning, progress tracking, and effective collaboration. These platforms help development teams organize their work, ensure transparency, and keep the project aligned with deadlines and contractual specifications. In practice, projects are structured into smaller work units such as tasks, user stories, or bugs. Each task is assigned to a team member along with a deadline.

For example, a task related to implementing a specific user interface feature might be assigned to a frontend developer, while a backend developer might be responsible for database integration. Sprint planning (typically in two-week intervals) ensures that the team focuses on specific deliverables, while task boards (e.g., "In Progress," "Blocked," "Done") provide real-time visibility into progress.

Both Jira and Azure DevOps also support *issue tracking*. Bugs or problems identified during development are logged into the system, assigned a priority, and delegated to responsible team members. This centralized tracking ensures that issues are visible, documented, and addressed systematically, reducing delays and maintaining quality standards.

By using these platforms, teams maintain organized workflows, promote accountability, and foster efficient communication. These tools also allow managers and clients to monitor progress against contractual milestones, ensuring that the project remains on track.

5.6.1 Access Rights and Stakeholder Visibility

To ensure accountability and protect contractual rights, access to Jira or Azure DevOps should be carefully structured:

- **Developers**: create, update, and close tasks, bugs, and user stories
- **Project Managers / Technical Leads**: monitor progress, adjust priorities, and ensure alignment with milestones
- **Quality Assurance (QA) Teams**: log defects, confirm fixes, and validate acceptance criteria
- **Clients or Client Representatives**: in many custom software contracts, limited access is granted to the client (observer or reporting role). This provides transparency and creates an audit trail, while still protecting sensitive internal data

Best Practice: The contract can expressly require the developer to provide the client with read-only access to Jira/DevOps boards, ensuring that the client can monitor progress without interfering in day-to-day management.

5.6.2 Legal Risks

Incomplete Documentation: If tasks and bugs are not properly logged, it may be difficult to prove whether contractual deliverables were completed.

Example: If the developer claims a feature was implemented, but no task or acceptance test exists in Jira, the client can contest its completion.

Access Restrictions: If the client is denied access to project management tools, disputes may arise over lack of transparency. Courts may view this as a breach of good faith in contract execution.

Alteration of Records: Task histories can be edited or deleted. Without proper governance, a party could manipulate records to hide delays or failures.

Confidentiality Risks: Granting the client unrestricted access may expose sensitive information about other projects or proprietary methodologies.

5.6.3 Evidentiary Value in Litigation

In case of dispute, Jira and Azure DevOps can provide powerful electronic evidence:

Task Histories: Timestamps of when tasks were created, assigned, and completed.

Bug Reports: Evidence of recurring problems, how long they remained unresolved, and whether they blocked milestones.

Sprint Reports / Burndown Charts: Show whether progress aligned with agreed contractual timelines.

User Access Logs: Demonstrate who had access to the system, who logged changes, and whether the client was informed of delays.

Courts increasingly accept project management logs as evidence of performance or non-performance. For this reason, contracts should specify that Jira/DevOps records are to be preserved and may be used as evidence in case of dispute.

5.7 Ensuring Compliance with Contractual Specifications

Ensuring compliance with contractual specifications is a critical aspect of the development phase, as it directly ties the project's deliverables to the standards and requirements agreed upon in the contract.

In practice, this means that the development team must work closely with the contract's Scope of Work (SoW), milestones, and quality benchmarks to ensure that each deliverable aligns with the client's expectations and the project's objectives. Ensuring compliance helps prevent disputes, maintains client satisfaction, and ensures that the project meets its legal obligations.

Throughout the development process, the team frequently references the contract's specifications to verify that all features, functionalities, and performance standards are being met. For example, if the contract specifies that the software should handle up to 10,000 concurrent users, the development team is responsible for building the application to support this capacity. This might involve conducting load testing and optimizing the system architecture to meet the performance requirements.

Project managers and technical leads play a key role in maintaining compliance by regularly comparing the development progress with the contractual specifications. They often conduct internal reviews to verify that each component of the software meets the required standards before moving on to the next phase. These reviews may involve code quality checks, performance testing, and feature validation to ensure that all work aligns with what was outlined in the contract.

Additionally, Quality Assurance (QA) specialists are essential in verifying compliance. The QA team conducts tests based on the acceptance criteria set forth in the contract, identifying any issues or deviations from the agreed specifications. This includes functional testing, performance testing, and security testing, among others. By catching issues early and ensuring that each deliverable meets the agreed standards, QA specialists help maintain compliance throughout the development process.

Regular updates and communication with the client are also important. The development team often holds progress meetings with the client to present completed components, gather feedback, and confirm that the work aligns with contractual specifications. This transparency helps ensure that both parties are satisfied with the project's progress and allows any minor adjustments to be addressed promptly, preventing potential conflicts.

In cases where adjustments to the original specifications are needed, the **change management** process outlined in the contract ensures that modifications are documented, approved, and aligned with any cost or timeline implications. By following these structured procedures and adhering to contractual requirements, the development team helps secure a successful outcome that meets both legal and client expectations.

5.8 Checklist: Development Phase Deliverables and Contractual Compliance

This checklist helps ensure that all development deliverables align with contractual requirements and maintain quality standards throughout the process.

1. **Review of Contractual Specifications**
   - Have all contractual specifications been reviewed and understood by the development team?
   - Is the Scope of Work (SoW) clearly defined and documented for each deliverable?
   - Are key performance requirements (e.g., scalability, security) referenced from the contract?
2. **Alignment with Scope of Work (SoW)**
   - Are all features and functionalities under development consistent with the SoW?
   - Have any additional features or requests been assessed for scope alignment and approved if needed?
   - Are all development tasks organized according to milestones or deliverables set in the contract?
3. **Coding Standards and Documentation**
   - Are coding standards and best practices being followed to ensure code quality and maintainability?
   - Is the code well-documented, with clear explanations for complex functions and integrations?
   - Is each developer documenting their work to support compliance with contractual standards?
4. **Testing and Quality Assurance**
   - Are unit tests conducted for individual components as they are developed?

- Is integration testing performed to confirm that components work together as expected?
- Are QA specialists conducting tests according to the acceptance criteria defined in the contract?
- Are performance and load tests being run to verify compliance with capacity or speed requirements?

5. **Code Reviews and Internal Audits**
    - Has each major code segment undergone peer review for consistency with contractual specifications?
    - Are technical leads or project managers conducting regular audits to verify quality?
    - Are any non-compliant sections flagged for revision before progressing further?
6. **Client Review and Feedback**
    - Are regular progress updates provided to the client, covering key milestones and deliverables?
    - Is client feedback incorporated into the development process as specified in the contract?
    - Are revisions made promptly to address any client concerns or feedback?
7. **Documentation of Completed Deliverables**
    - Are completed deliverables documented for client review and approval?
    - Are test results documented to provide evidence of compliance with performance and quality standards?
    - Is each deliverable submitted with supporting documentation as required by the contract?
8. **Change Management**
    - Are any requested changes documented and assessed for impact on cost, timeline, or scope?
    - Have all changes been approved in writing by both the client and the project manager?
    - Are adjustments incorporated into the project timeline to reflect approved changes?
9. **Final Compliance Review Before Milestone Completion**
    - Is each deliverable verified against contractual specifications before marking it as complete?
    - Has the project manager signed off on each deliverable, confirming it meets quality and functional requirements?
    - Are any outstanding issues documented, with clear plans for resolution?

5.9 Legal Risks Associated with the Development Phase

Although the Development Phase is often perceived as a purely technical stage, where software engineers translate design documents into working code, it is in fact one of the most legally sensitive stages of the entire project lifecycle. At this point, decisions made by developers, sometimes even small technical shortcuts, can generate far-reaching legal consequences. Unlike earlier phases, where risks are primarily contractual or organizational, here the risks are embedded in the very code that forms the product, making them harder to detect and more costly to remediate once the software is delivered.

From a legal perspective, the Development Phase is where **intellectual property**, **licensing**, **confidentiality**, **liability**, and **regulatory compliance converge**. Every line of code written or reused carries an implicit legal status: it may be original (and therefore protectable as the client's property); borrowed from open-source repositories (and subject to license obligations); or licensed from third parties (and subject to commercial terms). If these distinctions are blurred, the client may believe it owns a bespoke product, only to discover later that parts of the software are encumbered by licenses, shared with other clients, or even subject to disclosure obligations under copyleft rules.

The Development Phase also creates **compliance challenges**. Developers often integrate numerous external libraries and dependencies. While these accelerate delivery, they also introduce hidden risks: *shadow dependencies* may bring incompatible licenses or outdated, insecure components into the system without anyone's explicit awareness. Similarly, failing to renew or correctly scope commercial licenses can result in claims from software vendors or unexpected costs for the client.

Beyond intellectual property and licensing, development activities can endanger **confidentiality and trade secrets**. For example, developers may use real client data for testing and inadvertently commit it into public repositories, exposing sensitive information. Weak access controls around repositories and collaboration platforms can further magnify the risk of leaks.

Quality and liability are another legal dimension. Poor coding practices are not merely technical failings, they can translate into contractual breaches. For example, a failure to follow secure coding practices may allow SQL injection attacks or buffer overflows. If such vulnerabilities lead to data breaches, the developer and the client may both face damages claims, regulatory fines, and reputational loss.

Finally, the Development Phase is where **regulatory compliance must be embedded by design**. If developers ignore data protection requirements under GDPR, healthcare obligations under HIPAA, or payment security standards under PCI DSS, the software may be legally non-compliant from day one. In such cases, liability extends beyond contract law into statutory and regulatory domains, exposing both the client and the developer to administrative penalties or civil claims.

Key Insight: The Development Phase is not simply about writing code—it is about embedding legal compliance into the very fabric of the software. Lawyers, project managers, and developers must therefore treat this stage as a legally sensitive environment where intellectual property, licensing, confidentiality, liability, and regulatory standards must all be actively monitored.

5.9.1 Intellectual Property Risks

The development phase is where legal rights become inseparably intertwined with technical choices. Every file that enters the codebase—whether newly authored, reused from prior work, pulled from an open-source repository, or integrated via a commercial SDK—carries its own ownership and licensing terms. If these are not identified and governed from the outset, the client may receive software that it cannot lawfully exploit, transfer, or modify, and the developer may face infringement claims or breach-of-contract liability.

Three recurrent IP risk clusters dominate this phase:

1. **Unclear Ownership of Custom Code vs. Reused Components**

What happens: Teams rarely build in a vacuum. Developers may reuse "utility" functions, templates, or modules they created in earlier engagements (legacy code), or they may blend newly written, client-funded code with these prior assets. Unless the contract and repository hygiene make the boundaries explicit, ownership becomes blurred: which parts belong to the client as bespoke deliverables, and which remain the developer's pre-existing intellectual property?

Why it matters: Unclear ownership impedes maintenance, upgrades, and future re-procurement. A client that believes it "owns the software" may later discover that key modules are subject to the developer's retained rights, or even to a third party's rights, blocking adaptation, sublicensing, or sale of the solution.

Typical red flags:

- No written IP assignment for code "created during the project"
- Vague carve-outs for "tools" or "know-how" that are never enumerated
- Mixed repositories where bespoke code and legacy modules are interleaved without attribution

Prevention and allocation

IP assignment + carve-outs: assign to the client all code created *for* the project; enumerate the developer's pre-existing modules (with file paths) and grant the client a perpetual, worldwide license to use them within the delivered product.

Software Bill of Materials (SBOM): require a component-level inventory marking each item as *custom/new*, *pre-existing developer asset*, *open source*, or *third-party commercial*.

Repository discipline: separate folders/namespaces and headers indicating provenance; mandatory commit messages referencing the component category.

Responsible roles: Technical Lead (classification), Project Manager (process enforcement), Legal Counsel (contract language and review).

Evidence in litigation

Software Bill of Materials (SBOMs). An SBOM is essentially an "ingredients list" for the software, detailing every component that makes up the system. Just as a bill of materials in construction shows which materials were used and by whom they were supplied, an SBOM shows whether a module was custom-written for the client, reused from the developer's earlier work, taken from open-source repositories, or licensed from a vendor. In litigation, an SBOM can prove whether the developer delivered a genuinely bespoke system or whether hidden third-party elements were inserted.

Commit History. Modern software is stored in version-control systems (such as Git) which record every change with the author's name, date, and description. This history is the software equivalent of a notarial logbook: it shows who wrote what, when, and under what circumstances. In court, commit history can reveal, for example, that an entire file was copied from another project in a single transaction, suggesting reuse rather than original authorship.

File Headers and Copyright Notices. Many source code files contain notices at the top identifying copyright holders or licenses (e.g., "© 2018 Oracle" or "Licensed under GPL"). These function like title deeds: they indicate who originally owned the work. If such headers appear in the client's software, they are strong evidence that parts of the code were not authored exclusively for that client.

Schedules of Pre-Existing Components. Well-drafted contracts often include schedules listing modules that the developer declares as "pre-existing" or "background IP." This schedule sets the boundary between code that will belong to the client and code that remains with the developer but is licensed. In litigation, the absence of a disclosed module from this schedule can support the client's claim that its inclusion breached the contract.

Expert Code-Comparison Reports. Independent experts can compare two codebases—such as the client's software and an open-source library or another client's system—to determine the degree of similarity. These reports are the technical equivalent of handwriting or forensic accounting analyses: they translate complex technical patterns into quantified evidence of copying or overlap.

2. **Breach of Open-Source Obligations (e.g., hidden GPL components)**

What happens: Open-source libraries are ubiquitous and valuable. But licenses differ. "Permissive" licenses (MIT/Apache) impose minimal conditions; "copyleft" licenses (e.g., GPL) require that if GPL code is combined into a program and that program is *distributed*, recipients must receive the corresponding source code under GPL terms. If GPL or similarly restrictive code is embedded—intentionally or by dependency chain—and the compliance steps are skipped, the result can be forced disclosure obligations or infringement claims.

Why it matters: A client expecting a proprietary product can be compelled to disclose source code to recipients if GPL is embedded in a combined work distributed to them. Even where no disclosure is triggered (e.g., internal use only), non-compliance can derail audits, financings, or M&A transactions.

Typical red flags:

- No automated license scans; reliance on copy-paste without attribution
- Use of packages with unknown or conflicting licenses; "shadow dependencies"
- Absence of OSS compliance policy (no NOTICE files, no license file bundle, no source-offer mechanism)

Prevention and allocation

Automated scanning & approvals: integrate license scanners in CI (e.g., to flag copyleft or unknown licenses); require legal approval before adding new packages.

Contractual OSS governance: oblige the developer to (i) deliver an SBOM; (ii) comply with license obligations (attribution, source offers where applicable); and (iii) indemnify the client for OSS non-compliance introduced by the developer.

Substitution clause: if a restrictive component is discovered, the developer must replace it with a permissive/compatible alternative at no additional cost.

Responsible roles: Developer (selection), Compliance/Legal (license review), Project Manager (gates in the workflow), Client Representative (acceptance criteria).

Evidence in litigation

When disputes arise over whether software has been lawfully built and distributed, several categories of technical and documentary evidence become crucial. These are the software-world equivalent of contractual annexes or accounting records in commercial disputes: they reveal whether licensing obligations were met and whether the client was misled about the software's legal status.

License Scan Reports. Automated tools (e.g., Black Duck, Synopsys, FOSSID) can scan the codebase and generate reports listing all open-source and third-party components, along with their licenses. In litigation, such a report can demonstrate whether the software contained GPL code, MIT-licensed modules, or commercial libraries, and whether these were disclosed to the client. The absence of scans, where industry standards would expect them, may itself suggest negligence.

Third-Party Forensic Analyses. Independent experts can analyze delivered binaries or source code to identify external libraries and dependencies. This is similar to a forensic accounting audit: it provides an impartial, court-ready assessment of whether unlicensed or conflicting components were included.

NOTICE and License Bundles (or their absence). Many open-source licenses require that a NOTICE file or license text accompany the software when it is distributed. The presence of a proper bundle supports compliance, while its absence is strong evidence that obligations were ignored. For example, distributing Apache-licensed components without including the required NOTICE file can establish a breach of license terms.

Distribution Records Showing Recipients. Copyleft licenses (like GPL) only trigger obligations when the software is *distributed* to others. Distribution logs, delivery records, or evidence of software provided to affiliates or customers can therefore prove whether the duty to release source code was activated. Without such records, a developer might argue that the software was used only internally, which carries different legal consequences.

Correspondence About License Choices. Emails, internal tickets, or meeting notes showing discussions about license terms are highly probative. They can reveal whether the developer was aware of licensing restrictions, whether the client was informed, and whether conscious decisions were made to accept or disregard compliance obligations.

These evidentiary sources allow courts and arbitrators to reconstruct not only *what* components were used, but also *whether compliance duties were understood and respected.* Together, they provide the factual foundation for claims of copyright infringement, breach of contract, or professional negligence.

3. Unauthorized Use of Third-Party APIs or SDKs Beyond License Scope

What happens: Commercial SDKs and platform APIs (payments, maps, messaging, analytics, proprietary databases) accelerate delivery but come with binding terms: per-seat/per-server limits, geographic or field-of-use restrictions, "no caching" rules, or bans on certain data uses. Over-deployment, disallowed use cases, or silent key-sharing can breach those terms.

Why it matters: Breaches can trigger vendor claims for unpaid fees, termination of access, audit findings, or damages for contractual infringement—potentially causing outages for the client's production system.

Typical red flags:

- API keys reused across environments or clients; lack of rate-limit monitoring
- No record of seats/instances vs. licensed counts; unclear multi-tenant usage
- Ignored "no-store/no-republish" clauses (e.g., for map tiles, card data, or content)

Prevention and allocation

License responsibility split: contractually define who procures and pays for third-party licenses (client vs. developer), and who bears compliance.

Operational controls: separate API keys per environment/client; dashboards to monitor usage caps and entitlements; periodic vendor-license audits.

Contractual warranties & indemnities: developer warrants lawful integration and compliance with SDK/API terms; indemnity for breaches caused by developer's integration.

***Responsible roles*:** Procurement (license procurement), Legal (terms review), Technical Lead/DevOps (key management and metering), Project Manager (compliance checkpoints).

Evidence in litigation

When software incorporates external APIs or Software Development Kits (SDKs), compliance with the vendor's license terms becomes a central legal issue. In litigation, evidence must demonstrate whether the integration stayed within the permitted scope or crossed into unauthorized use. The following categories of evidence are commonly examined:

Vendor License Agreements and Usage Reports. The starting point is the contract between the developer (or client) and the API/SDK vendor. These agreements specify limits, such as "per server," "per user," or geographic restrictions. Accompanying usage reports from the vendor show the actual consumption. In disputes, comparing the license terms with usage data can establish whether the client exceeded entitlements, triggering liability or unpaid fees.

API Logs and Key Histories. Every call made to an API is logged, and API keys (unique identifiers) record who used the service, when, and for what purpose. In litigation, these logs can prove whether a developer reused one client's key across multiple projects, or whether usage exceeded the rate limits or scope permitted by the license. This is analogous to access logs in data protection cases—it shows precisely how and by whom the resource was consumed.

Architecture Documentation Showing Integration Patterns. System design documents, diagrams, or code comments often reveal *how* the API or SDK was integrated. For example, they may show that a payment gateway was used to store card data in violation of PCI DSS rules, or that a mapping API was cached locally despite a license prohibition. In litigation, these documents serve as technical blueprints demonstrating compliance or breach.

Audit or True-Up Correspondence. Many commercial API and SDK licenses include audit clauses, allowing vendors to review usage and invoice additional fees. Emails, letters, or formal audit reports generated during these "true-up" processes are strong evidence: they show whether the client or developer was already put on notice of overuse, whether corrective action was taken, and whether financial liabilities were acknowledged.

In disputes over third-party APIs or SDKs, evidence often mirrors financial and compliance audits: the license agreement sets the rules, logs and usage reports show behavior, architecture documents reveal design choices, and audit correspondence records the parties' awareness. Together, these elements establish whether the software stayed within the license scope or strayed into infringement and breach.

5.9.2 Licensing and Compliance Risks

Licensing and compliance risks arise when the software incorporates components that are governed by third-party terms like commercial licenses, open-source licenses, or platform usage policies. Because modern applications assemble dozens or hundreds of such components (often with their own sub-dependencies), lapses are easy to miss and costly to fix later. Two patterns are especially common:

1. **Failure to Obtain or Renew Licenses for Third-Party Components**

What happens: Developers integrate commercial SDKs, databases, fonts, reporting engines, or cloud services that require paid licenses (per user, per server, per CPU core, per environment, or per transaction). If the correct licenses are not purchased at Go-Live, or if renewals are missed, the running system is out of compliance.

Why it matters: Vendors can terminate access, throttle service, or demand back-fees and penalties. Business-critical functions (payments, document generation, analytics) may stop working, exposing the client to operational losses and breach of contract toward its own customers.

Real world examples (illustrative)

Per-server/instance shortfall: A reporting engine licensed for 2 production servers is silently deployed on 8 autoscaled nodes. The vendor audit later invoices for six unpaid instances plus penalties.

Expired runtime license: A commercial PDF library embedded in an ERP is not renewed. After the grace period, invoices and contracts cannot be generated, causing delivery failures and customer claims.

Prevention and allocation

Contractual allocation: Specify who procures and pays for third-party licenses (client vs. developer) and who is responsible for renewal tracking.

License registry: Maintain a central register (owned by the client) listing component, vendor, metric (per-user/server), count purchased, renewal date, and owner.

Operational controls: Meter usage (per user/server), segregate environments (dev/test/prod), and prohibit sharing keys across clients.

Acceptance gate: No Go-Live without a signed "license readiness" checklist.

Responsible Roles

Procurement (purchase & renewals), Legal (terms review), Project Manager (readiness gates), Technical Lead/DevOps (deployment metering).

Evidence in litigation

When disputes arise over whether software was properly licensed and maintained, several categories of evidence become central. For lawyers, these are the software-world equivalent of **invoices, renewal contracts, or correspondence with suppliers**: they show what was agreed, what was delivered, and whether the client or developer respected the scope of licensed rights.

Vendor License Agreements and Purchase Orders. These are the contracts and commercial orders that define what the client was entitled to use, such as "100 users," "2 production servers," or "12 months' support." In litigation, they are the baseline against which actual use is measured. If the license agreement says two servers but the system was deployed on eight, the documents provide clear evidence of overuse.

Renewal Notices. Vendors usually send reminders before a license expires. These notices show that the parties were warned about upcoming renewals. In court, they can prove that the developer or client had knowledge of the obligation but ignored it. For example, if reminders were sent 30 and 10 days before expiration and no renewal was made, this supports liability for operating the software without a valid license.

Usage and Telemetry Reports. Many software products and cloud services generate usage data how many users logged in, how many API calls were made, or how many servers were running. These reports act like utility bills: they measure what was consumed. In litigation, they demonstrate whether the client stayed within the licensed limits or exceeded them, supporting claims for unpaid fees or breach.

Audit or True-Up Correspondence. Vendors often conduct audits or "true-up" reviews to check compliance. Emails, letters, or reports from these processes are highly probative. They may show that the developer or client admitted over-deployment, promised to fix it, or disputed the findings. Courts can treat this correspondence as an acknowledgment of non-compliance.

Internal License Registry and Change Tickets. Some organizations keep an internal register of licenses and use service desk tickets to approve deployments. These act as contemporaneous business records. In disputes, they can prove whether licenses were tracked diligently or neglected. For example, a registry showing only "test licenses" purchased, combined with tickets approving a live production rollout, would strongly support a claim of breach.

Each of these items (license agreements, renewal notices, usage reports, audit correspondence, and internal records) provides a **paper trail of entitlement versus reality**. Together, they allow the court to determine whether the client lawfully used third-party software or whether hidden liabilities were created through expired, exceeded, or ignored license terms.

2. **"Shadow Dependencies" Creating Hidden License Conflicts**

What happens: A developer adds a convenient open-source library. That library, in turn, brings its own dependencies (and those bring others). These **transitive** or "shadow" dependencies can include restrictive licenses (e.g., GPL/AGPL) or incompatible terms (e.g., attribution or NOTICE obligations), which no one explicitly approved.

Why it matters: Hidden copyleft code can trigger source-disclosure duties upon distribution, undermining the client's proprietary model. Missing attribution/NOTICE files or incompatible mixing of licenses can constitute breach, leading to takedown demands or remedial rework.

Real world examples (illustrative)

Copyleft creep: A permissive library silently depends on a GPL component. When the proprietary application is distributed to affiliates, GPL obligations are triggered, exposing the client to compliance claims.

Attribution gap: A mobile app bundles several Apache-licensed components but ships without the required NOTICE file. Store review or a competitor flags the omission, forcing an urgent compliance release.

Prevention and allocation

- **Automated scanning in CI/CD**: Require license scans (e.g., Black Duck, FOSSID, Synopsys) at each build; block merges on high-risk findings
- **SBOM at each release**: Deliver a Software Bill of Materials including all **direct and transitive** dependencies and their licenses
- **Approval workflow**: Any new dependency (direct or transitive) that is copyleft or unknown must be reviewed by Legal/Compliance before use
- **Substitution clause**: If a restricted component is discovered, the developer must replace it with a compatible alternative at no additional cost and within a defined SLA

Responsible roles

Developer (dependency selection), Technical Lead (tooling and policy enforcement), Compliance/Legal (license review & approvals), Project Manager (release gates).

Evidence in litigation

When a dispute involves whether a piece of software uses open-source components correctly, certain technical records act as the **equivalent of annexes and correspondence in a commercial case**. They show exactly what was included, when, and under what terms.

License Scan Reports (with Dependency Trees). These are reports generated by automated tools that scan the software to detect all external components and their licenses. The "dependency tree" is like a family tree showing which components were directly added by developers and which came automatically with them. In court, these reports prove if restrictive licenses (like GPL) were present, even indirectly.

SBOMs (Software Bill of Materials) per Version. An SBOM is an inventory list of all components used in a specific version of the software. Having one for each version is like having a dated asset register—it shows exactly what was in the product at each release, which is critical for proving when a problematic component was introduced or removed.

Commit History Showing When/Why a Dependency Was Added. In software repositories, every change is logged with a date, author, and a short note. This history works like meeting minutes: it records who decided to add a component, when, and for what purpose. In litigation, it can prove whether the developer knowingly introduced a risky library.

Package Lockfiles (e.g., package-lock.json, pip.freeze). These files are generated automatically by software tools and list every component installed, including hidden "transitive dependencies" that come bundled with others. They are like a receipt that lists not only what you bought, but also the free items added without asking. In court, they prove the existence of components the developer might claim were "never added."

Correspondence About License Choices. Emails, tickets, or chat messages where developers discuss which components to use and whether their licenses are acceptable. This can reveal awareness of restrictions and whether the client was informed or kept in the dark.

Distribution Records. These show who received copies of the software and when. This is important because some licenses (like GPL) only impose obligations—such as providing the source code—once the software has been distributed to others.

Key Point for Lawyers: These artifacts (scan reports, SBOMs, commit logs, lockfiles, correspondence, and distribution records) build a timeline and paper trail that can prove:

1. **What** open-source components were included,
2. **When** they were introduced, and
3. **Whether** the developer complied with the licensing obligations.

Treat licensing like any other regulated inventory: **catalogue, approve, meter, renew**. Make the contract mirror the workflow. Determine who buys and renews licenses; who scans and approves dependencies; what happens if a prohibited license appears (substitution, indemnity, timelines). Preserve the artifacts (SBOMs, scan reports, audit logs): they are your proof if a dispute arises.

5.9.3 Confidentiality and Trade Secret Risks

Confidentiality and trade secret risks arise when sensitive client information, like business data, personal data, proprietary algorithms, or strategic plans, are mishandled during the software development process. Because development often involves collaborative tools and remote teams, the risk is not just accidental leakage, but also *structural exposure* through insecure storage or distribution practices.

1. **Developers Embedding Client's Confidential Data into Code Repositories**

What happens: To simulate real-world scenarios, developers sometimes copy actual client data (e.g., full customer lists, transaction histories, pricing models) into testing environments or even into code repositories. If these repositories are shared with external contractors or stored in the cloud, that data can be accessed by people who have no right to see it.

Why it matters: Embedding confidential or personal data into code systems transforms a technical repository into a potential *data breach.* For regulated data (GDPR, HIPAA, PCI DSS), this may trigger mandatory breach notifications, regulatory investigations, fines, and contractual liability. Even non-regulated trade secrets can lose protection if exposed without safeguards.

Real world Example

In 2019, a financial services vendor accidentally committed a database containing thousands of client Social Security numbers to a public GitHub repository. Regulators treated it as a reportable breach under state privacy laws.

In an M&A due diligence, a buyer discovered that proprietary pricing algorithms from a target's key customer had been stored in a shared developer repository accessible to dozens of unrelated contractors.

Prevention and allocation

Data minimization: Use anonymized or synthetic datasets for testing.

Access control: Private repositories with role-based permissions and two-factor authentication.

Contractual safeguards: Prohibit use of production data in development without written consent; require immediate removal if discovered.

Responsible roles

Developer (operational compliance), Information Security Officer (policy enforcement), Client's DPO or Legal Counsel (oversight and audits).

2. **Risk of Disclosure if Repositories Are Not Secured**

What happens: Even without sensitive data embedded, unsecured repositories can be a backdoor to the entire codebase. If credentials are weak, permissions overly broad, or repositories set to "public," malicious actors can copy, modify, or leak proprietary code.

Why it matters: The source code itself can be a trade secret. Exposure can destroy its legal protection and allow competitors to replicate the product without consequence. In regulated sectors, the code may also contain configuration files or API keys that open up wider system vulnerabilities.

Real world example

In 2021, a major software vendor had its source code stolen after attackers accessed poorly secured internal repositories—leading to IP theft and reputational damage.

A startup lost exclusive control over its AI training code after an ex-contractor downloaded it from an unsecured Bitbucket account and launched a competing product.

Prevention and allocation

Security controls: Enforce encryption, MFA, and least-privilege access to repositories.

Monitoring: Audit logs of repository access and alerts for unusual downloads.

Contract clauses: Require developer to maintain repositories in compliance with ISO/IEC 27001 or equivalent; indemnify client for breaches caused by inadequate security.

Responsible roles: DevOps Engineer (technical security), Information Security Officer (policy compliance), Project Manager (vendor oversight).

Evidence in litigation

When the dispute concerns a potential leak of confidential information or trade secrets during software development, the following categories of evidence serve as the software-world equivalent of **security camera footage, visitor logs, and internal memos** in a physical breach case. They help establish *what* was exposed, *who* had access, *how* it happened, and *whether safeguards were in place*.

Repository Access Logs

What they are: Digital records showing every access to the code repository, identifying the user account, IP address, date, time, and actions taken (viewed, cloned, downloaded).

Why they matter: In litigation, these logs can prove whether unauthorized individuals viewed or downloaded sensitive code or data. They can also link activity to specific employees, contractors, or external actors.

Example: Access logs that show that a former contractor downloaded the entire repository from an overseas IP address two days before resigning is a direct evidence of unauthorized copying.

Data Discovery Reports

What they are: Technical scans and analyses of repository contents to detect the presence of real client data (e.g., customer names, payment card details, trade secrets) and trace how it entered the repository.

Why they matter: They can prove whether confidential information was embedded in code or test files, intentionally or accidentally, and identify the commit or event that introduced it.

Example: A forensic report reveals that a database dump containing 50,000 customer records was committed to the repository by a junior developer for testing purposes.

Security Audit Reports

What they are: Independent or internal assessments of repository security configurations—covering access permissions, authentication controls, encryption, and alignment with contractual or industry standards (e.g., ISO/IEC 27001).

Why they matter: These reports demonstrate whether the developer maintained "reasonable security measures" as required by contract or law. Non-conformance strengthens claims of negligence.

Example: An audit shows the repository was set to "public" for three weeks, allowing anyone with the link to access sensitive files—evidence of inadequate security controls.

Screenshots / Archive Copies of Repositories

What they are: Static captures or full exports of repository contents at a specific point in time, preserving the exact state before changes or removals.

Why they matter: They serve as unalterable proof that confidential data or proprietary code was present and accessible, even if later deleted.

Example: Screenshots taken during an internal investigation show the client's proprietary algorithm in a public branch of the repository, captured before the developer removed it.

Correspondence

What it is: Emails, instant messages, or ticket notes documenting discussions about using real client data in testing or warning of repository vulnerabilities.

Why it matters: Such correspondence can reveal prior awareness of the risk, internal debates about compliance, or ignored security warnings. Courts may view this as evidence of willful disregard or contributory negligence.

Example: An internal email from the project manager warns that "production data must not be uploaded to the dev repository," followed by a developer's admission that it was done "for convenience."

Key Point for Lawyers: In confidentiality and trade secret cases, these artifacts provide a chronological, factual chain (from the decision to use or store data, to the technical state of the repository, to the moment of access) allowing the court to determine not just *if* a breach occurred, but also *how*, *by whom*, and *under what level of security*.

In trade secret and confidentiality disputes, the questions are **what data/code was exposed, who had access, and whether adequate safeguards existed**. Repository logs, audits, and contractual terms will often be decisive in proving or disproving liability.

5.9.4 Quality and Liability Risks

Quality and liability risks arise when the delivered software does not meet the security, functionality, or performance standards promised in the contract. These risks usually stem from two main problems:

1. **Poor Coding Standards Creating Security Vulnerabilities**

What it means: If developers fail to follow basic "secure coding" rules, they may leave openings in the software that attackers can exploit. Common examples include **SQL injection** where an attacker can send malicious commands directly to the database or **Buffer overflow** which is a coding error that can allow unauthorized code to run.

Why it matters legally: If these vulnerabilities are exploited, the client may suffer data loss, downtime, or even regulatory fines for violating data protection laws. In such cases, the developer can face damages for: a) **breach of contract** for failure to deliver a secure product as agreed; b) **negligence** for failure to exercise reasonable professional care.

How to prevent it: a) apply recognised standards (e.g., OWASP) for secure coding; b) use automated testing and code reviews before launch; c) conduct peer reviews of sensitive or complex code.

2. **Failure to Meet Contractual Specifications**

What it means: The delivered software does not have the promised features, performance, or integrations, including: a) missing critical modules; b) lower performance than agreed (e.g., supports only 3,000 simultaneous users instead of 10,000); c) significant delays in delivery.

Why it matters legally: These situations are clear **breaches of contract**. The client may claim: a) fixes at the developer's expense; b) liquidated damages for delays; c) compensation for financial losses caused by the defects.

How to prevent it: Test each contractual requirement before acceptance, hold milestone reviews before moving to the next development stage and require formal acceptance sign-off from the client for each delivery.

Evidence in litigation

When a dispute arises over the quality or conformity of the software, the following evidence is particularly valuable in court:

1. **Code Review and Testing Records** (reports from code reviews, automated security scans, and functional tests. These show whether vulnerabilities or defects were detected and how they were handled)
2. **Performance and Load Test Results** (data from simulations showing how many users or transactions the system can handle. This proves whether performance matched contractual promises)
3. **Defect Logs** (e.g., Jira, Azure DevOps records of bugs, their severity, and how long they remained unresolved. These can link delays or failures to specific issues in the development process)

4. **Acceptance Test Results and Sign-Offs** (documents showing which deliverables the client approved and which were rejected. This establishes whether the client accepted the product "as is" or flagged non-compliance)
5. **Change Requests and Waivers** (written agreements altering scope or timelines. These can prove that some "missing" features were actually agreed to be postponed or removed)
6. **Incident and Outage Reports** (logs and reports showing service downtime or failures after launch, which may be linked to poor code quality)

Key Point for Lawyers: In quality and liability disputes, the most persuasive evidence combines **technical proof** (test results, logs) with **contractual context** (what was promised, when it was due, and whether the client agreed to any changes).

5.9.5 Regulatory and Compliance Risks

Regulatory and compliance risks arise when the software is developed without meeting the legal and industry standards that apply to its intended use. These standards may come from laws, regulations, or mandatory industry frameworks. If ignored during development, they can create liabilities for both the client and the developer.

1. **Software Must Comply with Applicable Regulations**

What it means: Different industries and jurisdictions impose strict technical and procedural requirements on software. Common examples include: **GDPR** (General Data Protection Regulation in the EU) that governs how personal data must be collected, stored, and protected; **HIPAA** (Health Insurance Portability and Accountability Act in the U.S.) that sets rules for protecting health information; **PCI DSS** (Payment Card Industry Data Security Standard), a global requirement for handling credit card transactions securely.

Why it matters legally: If the software does not meet these standards, the organisation operating it can face fines, legal claims, and loss of business licences. The developer may also be liable if the non-compliance is due to design or coding decisions made during development.

How to prevent it: Identify all relevant regulations before development begins; apply "compliance by design" building features and safeguards to meet these rules from the start; conduct regular compliance reviews with legal and technical teams throughout the project.

2. **Liability When Requirements Are Ignored**

What it means: If the software's architecture (its underlying structure and design) does not include the safeguards needed for compliance, fixing it later can be extremely costly and sometimes impossible without a complete rebuild.

Why it matters legally: Both the client (who operates the non-compliant software) and the developer (who built it without meeting the requirements) can face regulatory fines, contractual claims between client and developer, and civil claims from affected individuals or businesses.

How to prevent it: a) include compliance requirements in the Statement of Work and acceptance criteria; b) involve compliance officers and legal advisors in the design phase; c) require formal compliance sign-off before deployment.

Evidence in litigation

When a dispute or regulatory investigation arises, the following evidence can be decisive:

Regulatory Requirement Analysis. Documents created before development showing which laws and standards apply, proving the parties understood their obligations.

Design and Architecture Documentation. System diagrams and technical specifications showing whether compliance measures (encryption, access controls, logging) were built into the system.

Compliance Checklists and Audit Reports. Records of internal or external audits confirming (or denying) that requirements were met.

Data Protection Impact Assessments (DPIAs). For GDPR and similar laws, formal assessments showing how personal data risks were evaluated and addressed.

Security and Access Logs. Evidence that required controls (e.g., encryption, restricted access) were implemented and used in practice.

Correspondence on Compliance Decisions. Emails or meeting notes where compliance risks were discussed, showing whether they were addressed or ignored.

Regulatory and compliance disputes turn on whether obligations were identified, built into the software, and verified before launch. The strongest cases are supported by a clear paper trail linking legal requirements to specific technical measures and tests.

Development Phase Legal Risks

Table 5.1 Responsibility Matrix—Development Phase Legal Risks

Risk Category	*Responsible Role(s)*	*Preventive Measures*	*Evidence in Litigation*
Intellectual Property	Developer, Project Manager, Legal Counsel	• Contractual IP assignment clauses • Software Bill of Materials (SBOM) • Restrict reuse of legacy code	• SBOM showing provenance • Code comparison by forensic expert • Contracts with IP assignment
Licensing & Compliance	Developer, Compliance Officer, Legal Counsel	• Automated license scanning (Black Duck, Synopsys) • License responsibility clauses • Regular audits of third-party libraries	• License scan reports • Audit logs of imported components • Vendor license agreements
Confidentiality & Trade Secrets	Developer, Information Security Officer, Client's DPO/Legal Counsel	• Use anonymized test data • Secure repositories with MFA • NDA for all contributors	• Repository access logs • Security audit reports • Evidence of data leaks
Quality & Liability	Development Team, QA, Technical Lead, Legal Counsel	• Secure coding standards (OWASP) • Peer code reviews • Penetration and load testing • SLA clauses in contract	• Test reports and QA logs • Bug reports in Jira/DevOps • SLA performance metrics
Regulatory Compliance	Developer, Compliance Officer, Data Protection Officer (DPO), Legal Counsel	• Privacy by Design (GDPR, HIPAA, PCI DSS) • Compliance checklists before release • External certification if required	• Regulatory audit results • Privacy/Data Protection Impact Assessments (DPIAs) • Certification reports

CHAPTER 6

Testing Phase

6.1 Importance of Testing

The importance of the Testing Phase in the Software Development Lifecycle (SDLC) cannot be overstated. It is the decisive moment where all the planning, design, and development efforts are put to the test, and where the software must prove that it functions as intended. This is not merely a technical check, it is the formal process of validating that the product meets the agreed contractual specifications in terms of functionality, performance, and security.

Testing serves as the project's quality gate. It ensures that defects, bugs, or performance issues are identified before deployment, when fixing them is far less costly and disruptive. For example, in the case of a financial trading platform, failing to detect a calculation error before launch could result in erroneous trades, regulatory fines, and severe reputational damage. Similarly, in a healthcare application, untested data handling could lead to breaches of patient confidentiality and violations of HIPAA or GDPR.

From a contractual standpoint, testing provides an objective benchmark for determining whether the developer has fulfilled their obligations. Most well-drafted software agreements contain **Acceptance Criteria**, which set measurable standards for performance, security, and usability. These criteria might include the ability to handle a specified number of concurrent users, process transactions within a given time frame, encrypt sensitive data, or meet accessibility standards. Passing the agreed acceptance tests is often a condition precedent for milestone payments or final project acceptance.

For clients, comprehensive testing acts as a safeguard, confirming that they are receiving the product they contracted for and that it will integrate seamlessly into their business operations. For developers, it is an opportunity to demonstrate compliance, protect against unwarranted claims, and document that the delivered product meets industry standards.

In legally binding relationships, the absence of thorough testing can turn into a liability nightmare. Without documented proof that the software passed agreed tests, disputes may arise over whether the product is "fit for purpose." On the other hand, a well-executed testing phase, with

 DOI: 10.4324/9781003669609-6

detailed reports and signed acceptance documents, provides both parties with the confidence and legal security needed to move into deployment.

In short, testing is not simply a technical exercise, it is a critical stage of contractual risk management, operational readiness, and trust building between client and developer. It is the final assurance that the software is ready for real-world use, legally defensible, and technically sound.

Sample contract clauses:

> The Client shall have the right to conduct Acceptance Testing upon completion of each major deliverable as defined in the project Scope of Work. The Developer agrees that each deliverable shall meet the performance, functionality, and security specifications outlined in the Requirement Specification Document and comply with the standards specified in this Agreement. Acceptance shall be based on the successful completion of testing against the following criteria: i) **functionality**: Each feature and module shall perform as specified in the Requirement Specification Document without deviations, including but not limited to [list key functionalities, such as real-time data processing, automated reporting, etc.]; ii) **performance**: The software shall meet the agreed performance benchmarks, including but not limited to [e.g., response time under load, data processing speed], as detailed in Appendix B of this Agreement; iii) **security**: The software shall comply with all security requirements set forth in the contract, including data encryption, access control, and vulnerability protections as specified under applicable standards [e.g., GDPR]; iv) **usability**: The user interface shall be intuitive and meet usability standards defined in the Requirement Specification Document, including [specific criteria related to user experience or accessibility].
>
> Upon receipt of the deliverable, the Client shall have [X] business days to conduct Acceptance Testing and provide a written report to the Developer detailing any defects or deviations from the Acceptance Criteria. The Developer shall correct any identified issues within [Y] business days at no additional cost to the Client. Final acceptance of each deliverable shall be confirmed in writing by the Client upon successful completion of all tests. Failure to meet the Acceptance Criteria may result in the withholding of payments, as specified in the Payment Terms, or constitute grounds for contract termination if uncorrected within the stipulated period.

6.2 Main Stages of Testing

Testing is the process that proves whether the Acceptance Criteria have been met. For example, a contract may state that the software must support a specific number of users concurrently or handle transactions within a certain time frame. Testing confirms these capabilities, and failure to pass these tests could constitute a breach of contract, entitling the client to seek remedies such as rework at the developer's expense or even contract termination in severe cases.

Additionally, testing minimizes **liability risks**. By thoroughly testing the software, developers can identify and fix potential issues before the software goes live, reducing the chances of future legal claims if the software fails to perform. A well-documented testing process also serves as evidence that the developer took all reasonable measures to ensure quality, which can be crucial in the event of a dispute.

Testing is essential not only for functionality but also for **compliance** with any regulatory requirements outlined in the contract. In conclusion, testing within the SDLC is a fundamental aspect of risk management, legal compliance, and quality assurance. It protects both the client and developer by ensuring that the software fulfills its contractual promises and is ready for deployment, minimizing the likelihood of future disputes and legal challenges.

In real-world software projects, the Testing Phase is not a single event, but a structured, multi-stage process designed to validate the software from different perspectives. Each stage has its own objectives, methods, responsible parties, and contractual implications. This phase has generally two main stages: **Developer Testing** and **Client Testing**. Typically, the development team conducts initial testing to verify that the software meets the specified requirements before it is handed over to the client for final testing and acceptance.

6.2.1 Developer Testing

Developer Testing includes unit, integration, and system tests to catch any bugs, performance issues, or functional gaps early on. During this stage, the development team works to ensure that each module operates correctly, that components work together seamlessly, and that the software meets the baseline requirements set in the contract.

1. **Unit Testing**

Unit testing is the very first safeguard in ensuring software quality. Its purpose is to verify that individual components or modules work correctly in complete isolation, before they are combined with other parts of the system. This stage is entirely under the control of the development team and serves as the technical foundation upon which all subsequent testing relies.

In practice, after writing a piece of code, for example, a function that calculates tax rates in an e-commerce platform, the developer immediately runs a series of unit tests to ensure that the logic produces the correct output for a variety of input scenarios. If the tax calculation should return 19% for standard goods and 9% for certain food items, the unit tests will verify both rules individually and flag any deviation instantly.

At this stage, there is **no integration with other modules**. The purpose is to validate the correctness of the smallest building blocks before they interact with the rest of the system. Each unit test typically runs in seconds or minutes, and testing continues throughout the entire development cycle as new code is added.

While the client has no direct involvement at this point, the process is not without contractual relevance. Maintaining structured, time-stamped logs of passed unit tests provides **early evidence of due diligence**. If a dispute arises later over a defect, the developer can demonstrate that the individual component in question was functioning correctly when originally delivered.

Legal risk

If unit testing is skipped, poorly executed, or undocumented, defects that could have been detected early may emerge later during integration or user acceptance testing. At this stage fixing them is far more expensive and time-consuming. From a contractual standpoint, this exposes the developer to claims of breach of quality standards, delays in delivery, or even the imposition of penalty clauses if defects affect agreed milestones. In jurisdictions where "reasonable skill and care" is a contractual obligation, lack of unit testing can be used as evidence that the developer failed to meet professional standards.

Evidence in litigation

Key evidence that can be retained from the unit testing stage includes:

- **Automated Test Reports**: Generated by tools like JUnit or pytest, showing test case IDs, execution time, and pass/fail status
- **Version-Controlled Test Scripts**: Unit test files stored in the same repository as the source code, with commit history proving when they were created or updated
- **Execution Logs**: Time-stamped logs showing test runs and outcomes, ideally linked to specific code commits
- **Defect Fix Records**: Documentation of issues identified at the unit level and the code changes applied to resolve them

By preserving this evidence, developers strengthen their legal position in demonstrating that early quality assurance steps were performed in accordance with contractual and industry standards.

Unit testing summary

Objective: Verify that individual components or modules function correctly in isolation.

Responsible Party: Developer / Development Team.

Client Involvement: None at this stage.

Process: After writing a piece of code, the developer immediately runs unit tests (often automated) to ensure that the logic produces the expected results. These tests are usually created and maintained by the development team and run continuously through tools like JUnit, NUnit, or pytest.

Integration Moment: None yet—tests are on isolated code, not on integrated modules.

Typical Duration: Ongoing throughout development; each unit test runs in seconds or minutes.

Contractual Note: Although this stage is internal, maintaining logs of passed unit tests can serve as early evidence of due diligence in the event of a defect dispute.

2. **Integration Testing—Verifying Module Interactions**

Integration Testing is the next critical layer in the quality assurance process, designed to confirm that different modules or services communicate and work together as intended. Unlike unit testing, which focuses on isolated components, integration testing validates the flow of data and functionality across interconnected parts of the system. In practice, once modules have passed unit testing, they are progressively combined, and their interactions are tested.

For example, in a logistics management platform, the **Order Management** module must send order data to the **Inventory Tracking** module, which then updates stock levels and communicates with the **Delivery Scheduling** module. Integration testing ensures that these handoffs occur correctly and that the data remains consistent across modules. In distributed systems, this often involves testing API calls, message queues, and service orchestration to ensure that services interact seamlessly under various scenarios.

Integration is typically performed incrementally (known as continuous integration) where small sets of modules are connected and tested as they are developed. Larger, more comprehensive integration cycles are scheduled at predefined project milestones, ensuring that the entire system remains stable as new features are introduced. Depending on the complexity of the software, integration testing can take anywhere from several days to multiple weeks.

While the client's direct involvement is minimal at this stage, they are sometimes informed of major integration milestones, especially if the contract specifies key interoperability requirements or integration with third-party systems. From a contractual standpoint, if specific integration points (e.g., with a payment gateway, ERP system, or government database) are stated in the Scope of Work, successful integration testing is a contractual obligation.

Legal risk

If integration testing is skipped, rushed, or insufficiently documented, functional breakdowns may only become visible during User Acceptance Testing or post-deployment, when the cost and impact of fixing them are significantly higher. Failure to achieve successful integration with third-party systems named in the contract can constitute a material breach, leading to withheld milestone payments, contractual penalties, or termination rights. Moreover, in regulated industries, a failed integration with mandatory systems (e.g., tax reporting APIs, patient databases) can result in compliance violations and regulatory fines.

Evidence in litigation

Key evidence that can be retained from the integration testing stage includes:

- **Integration Test Reports**: Detailed results showing which modules were tested together, test case IDs, execution outcomes, and timestamps
- **API Call Logs**: Records of request/response exchanges between modules or third-party systems, demonstrating successful communication and error handling
- **Service Orchestration Diagrams**: Updated architectural diagrams showing how services are connected, reflecting the actual implementation at the time of testing.
- **Defect and Resolution Logs**: Documentation of integration issues found, steps taken to resolve them, and verification that fixes were successful
- **Third-Party Certification or Confirmation**: Where applicable, written confirmation from third-party service providers that the integration meets their technical and operational requirements

By preserving this evidence, both the developer and the client can prove that integration testing was conducted in line with contractual obligations, reducing the risk of disputes over interoperability or system stability.

Particular Case: Multi-Vendor Integration

In some projects, integration testing involves software developed by different vendors, for example, one developer builds a CRM system while another implements Microsoft Dynamics 365 Business Central. In such cases:

- **Each vendor** must ensure their system meets functional specifications in isolation and is capable of exchanging data exactly as per the integration requirements

- **Joint integration sessions** should be scheduled, with both vendors present to test end-to-end workflows, data mapping, and error handling
- **Clear interface specifications** including API endpoints, data formats, and field mappings, and trigger conditions must be agreed in advance and maintained under version control
- **An integration coordinator or project manager** should oversee testing, maintain consolidated defect logs, and ensure accountability for each issue

Without clear responsibilities, disputes may arise where each vendor blames the other for defects, causing delays and increased costs. To mitigate this risk, contracts should define ownership for each integration point, require shared logging/monitoring of all transactions, and establish a process for independent testing to resolve responsibility disputes.

Sample contract clauses: **integration responsibility and dispute resolution**:

Ownership of Integration Points

Each Developer shall be solely responsible for the development, configuration, and maintenance of its designated system components and for ensuring that such components interact with other systems in accordance with the agreed Integration Specification Document, annexed to this Agreement as *Annex [X]*.The Integration Specification Document shall clearly identify each integration point, the system(s) involved, and the Developer responsible for ensuring successful operation of that integration point.

Shared Logging and Monitoring

The Developer shall implement and maintain shared logging and monitoring mechanisms for all integration transactions, including API calls, data exchanges, error messages, and timestamps. Such logs shall be stored in a secure, mutually accessible repository for a minimum period of [12] months from the date of each transaction and shall be admissible as evidence in determining defect ownership.

Cooperation and Testing

The Developers shall cooperate fully in conducting integration testing according to the joint test plan approved by the Client. This includes participation in joint testing sessions, prompt correction of identified defects, and retesting as necessary to confirm compliance with the Integration Specification Document.

Independent Testing in Case of Dispute

In the event of a dispute as to which Developer is responsible for an integration defect, the Client may appoint an independent testing provider to perform diagnostic tests. The Developer agree to provide the independent tester with all necessary access, documentation, and technical assistance. The independent tester's written findings shall be deemed binding for the purposes of allocating responsibility for corrective action and associated costs.

Costs and Remedies

The Developer found responsible for the defect, whether by mutual agreement or independent testing, shall bear all costs of remediation, including retesting, and shall not be entitled to any extension of deadlines or additional compensation in respect of such remediation.

Integration testing summary

Objective: Confirm that different modules or services communicate and work together as intended.

Responsible Party: Development Team / QA Engineers.

Client Involvement: Minimal; sometimes informed of major integration milestones.

Process: Once modules are unit-tested, they are combined progressively, and their interactions are tested—e.g., the Order Management module sending data to Inventory and receiving confirmations back. In distributed systems, this often involves API calls and service orchestration testing.

Integration Moment: Partial integrations happen iteratively (continuous integration). Major integration cycles occur at predefined milestones.

Typical Duration: Several days to weeks depending on system complexity.

Contractual Note: Failures here may indicate design or requirement misalignment; if a contract specifies specific integration points or third-party APIs, successful integration testing is part of fulfilling acceptance criteria.

3. **System Testing—The First End-to-End Validation**

System Testing is the first true end-to-end validation of the complete, integrated software. Its purpose is to ensure that the fully assembled system (with all modules, components, and integrations in place) meets the functional and non-functional requirements defined in the contract. Unlike unit or integration testing, which focus on isolated parts or specific connections, system testing evaluates the software as a whole, in an environment that closely mirrors production.

In practice, the **QA team** executes comprehensive test cases covering all major functionalities, performance benchmarks, and security features. This includes:

- **Functional Testing**: Verifying that the system performs each required function as described in the specifications
- **Performance Testing**: Assessing speed, responsiveness, and stability under expected and peak loads

- **Security Testing**: Checking access controls, data encryption, and resistance to common vulnerabilities

For example, in a hospital management system, system testing would verify that patient registration, appointment scheduling, billing, and medical record retrieval all work together smoothly, with correct data flowing between them, while also ensuring compliance with HIPAA or GDPR data protection requirements.

At this stage, the **client's involvement** is generally limited to providing sample data, reviewing test plans, and being informed of progress. Testing is carried out in a controlled environment designed to replicate the production setup, ensuring that results are realistic. Depending on project size, system testing typically lasts **1–3 weeks for medium-scale applications** and significantly longer for enterprise systems.

From a contractual perspective, system testing represents the **first formal checkpoint** for verifying overall contractual compliance. All test logs, defect reports, and remediation records from this stage become critical evidence in demonstrating that the delivered system was tested thoroughly before moving to client acceptance.

Legal risk

If system testing is incomplete, poorly documented, or conducted in an environment that does not accurately mirror production, defects may go undetected until the software is live, potentially causing operational failures, security breaches, or regulatory violations. From a legal standpoint:

- The **developer** risks claims of breach of contract if the delivered system fails to meet the agreed functional or performance standards, especially if those could have been detected during system testing
- The **client** risks accepting a system that appears functional in a test environment but fails in production, making it harder to prove non-compliance later
- In regulated industries, skipping or inadequately performing compliance-related tests can result in fines and liabilities for both parties

Evidence in litigation

Key evidence that can be retained from the system testing stage includes:

- **System Test Reports**: Detailing all test cases executed, expected results, actual results, and pass/fail status
- **Performance Benchmark Logs**: Showing load testing results, response times, and stability metrics under different conditions

- **Security Test Results**: Evidence of penetration testing, vulnerability scans, and validation of encryption and access control measures
- **Defect Tracking Records**: Documentation of issues found during system testing, their resolution steps, and confirmation of successful fixes
- **Environment Configuration Records**: Specifications of the test environment to prove it accurately reflected the production setup

Maintaining this evidence ensures that both the developer and client can demonstrate that system testing was executed in good faith, aligned with the contractual requirements, and that any disputes over system readiness can be resolved with objective proof.

System testing summary

Objective: Ensure that the complete, integrated system meets the specified functional and non-functional requirements.

Responsible Party: QA Team / Test Engineers.

Client Involvement: Usually informed of test plans; may provide data samples.

Process: The QA team executes test cases covering all major functionalities, performance benchmarks, and security features. This includes functional testing (does it work?); performance testing (does it work fast enough?); and security testing (is it safe?).

Integration Moment: Full system is now operational; tests run in an environment mirroring production.

Typical Duration: 1–3 weeks for medium projects; longer for enterprise systems.

Contractual Note: This is the first formal checkpoint where evidence (test logs, defect reports) should be stored as proof of contractual compliance.

4. **Security Testing—Protecting Data and Compliance**

Security Testing is the phase dedicated to identifying vulnerabilities, verifying that the system's security controls are effective, and ensuring compliance with applicable regulations such as **GDPR**, **HIPAA**, or **PCI DSS**. The objective is not only to protect sensitive data from breaches but also to safeguard the organisation from regulatory penalties, reputational damage, and contractual disputes.

In practice, **security specialists**, often supported by external cybersecurity auditors, execute a combination of:

- **Penetration Testing**: Simulating real-world attacks to assess how well the system withstands intrusion attempts
- **Vulnerability Scanning**: Using automated tools to detect known weaknesses in software components, configurations, or dependencies
- **Secure Code Review**: Examining the source code to identify insecure coding practices and logic flaws
- **Security Feature Verification**: Ensuring encryption is properly implemented, access controls are role-based and enforced, and audit logs are complete and tamper-proof

For example, in an online healthcare platform, security testing would validate that patient records are encrypted in storage and in transit, that only authorised users can access sensitive medical data, and that every access attempt is logged for audit purposes in compliance with HIPAA requirements.

Security testing is ideally performed **before UAT but after all core functionality is stable**, so that vulnerabilities are identified early enough to be addressed without delaying deployment. Depending on the system's complexity and criticality, this phase typically lasts **5–10 business days**.

From a contractual standpoint, in regulated industries it is common for agreements to require **documented security testing results** before the system can be approved for go-live. These reports are often an explicit acceptance criterion and may need to be shared with regulatory bodies or compliance auditors.

Sample contract clause—security testing obligations:

Scope of Security Testing

The Developer shall perform comprehensive Security Testing of the Deliverable prior to User Acceptance Testing (UAT) and before any deployment into the production environment. Security Testing shall include, at a minimum: (a) penetration testing simulating realistic threat scenarios; (b) automated and manual vulnerability scanning of all system components; (c) secure code review of critical modules; and (d) verification of encryption, access controls, and audit logging features.

Compliance Requirements

All Security Testing shall be conducted in accordance with applicable industry standards and regulations, including [GDPR / HIPAA / PCI DSS], as specified in *Annex [Security Standards]*. The Developer shall ensure that the Deliverable meets or exceeds the security requirements set forth in the Scope of Work and these standards.

Testing Methodology and Approval

Prior to execution, the Developer shall submit the Security Testing plan, including tools, methodologies, and test cases, for Client review and approval. The Client reserves the right to require adjustments to align with regulatory or organisational requirements.

Reporting and Documentation

Upon completion of Security Testing, the Developer shall deliver to the Client a Security Test Report containing: (a) a list of all vulnerabilities identified, categorised by severity; (b) recommendations for remediation; (c) evidence of compliance with contractual and regulatory requirements; and (d) proof of retesting and closure for all resolved vulnerabilities.

Remediation Obligations

The Developer shall remedy all *critical* and *high-severity* vulnerabilities before deployment, at no additional cost to the Client. Medium- and low-severity issues shall be addressed according to the remediation schedule agreed in writing by both Parties.

Right to Independent Security Audit

The Client may, at its discretion, appoint an independent security auditor to review the Security Testing process and results. The Developer shall provide full access to relevant systems, documentation, and testing environments for this purpose.

Failure to Meet Security Standards

If the Deliverable fails to meet the agreed security standards or contains unremediated vulnerabilities at the time of deployment: (a) the Client may withhold acceptance and related milestone payments; (b) the Developer shall bear all costs associated with additional testing and remediation; and (c) repeated failure after [two] remediation cycles may constitute grounds for termination for cause under Clause [Termination for Cause].

Evidence in Dispute Resolution

The Parties agree that the Security Test Report, vulnerability scan logs, and remediation evidence shall be admissible as conclusive proof in any dispute resolution proceedings under Clause [Dispute Resolution], for the purpose of determining compliance with this Clause [X].

Legal risk

- **For the developer**: Delivering a system with unaddressed vulnerabilities can result in claims for breach of contract, breach of warranty, and—in regulated industries—liability for regulatory fines. If the system is later compromised, the absence of thorough security testing can be used as evidence of negligence
- **For the client**: Accepting a system without reviewing and approving security testing results may waive their right to claim non-compliance later, especially if the contract specifies that acceptance confirms readiness for regulatory use

- **For both parties**: If the scope and methodology of security testing are not clearly defined in the contract, disputes may arise over whether vulnerabilities were within the agreed testing parameters or beyond scope

Evidence in litigation

To strengthen contractual enforceability and legal defensibility, the following should be retained:

- **Security Test Reports**: Detailing penetration test scenarios, vulnerabilities found, and remediation status
- **Vulnerability Scan Logs**: Including date/time stamps, tool versions, and scan results
- **Code Review Reports**: Highlighting identified security flaws and corrective measures applied
- **Access Control and Encryption Verification**: Proof that access restrictions and encryption methods meet contractual and regulatory standards
- **Remediation Evidence**: Documentation of fixes applied to vulnerabilities, with confirmation of retesting and closure

Maintaining this evidence ensures that both developer and client can demonstrate that security testing was thorough, aligned with contractual obligations, and compliant with regulatory standards.

Security testing summary

Objective: Identify vulnerabilities and ensure compliance with applicable regulations (e.g., GDPR, HIPAA, PCI DSS).

Responsible Party: Security Specialists / External Auditors.

Client Involvement: Approves security testing scope and methods, especially for sensitive systems.

Process: Includes penetration testing, vulnerability scanning, code review, and verification of encryption, access controls, and audit logging.

Integration Moment: Ideally performed before UAT but after all core functionality is stable.

Typical Duration: 5–10 business days, depending on system criticality.

Contractual Note: Contracts for regulated industries often require documented security testing results before deployment.

5. **Regression Testing—Ensuring Fixes Don't Break Other Parts**

Regression Testing is the safeguard that ensures new fixes, updates, or enhancements do not inadvertently introduce defects into existing functionality. It is the quality assurance net that catches "side effects," meaning issues that may appear in areas of the system unrelated to the change that was made. In practice, regression testing is performed both **continuously during development** and **immediately after defect fixes** identified during UAT, integration testing, or post-integration with third-party services. The **QA team** or developers run automated regression suites for speed and coverage, while manual regression testing is reserved for business-critical workflows where human validation is essential.

For example, in an online banking application, fixing a defect in the fund transfer module might unexpectedly disrupt account balance updates or transaction history displays. Regression testing verifies that these unaffected areas still function correctly after the fix.

The **client's involvement** is indirect but significant. While they do not perform regression testing themselves, they benefit directly from the assurance that the system remains stable and consistent after changes.

From a contractual standpoint, some agreements explicitly require documented regression testing after **any** change request or bug fix, as part of the quality control process to preserve system integrity.

Sample contract clause—regression testing after changes or defect fixes:

Mandatory Regression Testing

The Developer shall perform regression testing after any change to the Deliverable, including (without limitation) defect fixes, code updates, configuration changes, and implementation of approved Change Requests, to ensure that no new defects are introduced into previously functioning parts of the system.

Testing Scope

Regression testing shall cover: (a) all functionalities directly affected by the change; and (b) all dependent or related functionalities as identified in the Requirements Traceability Matrix and/or Integration Specification Document.

Documentation Requirements

The Developer shall maintain complete and accurate records of all regression tests performed, including: regression test plans and scenarios; execution results with pass/fail status for each test case; automated test logs (where applicable); defect reports for any issues identified and evidence of their resolution.

Client Notification and Access

Upon completion of regression testing, the Developer shall provide the Client with the regression test report and grant the Client (or its appointed representative) access to all relevant logs, defect reports, and change logs upon request.

Sign-Off

No Deliverable, update, or fix shall be considered complete until regression testing has been successfully executed and documented, and the results have been approved in writing by the Client or its authorized representative.

Failure to Perform Regression Testing

If the Developer fails to perform or document regression testing as required under this Clause [X], and a defect subsequently arises that could reasonably have been detected through such testing, the Developer shall: (a) remedy such defect at its sole cost and expense; (b) bear the costs of any additional testing or remediation required; and (c) have no entitlement to additional time or payment in connection with such remedial work.

Legal risk

Skipping or inadequately performing regression testing can lead to serious operational and contractual consequences:

- **For the developer**: New defects caused by recent changes may result in breach of warranty claims, especially if the software was previously accepted but subsequent updates introduced failures
- **For the client**: If regression testing is not contractually required or documented, proving that a defect was introduced by a specific change may be difficult, limiting the ability to claim remedies
- **For both parties**: Without regression testing, disputes may arise over whether an issue was pre-existing or caused by recent changes, prolonging resolution and increasing costs

Evidence in litigation

Key evidence that can be retained from regression testing includes:

- **Regression Test Reports**: Detailed execution results for each test case, indicating whether functionality was preserved after the change
- **Change Logs**: Records of code modifications, linked to the regression tests executed for those changes
- **Automated Test Suite Logs**: Time-stamped evidence from tools such as Selenium, Cypress, or JUnit, proving that regression checks were executed successfully
- **Defect Tracking Records**: Documentation of defects discovered during regression testing, their resolution, and retesting confirmation
- **Sign-Off Records**: Approval from QA leads or project managers confirming that regression testing was completed for a specific release or fix

Maintaining this evidence ensures that both the developer and client can demonstrate diligence in preserving system integrity, reducing disputes over post-fix defects and clarifying responsibility in case of failure.

Regression testing summary

Objective: Confirm that recent fixes or updates have not introduced new defects in existing functionality.

Responsible Party: QA Team / Developers (for automated regression tests).

Client Involvement: Indirect—client benefits from stability assurance.

Process: Automated regression tests are preferred for speed; manual regression testing is used for critical workflows. This often follows defect fixes during UAT or after integration with third-party services.

Integration Moment: Done continuously throughout development and after UAT fixes.

Typical Duration: Hours to days, depending on scope.

Contractual Note: Some contracts require documented regression testing after any change request or bug fix, to preserve system integrity.

6. **Performance and Load Testing – Proving Scalability**

Performance and Load Testing is the phase in which the system is pushed to its operational limits to confirm that it can handle the expected user load, data volume, and transaction throughput under both normal and stress conditions. The goal is to prove that the application will remain stable, responsive, and reliable during peak usage, as defined in the contractual performance benchmarks.

In practice, **QA performance engineers** or developers use specialized tools such as **JMeter, LoadRunner**, or **Gatling** to simulate real-world traffic patterns, sudden spikes in usage, and prolonged high-load conditions. These simulations are designed to identify bottlenecks, memory leaks, or resource contention issues before the system goes live.

For example, in a national e-commerce platform, performance and load testing might simulate 50,000 concurrent users browsing products, placing orders, and processing payments, all while inventory updates and order confirmations happen in real time. The tests would measure page load times, API response times, transaction processing speed, and system stability over extended periods.

Performance and load testing is typically conducted **after full integration and before UAT**, though in large projects it may also run in parallel with functional testing to allow early detection of scaling issues. Depending on scope, this phase usually lasts **3–7 days** for comprehensive analysis.

From a contractual standpoint, the defined performance benchmarks (such as maximum response times, supported concurrent users, or transaction throughput) must be explicitly stated in the Scope of Work or acceptance criteria. Failure to meet these can be a valid basis for withholding acceptance or triggering contractual remedies.

Legal risk

- **For the developer**: Delivering a system that fails to meet contractual performance benchmarks may constitute a material breach, entitling the client to withhold payments, demand rework, or terminate the contract. If benchmarks are not defined precisely, the developer risks being held to unrealistic or subjective standards
- **For the client**: If performance requirements are vague or absent from the contract, the ability to enforce remedies for slow or unstable performance is significantly weakened
- **For both parties**: Poor documentation of test methodology and environment can lead to disputes over whether a failure was due to the system itself or to an unrealistic test setup

Evidence in litigation

Key evidence from the performance and load testing stage includes:

- **Performance Test Reports**: Detailed results showing each test scenario, load level, measured performance metrics, and whether benchmarks were met
- **System Resource Logs**: CPU, memory, disk, and network usage data during load tests
- **Error and Bottleneck Analysis**: Documentation of failed transactions, slow queries, or component failures under load
- **Environment Configuration Records**: Specifications of the hardware, software, and network setup used during testing to prove conditions were realistic and aligned with contractual expectations
- **Benchmark Verification**: Comparative evidence showing actual performance metrics against contractual performance criteria

Maintaining this evidence ensures that both client and developer can prove whether performance obligations were met, reducing disputes over system readiness and scalability.

Sample contract clause—performance and load testing obligations:

Performance Benchmarks

The Deliverable shall meet the performance and scalability benchmarks specified in *Annex [Performance Criteria]*, including but not limited to: (a) maximum average response time under normal load: [X] seconds; (b) maximum average response time under peak load: [Y] seconds; (c) supported concurrent users: minimum [Z] users without performance degradation; (d) transaction throughput: minimum [N] transactions per second; and(e) system stability under continuous peak load for at least [T] hours without critical failures.

Testing Obligations

The Developer shall conduct Performance and Load Testing after full integration of the system and before commencement of UAT. Testing shall be executed in an environment that accurately replicates the agreed production configuration in terms of hardware, software, network, and data volumes.

Tools and Methodology

Performance and Load Testing shall be conducted using industry-standard tools such as [JMeter / LoadRunner / Gatling] or equivalent. The test plan shall include test scenarios, data sets, expected results, and load profiles as approved in writing by the Client prior to execution.

Reporting and Documentation

The Developer shall deliver a comprehensive Performance Test Report within [X] Business Days of completing the tests, including: (a) description of each test scenario executed; (b) load levels and duration of each test; (c) actual measured metrics versus contractual benchmarks; (d) identification of bottlenecks or failures; and (e) system resource utilization logs.

Failure to Meet Benchmarks

If the Deliverable fails to meet any contractual performance benchmark: (a) the Developer shall, at its sole cost, perform all necessary remediation to achieve compliance within [Y] Business Days; (b) the Developer shall re-execute performance and load tests until all benchmarks are met; (c) no additional payment shall be due for remediation work; and (d) milestone payments linked to performance acceptance may be withheld until compliance is demonstrated.

Repeated Failures

If the Deliverable fails to meet the agreed benchmarks after [two] consecutive remediation attempts, the Client may, without prejudice to other remedies available under this Agreement: (a) apply liquidated damages in the amount of [•] per calendar day until benchmarks are met; (b) engage a third-party performance optimization specialist at the Developer's expense; or (c) terminate this Agreement for cause under Clause [Termination for Cause].

Evidence in Dispute Resolution

The Parties agree that the Performance Test Report, supporting logs, and the approved test plan shall be admissible as conclusive evidence of whether the Deliverable met or failed the agreed performance benchmarks in any dispute resolution process under Clause [Dispute Resolution].

Performance and load testing summary

Objective: Validate that the system can handle the expected user load, data volume, and transaction throughput under stress conditions.

Responsible Party: QA Performance Engineers / Developers.

Client Involvement: May specify performance benchmarks and review results.

Process: Tools like JMeter, LoadRunner, or Gatling simulate heavy loads, spikes in traffic, and long-term operation to identify bottlenecks.

Integration Moment: Done after full integration and before UAT or as a parallel activity.

Typical Duration: 3–7 days for comprehensive analysis.

Contractual Note: Performance failures can be grounds for withholding acceptance; benchmarks should be explicitly stated in the contract.

6.2.2 Client Testing

1. **User Acceptance Testing (UAT)—Client's Validation**

User Acceptance Testing (UAT) is the decisive stage in the Software Development Lifecycle where the Client (or the designated end-users) verifies that the software meets real-world business needs and the contractual acceptance criteria. Unlike earlier testing phases focused on technical compliance, UAT validates *operational suitability*: whether the system works in the way the client's teams will actually use it.

In practice, the **client or product owner** runs predefined test scenarios, often using real or representative operational data, to simulate day-to-day processes. For example, in a retail ERP implementation, UAT might include creating purchase orders, processing sales transactions, updating inventory levels, and generating financial reports, all within the same workflow the business will follow after Go-Live.

The **developer's role** is to provide a stable, integrated release candidate in a controlled test environment, assist with test data setup, and promptly address any defects identified. The **QA team and project manager** facilitate the process by tracking issues, coordinating fixes, and ensuring that retesting is performed after corrections.

If the software passes all agreed test scenarios and meets the contractual acceptance criteria, the client issues a formal sign-off, triggering milestone payments, deployment authorization, and, where applicable, the transfer of intellectual property rights as set out in the agreement.

However, if the software fails UAT, meaning it does not perform as expected, contains critical defects, or does not comply with the agreed requirements, the process shifts into a **defect resolution and retesting cycle**. In such cases:

- The **client** must issue a written *rejection notice*, detailing the failed test cases, the specific contractual criteria not met, and any associated evidence (screenshots, logs, reports)
- The **developer** is obligated to remedy the identified defects within the timeframe stated in the contract, at no additional cost to the client, and to provide a new release candidate for retesting
- The **QA team and project manager** coordinate the retesting process, ensuring that fixes are verified and that no new defects have been introduced (regression testing)

Contractually, repeated failure to pass UAT within the agreed number of retesting cycles may entitle the client to:

- Withhold or reduce milestone payments until acceptance is achieved
- Apply contractual penalties or liquidated damages for delay
- Terminate the contract for cause, if the failure is material and remains uncorrected after the cure period

From a legal perspective, well-documented UAT results (whether pass or fail) are critical. They provide objective evidence of compliance or breach, forming the basis for enforcement of remedies, claims for damages, or defense against unfounded rejection.

UAT typically lasts **5–30 business days**, as stipulated in the contract, with duration depending on system size, complexity, and the number of scenarios to be validated. The results of UAT form the formal basis for project acceptance. The sign-off document produced at the end of this stage is often a contractual precondition for milestone payment, go-live authorization, or the transfer of intellectual property rights.

Go-Live

In real-world IT projects, **go-live** occurs immediately after successful completion of UAT, when the client and developer agree that the system is sufficiently stable for production use. This moment marks the **operational handover** from the development/testing environment to the client's live business environment.

Legal and Contractual Implications

Go-live is not Final Acceptance. It signifies that the system has met the minimum contractual acceptance criteria verified in UAT, but it is still subject to ongoing observation and defect resolution obligations.

Start of the Final Acceptance Period. Most contracts define a stabilization or warranty period, typically 30 to 180 days, during which the client uses the system in production, and the developer is obliged to fix, at no additional cost, any defects that prevent the system from meeting the agreed acceptance criteria.

Payment Triggers. Go-live often triggers partial release of milestone payments (e.g., 70–90% of the final payment), with the remaining balance payable upon Final Acceptance.

Intellectual Property Transfer. In some contracts, IP rights transfer partially at go-live and fully at Final Acceptance; in others, transfer occurs only at Final Acceptance to ensure the developer's leverage for defect resolution.

Client's Obligations Between Go-Live and Final Acceptance

Operational Use: The client must use the system in real business conditions as intended and must not introduce unapproved changes that could affect performance or stability.

Defect Reporting: The client must promptly notify the developer of any defects discovered, providing sufficient detail (steps to reproduce, screenshots, logs) to enable efficient resolution.

Cooperation: The client must provide timely access to the production environment, relevant data, and key personnel to facilitate defect investigation and remediation.

Acceptance Testing of Fixes: The client must test and confirm fixes provided during this period, ensuring that resolution is formally documented.

By clearly defining the obligations and rights of both parties between go-live and final acceptance, contracts avoid disputes over defect responsibility, payment delays, and the scope of post-go-live changes.

Sample contract clause—failure to pass User Acceptance Testing (UAT):

UAT Failure Notification

If the Deliverable fails to meet any of the agreed Acceptance Criteria during UAT, the Client shall issue a written *UAT Rejection Notice* to the Developer within [X] Business Days of completing UAT. The notice shall identify: (a) the failed test cases; (b) the specific Acceptance Criteria not met; and (c) supporting evidence such as logs, screenshots, or test reports.

Defect Resolution Obligations

Upon receipt of the UAT Rejection Notice, the Developer shall, at its sole cost and without undue delay, remedy the identified defects and provide an updated version of the Deliverable for retesting. The remedial work shall be completed within [Y] Business Days unless otherwise agreed in writing by the Parties.

Retesting Procedure

The Client shall re-execute only the failed test cases and any impacted workflows (including regression tests) within [Z] Business Days after delivery of the corrected version. If the Deliverable passes all re-executed test cases, the Client shall issue a *UAT Acceptance Certificate*.

Repeated Failures

If the Deliverable fails UAT on more than [two] consecutive occasions for the same material defect(s), the Client may, without prejudice to other remedies available under this Agreement or at law: (a) withhold milestone payments until Acceptance is achieved; (b) apply liquidated damages as specified in Clause [Liquidated Damages]; or (c) terminate this Agreement for cause pursuant to Clause [Termination for Cause].

No Additional Payment for Remedial Work

All corrective actions, retesting, and associated costs required for the Deliverable to meet the Acceptance Criteria shall be borne exclusively by the Developer, unless the failure is directly attributable to changes requested by the Client outside the agreed Scope of Work.

Evidence and Record-Keeping

All UAT results, defect reports, communications, and retesting records shall be retained by both Parties for a minimum of [12] months from the date of Acceptance or contract termination. These records shall be admissible as evidence in any dispute resolution proceedings under Clause [Dispute Resolution].

Legal risk

If UAT is not conducted thoroughly, both parties face significant risks:

- **For the client**: Accepting the system without comprehensive validation may forfeit the right to claim defects later, especially if the contract contains a "deemed acceptance" clause triggered by silence or delayed feedback
- **For the developer**: Failing to meet contractual acceptance criteria during UAT can result in withheld payments, forced rework at their expense, or even termination of the agreement
- **For both parties**: If UAT criteria are vaguely defined or missing from the contract, disputes may arise over whether a defect is a breach of scope or an out-of-scope change request, leading to cost and schedule conflicts

Evidence in litigation

To protect both parties and ensure enforceability, the following UAT evidence should be retained:

- **Signed UAT Test Plans**: Document listing all agreed scenarios, expected results, and acceptance criteria

- **Test Execution Logs**: Records showing which scenarios were executed, by whom, when, and the outcome of each test
- **Defect Reports**: Detailed descriptions of defects found, their severity, and resolution status
- **Retesting Confirmation**: Evidence that fixes were applied and verified before sign-off
- **Formal Acceptance or Rejection Notices**: Signed documents confirming acceptance or specifying reasons for rejection, within the contractual timeframe

Maintaining this evidence ensures that UAT is not only a functional checkpoint but also a legally defensible process. In the event of a dispute, these records can demonstrate compliance with contractual terms and clarify whether issues raised after acceptance are warranty defects or new requirements.

User Acceptance Testing (UAT) summary

Objective: Allow the client or designated end-users to verify that the software meets their real-world needs and contractual acceptance criteria.

Responsible Party: Client / Product Owner, with support from QA Team and Project Manager.

Developer's Role: Provide the test environment, assist with test data setup, fix defects found.

Process: The client executes agreed test scenarios, often using real or representative operational data. Feedback is documented and shared with the development team for corrections.

Integration Moment: UAT is performed on a stable, integrated version (often called a release candidate).

Typical Duration: Usually 5–15 business days as per contract, depending on system size and complexity.

Contractual Note: UAT results form the basis for formal acceptance. Sign-off here is often a precondition for milestone payment or deployment.

Final Acceptance and Sign-Off

Final Acceptance and Sign-Off is the closing phase of the Software Development Lifecycle from a contractual perspective. It formalizes that the delivered software meets all agreed functional, performance, and compliance requirements, and that it is ready for production deployment. This stage is not a technical test, but rather a **contractual and evidentiary milestone** confirming that all obligations have been fulfilled.

In practice, the **client**, coordinated by the **project manager**, reviews all testing evidence, including results from system testing, UAT, regression testing, performance testing, and security testing, alongside supporting documents such as defect resolution logs, compliance certificates, and user manuals. The **developer's role** is to provide complete and accurate documentation, ensuring that every acceptance criterion in the contract is demonstrably met.

For example, in an ERP deployment for a multinational company, final acceptance may involve verifying that all financial reports comply with local tax regulations, that all integrations with third-party payment providers are functional, and that no open critical defects remain unresolved. Only after these verifications are complete does the client issue a **Final Acceptance Certificate**.

Sign-off typically occurs **just before production deployment** and is completed within **1–5 business days**, depending on the scale of the system and the complexity of the contractual acceptance criteria. In most contracts, final acceptance **triggers the release of final milestone payments**, the **transfer of intellectual property rights**, and/or the **start of the maintenance and support period**.

Conditional Acceptance—Acceptance with Reservations

In some software projects, the parties may agree to a **Conditional Acceptance**, whereby the client formally confirms that the deliverable is stable and functional enough to be put into operation, but expressly identifies a set of minor defects or outstanding enhancements. These items are recorded in a list attached to the acceptance certificate, together with clear deadlines for remediation, at no additional cost to the client.

Conditional Acceptance is particularly useful when project timelines require a go-live before every detail is perfected, yet both parties want to maintain a clear contractual framework for completing the outstanding work. Under this arrangement, the developer remains obligated to deliver the agreed fixes within the specified timeframe, while the client reserves the right to impose penalties or withhold final payment if the remediation deadlines are not met.

Legal risk

- **For the developer**: If final acceptance is delayed or withheld due to incomplete documentation or outstanding defects, milestone payments may be postponed, and IP rights may not transfer. Repeated delays can expose the developer to claims of breach of contract
- **For the client**: Signing final acceptance without thorough verification may waive the right to raise certain defect claims later, especially if the contract contains a "final acceptance is conclusive" clause

- **For both parties**: If acceptance criteria are vague or not explicitly documented, disputes may arise over whether the software has been fully delivered, potentially delaying deployment and payments

Evidence in litigation

Key evidence to retain from the final acceptance stage includes:

- **Final Acceptance Certificate**: Signed by the client, confirming that all contractual obligations have been met
- **Testing Summary Reports**: Consolidated results from all testing phases, proving compliance with acceptance criteria
- **Defect Closure Reports**: Evidence that all critical and high-severity issues have been resolved and retested
- **Compliance and Regulatory Certificates**: Proof that the software meets applicable legal and industry standards (e.g., GDPR, HIPAA)
- **Handover Documentation**: Manuals, training materials, and configuration records provided to the client

Maintaining this evidence ensures that both parties have a clear contractual endpoint and that any future disputes over delivery, payment, or ownership can be resolved with documented proof of acceptance.

Final acceptance summary

Objective: Formalize that the software meets all contractual obligations and is ready for deployment.

Responsible Party: Client, with Project Manager coordinating.

Developer's Role: Provide all required documentation (test results, defect resolutions, compliance reports).

Process: Client reviews all testing evidence, confirms that acceptance criteria are met, and issues a formal sign-off document.

Integration Moment: Sign-off typically precedes production deployment.

Typical Duration: 1–5 business days.

Contractual Note: Sign-off often triggers final payment and the transfer of IP rights or maintenance responsibilities.

6.2.3 Final Acceptance Checklist

This checklist ensures that **before issuing Final Acceptance**, the client verifies that the software is fully compliant with contractual obligations, operational needs, and legal requirements. It is structured for use both in contract negotiations and in project closure.

1. **Contractual Prerequisites Verification**
   - All deliverables listed in the **Scope of Work (SoW)** have been provided
   - All testing phases (System Testing, UAT, Regression, Performance, Security) have been completed successfully, with signed test reports
   - All critical and high-severity defects have been resolved, retested, and closed in the defect tracking system
   - All approved change requests have been implemented, tested, and accepted by the client
   - No outstanding contractual obligations remain other than post-acceptance warranty/support

Evidence to Retain: Signed test reports, defect closure logs, change request approvals, contractual compliance checklist.

2. **Documentation Delivery** *(To be completed before Final Acceptance review)*
   - **Technical Documentation**:
     - System architecture diagrams, module specifications, database schemas, API documentation, data flow diagrams
     - Version numbers and build references match the final tested release
   - **Operational Documentation**:
     - End-user manuals, administrator guides, configuration instructions, standard operating procedures
   - **Maintenance & Support Documentation**:
     - Backup and recovery procedures, disaster recovery plan, monitoring guidelines, escalation procedures
   - **Compliance & Regulatory Documentation**:
     - Certificates and audit reports proving GDPR, HIPAA, PCI DSS, or other contractual compliance

Evidence to Retain: Document delivery acknowledgment, version control logs, compliance certificates, read-only access to final documentation repository.

3. **Training Delivery**
   - End-user training covering standard workflows, navigation, and operational tasks

- Administrator/technical training for internal IT staff, including configuration, troubleshooting, and escalation
- All training materials provided in durable form (slides, manuals, recordings)
- Attendance records signed by participants
- Post-training Q&A or feedback session completed

Evidence to Retain: Training agenda, participant list with signatures, feedback forms, archive of materials.

4. **Operational Validation**
   - The system has been running in production for the entire **Final Acceptance Period** defined in the contract (e.g., 30–180 days)
   - All issues reported during this period have been resolved, retested, and documented
   - SLAs for performance, availability, and security have been consistently met
   - No new critical or high-severity defects remain open

Evidence to Retain: Production logs, incident and resolution reports, SLA compliance dashboard.

5. **Integration and Interoperability Checks**
   - All third-party integrations are operational and stable
   - Data flows between integrated systems are complete, accurate, and secure
   - Cross-system security controls (authentication, encryption) are functioning
   - Test logs and transaction monitoring confirm interoperability without errors

Evidence to Retain: Integration test reports, API call logs, cross-system audit trails.

6. **Financial and Contractual Conditions**
   - All acceptance criteria from the contract are objectively verified as met
   - The **Final Acceptance Certificate** template is completed and ready for signature
   - Milestone payment amounts are confirmed and linked to the acceptance date
   - IP transfer clauses (if applicable) are ready to be executed upon signing

Evidence to Retain: Draft final acceptance certificate, payment release form, IP assignment documentation.

7. **Handover & Transition Readiness**
    - Access credentials for production systems have been transferred securely
    - All licensing keys, activation codes, and third-party credentials are documented and provided
    - Support contact points, escalation matrix, and maintenance schedules are confirmed
    - Warranty/support obligations are documented, with start and end dates clearly defined

Evidence to Retain: Credential transfer logs, signed handover form, support agreement annex.

8. **Formal Review Meeting**
    - Final review meeting held with client, developer, and project manager present
    - All evidence and documentation reviewed and confirmed
    - Any remaining minor issues documented in a **Post-Acceptance Remediation List** with deadlines
    - Agreement that no further acceptance conditions remain unmet

Evidence to Retain: Meeting minutes, signed remediation list (if applicable).

9. **Formal Sign-Off**
    - The **Final Acceptance Certificate** is signed by authorized representatives of both parties
    - Copies of the signed certificate are stored in both contractual and project archives
    - Notification of acceptance sent to all relevant project stakeholders

Evidence to Retain: Signed certificate, acceptance notification email, archive of acceptance package.

6.2.4 Template – Final Acceptance Certificate

Project Name: ______________________________

Contract No.: ______________________________

Client: ____________________________________

Developer: ______________________________

Date of Certificate: ________________________

Final Acceptance Date: ____________________

1. **Background**

This Final Acceptance Certificate is issued pursuant to Clause [X] of the Agreement dated [•] between the Client and the Developer for the delivery of [Project Description].

2. **Scope of Acceptance**

The Client confirms that:

1. All deliverables listed in the Scope of Work have been provided.
2. All contractual Acceptance Criteria have been met.
3. All critical and high-severity defects identified during the Final Acceptance Period have been resolved and retested.
4. All agreed documentation (technical, operational, maintenance, compliance) has been delivered.
5. All training sessions specified in the Agreement have been completed, and training materials have been received.

3. **Effect of Final Acceptance**

By signing this Certificate:

- The Deliverables are deemed fully accepted
- The Final Acceptance Date is established as the start of the warranty/support period under Clause [•] of the Agreement
- The final milestone payment of [amount/currency] becomes due in accordance with Clause [•]
- Intellectual property rights transfer as specified in Clause [•] of the Agreement

4. **Attachments**

- Final Testing Summary Report
- Defect Closure Report
- Documentation Delivery Acknowledgment
- Training Completion Record

6.2.5 Template – Conditional Acceptance Certificate

Project Name: ___________________________

Contract No.: ___________________________

Client: ______________________________

Developer: ______________________________

Date of Certificate: ______________________

Conditional Acceptance Date: ______________

1. **Background**

This Conditional Acceptance Certificate is issued pursuant to Clause [X] of the Agreement dated [•] between the Client and the Developer for the delivery of [Project Description].

2. **Scope of Conditional Acceptance**

The Client confirms that:

1. The deliverables listed in the Scope of Work have been substantially provided, and the system is operational in the production environment.
2. All contractual acceptance criteria for **critical** functionalities have been met, enabling go-live.
3. Certain non-critical items remain outstanding, as identified in *Annex A – Outstanding Items List*, but they do not prevent operational use of the system.
4. All agreed documentation necessary for go-live (technical, operational, maintenance, compliance) has been delivered.
5. All training sessions required for go-live have been completed, and the related training materials have been received.

3. **Outstanding Items and Deadlines** ***(Annex A)***

The following items are excluded from unconditional acceptance and must be completed by the Developer at no additional cost:

Ref. No.	Description of Outstanding Item	Severity	Completion Deadline	Evidence of Completion
1				
2				

4. **Effect of Conditional Acceptance**

By signing this Certificate:

- The Conditional Acceptance Date marks the start of the Final Acceptance Period defined in Clause [•] of the Agreement
- The Client will release partial payment of [amount/currency], representing [X]% of the final milestone. The balance will be

released upon full completion and approval of the items listed in Annex A

- The Developer undertakes to complete all outstanding items in Annex A by the agreed deadlines. Failure to do so will entitle the Client to exercise contractual remedies, including withholding the remaining payment, applying penalties, or extending the warranty period

5. **Attachments**

- Annex A – Outstanding Items List
- Conditional Acceptance Test Summary Report
- Go-Live Readiness Confirmation
- Documentation Delivery Acknowledgment
- Training Completion Record

6.2.6 Template – Final Acceptance Rejection Notice

Project Name: ______________________________

Contract No.: ______________________________

Client: ____________________________________

Developer: _________________________________

Date of Notice: _____________________________

1. **Background**

This Final Acceptance Rejection Notice is issued pursuant to Clause [X] of the Agreement dated [•] between the Client and the Developer for the delivery of [Project Description].

2. **Reason for Rejection**

Following the Final Acceptance Review conducted on [date], the Client has determined that the Deliverables do not meet the contractual Acceptance Criteria for the following reasons:

Ref. No.	Description of Non-Compliance	Severity Level	Contract/ Annex Reference	Evidence/ Attachment
1				
2				
3				

3. **Remediation Requirements**

The Developer is required to remedy the above deficiencies within **[X] Business Days** from receipt of this Notice and resubmit the Deliverables for review.

Failure to remedy within the specified period may result in the application of contractual remedies under Clause [•], including but not limited to: withholding of payments; application of liquidated damages; termination for cause.

4. **Attachments**
   - Final Testing Results highlighting non-compliance
   - Defect Reports with evidence (screenshots, logs)
   - Relevant contract clause references

CHAPTER 7

Deployment Phase

7.1 Overview of the Deployment Phase

The Deployment Phase is essentially the Go-Live process, marking the point at which the software is installed, configured, and activated in the client's production environment, becoming available for actual end users.

From both a technical and legal perspective, the Go-Live date is a determinative contractual milestone that must be expressly set out in the agreement. In well-drafted software contracts, the Go-Live date is not left as an open-ended event; instead, it is defined as a fixed calendar date or as a date triggered by the completion of specified preconditions, most notably, successful User Acceptance Testing (UAT) and formal client sign-off.

The Go-Live event triggers a cascade of contractual consequences. First, it often serves as the point at which the developer's primary delivery obligations are considered substantially fulfilled, enabling the release of final or substantial payment instalments as specified in the payment schedule.

Second, it commonly marks the commencement of the warranty period, during which the developer is legally bound to correct defects, ensure performance standards are met, and apply any required security patches without additional cost to the client.

Third, Go-Live frequently activates post-deployment support obligations, such as providing technical assistance, user support, performance monitoring, or system optimization during a defined stabilization period.

Fourth, the Go-Live date may also be tied to service-level obligations (e.g., uptime, response times) if such SLAs are part of the contract, meaning that failure to meet these standards post-launch could result in penalties, service credits, or even termination rights for the client.

Given these significant legal and financial consequences, the Go-Live date must be treated as a contractual anchor point. Its inclusion in the agreement ensures clarity, prevents disputes over whether delivery obligations have been met, and aligns both parties on the precise moment when operational use begins and the associated rights and duties take effect. In short, Go-Live is not merely a technical switchover; it is a legally determinative event with immediate and enforceable implications for both parties.

 DOI: 10.4324/9781003669609-7

Table 7.1 Key Parties Deployment Phase Roles and Responsibilities

Sub-Phase	*Timing*	*Developer*	*Client (Business & IT/Ops)*	*Project Manager (PMO)*	*Technology Lawyer*
Pre-Go-Live Readiness & Environment Freeze	T-20 to T-10	Complete integration, performance, security tests; fix UAT defects; freeze code; produce deployment runbooks & rollback plan; deliver final docs & training materials.	Provision production infra; confirm sizing, backups, monitoring access; approve freeze window; ensure licenses/credentials available.	Lock the plan; align calendars; confirm prerequisites; run readiness checklist; schedule cutover war-room.	Confirm contractual preconditions to Go-Live (UAT sign-off, SLAs, approvals); review risk register; verify change orders.
Data Migration Rehearsal & Validation	T-15 to T-7	Execute dry-run migration; reconcile records; tune scripts; produce reconciliation report & defect log.	Provide clean, approved data extracts; validate sample outputs; sign data mapping & acceptance memo.	Coordinate rehearsal; track defects to closure; publish readiness scorecard.	Confirm data protection, retention, and transfer compliance (e.g., GDPR), note any residual risks in a short memo.
Final UAT Closure & Go/No-Go Criteria	T-7 to T-3	Demonstrate fixes; present test evidence vs acceptance criteria; update risk/issue list with mitigations.	Issue formal UAT sign-off (or documented reservations with remediation plan); confirm business readiness.	Chair Go/No-Go meeting; record decisions; circulate cutover checklist.	Verify that UAT sign-off meets contract; confirm any conditional acceptance wording.

Cutover Planning & Communications	T-5 to T-1	Finalize step-by-step deployment script, rollback triggers, and verification checks; assign on-call roles.	Approve downtime window; notify stakeholders & customers; staff on-call SMEs (DBA, network).	Publish comms plan (who/when/how); align escalation bridges; run "cutover drill."	Review customer notices (if legally required) and outage disclaimers; check SLA activation rules.
Go-Live Execution (Cutover)	T0 (and T-1 nightly window)	Execute deployment; run smoke tests; enable monitoring/alerts; complete deployment checklist; declare provisional success or trigger rollback.	Validate business-critical transactions in production; confirm access & permissions; approve "open for business."	Lead war-room; time-box verification steps; log every decision & timestamp; coordinate rollback if needed.	Standby for urgent terms clarification (SLAs, force majeure, notifications).
Hypercare / Stabilization	T+1 to T+30 (typ.)	Triage & fix P1–P3 defects within agreed SLAs; tune performance; deliver daily status; hand over to steady-state support.	Report incidents promptly; provide logs & reproducible cases; avoid out-of-process changes; approve urgent fixes.	Run daily triage; track SLA compliance; publish burn-down of defects; manage stakeholder updates.	Verify warranty start, SLA enforcement, and any service credits; ensure incident records meet evidentiary standards.
Final Acceptance & Closure	Typically T+14 to T+45	Provide defect closure report, performance evidence, compliance pack; deliver as-built docs; complete knowledge transfer.	Conduct acceptance tests in production; issue Final Acceptance Certificate or Rejection/ Conditional Acceptance with cure list; release payments per contract.	Orchestrate closure meeting; confirm all deliverables received; archive project artifacts.	Review and approve Final Acceptance form; confirm IP transfer, warranty terms, and any remaining liabilities.

Note: Use the **T** notation as reference: **T-x** = days before Go-Live; **T0** = Go-Live day; **T+x** = days after Go-Live.

After Go-Live, the developer transitions into a new phase of contractual obligations, where their role shifts from active construction of the software to ensuring its stability, performance, and conformity to agreed standards under live operational conditions.

This period is often governed by a warranty clause and/or a post-deployment support agreement. The developer may be obligated to correct defects identified during the stabilization period, apply security patches, fine-tune performance, and provide technical assistance to users. These obligations are typically time-bound, with defined response and resolution times based on the severity of the issue. If service-level agreements are in place, the developer must also maintain agreed uptime and performance metrics, with penalties or service credits applying in cases of non-compliance.

From the client's perspective, Go-Live also marks the start of a new set of responsibilities. The client must ensure that the production environment is prepared and that necessary infrastructure, such as servers, network access, and security configurations, is properly maintained to support the software's operation.

The client is also generally responsible for providing timely feedback on issues, granting the developer necessary access for troubleshooting, and adhering to any usage guidelines outlined in the contract to preserve warranty rights.

Furthermore, the client must process final acceptance testing in the live environment within the agreed timeframe, pay any remaining contractual instalments tied to Go-Live, and document any defects or performance deviations according to the agreed reporting procedures.

In essence, Go-Live shifts the contractual relationship from one focused on *delivery* to one focused on *performance assurance and operational stability*. Both parties carry critical, interdependent obligations during this phase, and failure by either side to meet these obligations, whether it is the developer's duty to remedy defects or the client's duty to provide operational cooperation, can lead to disputes, delays in final acceptance, and potentially financial consequences.

Deployment encompasses all technical and operational activities required to make the software fully operational, including final testing, configuration, data migration, and user setup. Specific deployment strategies, such as phased, parallel, or "big bang" deployment, may be applied based on the project's complexity and the agreed terms.

The Deployment Phase thus represents not only the technical transition of software to an active state but also a formal acknowledgment of contractual fulfilment by the developer, setting in motion the post-deployment obligations and rights of both parties.

7.2 Stakeholders Roles in Preparing for Go-Live

Preparing for Go-Live is a decisive stage in the software development lifecycle, where all stakeholders converge to transition the system from a controlled development or staging environment into live, operational use. Technically, this phase ensures that the product is stable, secure, and configured for production. Legally, it represents the point at which multiple contractual conditions must be satisfied before Go-Live can lawfully occur. This includes the completion of User Acceptance Testing (UAT), formal client sign-off, readiness of the operational environment, and the fulfilment of any preconditions expressly set out in the contract.

7.2.1 Developer's Role and Obligations

The developer bears the **primary and overarching responsibility** for ensuring that the software is fully prepared for deployment into the client's live, operational environment. This obligation extends far beyond simply completing the coding work; it encompasses a comprehensive verification process designed to confirm that the delivered system is technically, functionally, and operationally ready to perform under real-world conditions.

In practice, this means that before the software can proceed to Go-Live, the developer must ensure that every component, integration point, and feature functions in accordance with the contractual specifications, the agreed acceptance criteria, and applicable regulatory or industry standards.

This responsibility requires the developer to conduct and document a full readiness assessment, including rigorous integration testing to validate the interaction of all modules, performance and load testing under simulated production conditions to verify system stability at scale, and security checks to confirm that the implemented safeguards meet or exceed contractual and statutory requirements.This process includes:

- ***Final integration testing*** to confirm that all modules and components work together as intended
- ***Load and stress testing*** under simulated production conditions to validate performance under peak usage
- ***Verification of security controls***, ensuring that all data protection, access control, and encryption mechanisms meet contractual and regulatory standards
- ***Defect correction*** for all issues identified during User Acceptance Testing (UAT), supported by formal resolution records

Equally critical is the provision of complete and accurate documentation, covering every operational aspect of the system: installation and configuration procedures, step-by-step user operation instructions, troubleshooting guides, and maintenance protocols. In practice, the developer must deliver comprehensive documentation as part of the deployment package. This includes:

- ***Installation and configuration guides*** for system administrators
- ***User operation manuals*** detailing day-to-day use
- ***Troubleshooting guides*** for common errors and issues
- ***Maintenance procedures*** to ensure ongoing system stability

Where the contract specifies **readiness criteria** like defined performance benchmarks, successful data migration validation, or industry compliance standards, the developer must provide **objective evidence** of compliance. This can include signed test reports, benchmark data, security audit logs, and migration checklists.

Legal risks for the developer

Failure to meet Go-Live readiness obligations can result in:

- *Claims of breach of contract* for delivering software that does not meet specifications
- *Delay-related damages* if missed deployment dates cause operational losses for the client
- *Regulatory liability* if inadequate security measures lead to compliance violations (e.g., GDPR fines)
- *Termination rights for the client* if the breach is considered material

Evidence in litigation

In the event of a dispute or litigation, contemporaneous technical and procedural documentation becomes critical in proving compliance. Key evidence may include:

- UAT sign-off forms confirming client approval
- Performance and security test reports
- Change logs and defect resolution records
- Data migration validation reports
- Internal QA and audit documentation

Producing this evidence not only protects the developer in legal proceedings but also strengthens their position in negotiations, mediations, or arbitration by providing an objective record of meeting contractual obligations.

7.2.1.1 Frequent Litigation Issues in the Preparing for Go-Live Stage

1. **Failure to Meet Performance Benchmarks**

Typical dispute. In final performance testing, the system misses contractually stated thresholds (throughput, response time, concurrency), forcing a Go-Live delay.

Example. An online banking platform agreed at ≥10,000 Transactions Per Second (TPS) achieves only ~6,500 TPS under peak test.

Legal theories raised by the client. Breach of express warranty; failure of a condition precedent to Go-Live; liquidated damages for delay.

2. **Unresolved Critical Defects After UAT**

Typical dispute. High-severity defects logged in UAT remain open when the developer asks to proceed to Go-Live.

Example. In an ERP rollout, invoice totals occasionally miscalculate taxes, but the developer labels it "post-Go-Live cosmetic."

Legal theories raised by the client. Breach of acceptance criteria; failure to exercise reasonable skill and care; attempted premature tender of delivery.

3. **Inadequate Security Hardening or Compliance Readiness**

Typical dispute. Pen-test or vulnerability scan identifies critical findings (e.g., broken access control, missing encryption at rest) shortly before Go-Live.

Example. A healthcare app fails to meet encryption and audit-logging controls promised for HIPAA/GDPR.

Legal theories raised by the client. Breach of statutory/compliance warranties; misrepresentation if compliance claims were used to secure the deal; indemnity triggers for regulatory exposure.

4. **Incomplete or Defective Data Migration**

Typical dispute. Migration rehearsal reveals lost, corrupted, or unmapped fields; the developer insists the client's legacy data was "dirty."

Example. Customer birthdates and VAT numbers are malformed in production-like rehearsal, breaking invoicing.

Legal theories raised by the client. Breach of migration obligations; negligent services; failure to follow agreed mapping and validation steps.

5. **Insufficient Documentation and Training Delivery**

Typical dispute. The software may run, but the developer has not delivered installation guides, run-books, or admin/user manuals promised pre-Go-Live; training is curtailed.

Example. Ops cannot execute failover because the run-book is missing; Go-Live stalls.

Legal theories raised by the client. Failure to deliver all contract deliverables; breach of condition precedent to acceptance; consequential delay.

6. **Environment Mismatch and "It Works on Our Machine"**

Typical dispute. Software passes in the developer's lab but fails in the client's staging due to unaligned versions, infra sizing, or missing dependencies.

Example. The application is designed to work with a newer database version than the one installed in the client's staging environment, causing errors when certain features are executed.

Legal theories raised by the client. Breach of obligation to ensure compatibility with the **specified target environment**; failure to follow deployment prerequisites.

7. **Attempted Unapproved Scope Substitution**

Typical dispute. Developer swaps committed features for "equivalent" alternatives to stay on schedule, meaning the developer changes a promised feature to a simpler version without the client's full agreement, claiming it will save time or meet deadlines.

Example. The contract specifies a "single sign-on" login so users can access the system with their company account, but instead the developer delivers a basic login with username and password, saying the advanced login will be added later.

Legal theories raised by the client. Breach of contract/specifications; non-conforming tender; repudiatory breach if material.

Evidence. Original specs vs. delivered feature parity analysis; emails proposing substitutions; lack of signed change orders; demo recordings and acceptance test results.

Preventive drafting. Require **formal change control** for any deviation; forbid unilateral substitutions; tie payments to **feature-level acceptance**.

8. **Schedule Slippage and Liquidated Damages**

Typical dispute. The developer misses the readiness date; client seeks damages or claims downstream loss.

Example. Retail launch tied to holiday season slips past the contractual freeze date.

Legal theories raised by the client. Breach of time obligations; liquidated damages enforcement; debates over excusable delay/force majeure.

9. **Poor Handover to Operations**

Typical dispute. The client's operations team cannot properly run or support the system because the developer did not provide the necessary monitoring tools, instructions, or emergency procedures.

Example. After launch, there are no system checks or dashboards to track performance, and a major system failure happens on the first day without any clear way to detect or fix the problem quickly.

Legal theories raised by the client. Breach of deliverables relating to operability/supportability; failure to meet implied duties of professional skill.

Evidence. Monitoring dashboards, alert rules; handover checklist, knowledge-transfer session records; post-cutover incident timeline and root-cause analysis.

Preventive drafting. Mandate **operational readiness criteria** (monitoring, logging, alerts, runbooks, KT sessions) as ***conditions precedent*** *to Go-Live.*

7.2.2 Client's Role and Obligations

The client plays a decisive role in ensuring that the software can be successfully transitioned from the development or staging environment into the live, operational environment. While the developer bears primary responsibility for building and verifying the system, the client's obligations are equally critical and are often contractual conditions precedent to Go-Live. Failure by the client to discharge these duties can delay deployment, trigger cost overruns, or even shift liability for post-deployment defects or operational failures back onto the client.

The client's obligations in the Preparing for Go-Live stage are not passive; they require active engagement, timely approvals, and the provisioning of all resources, infrastructure, and information necessary for deployment. In many contracts, these obligations are expressly tied to readiness milestones, meaning that without the client's cooperation, Go-Live cannot occur, and the developer's delivery obligations may be deemed suspended until the client meets its own commitments.

The client must ensure that the production environment is ready, compatible, and properly configured to host the software in accordance with the technical specifications agreed in the contract. This typically includes:

- Provisioning and configuring all necessary hardware, network infrastructure, storage, and connectivity as per the agreed deployment architecture
- Ensuring that all prerequisite software components (e.g., operating systems, middleware, databases) are installed, licensed, and configured to the versions required by the system
- Providing secure access credentials, VPN connections, or other means of system access to the developer's deployment team
- Completing all environmental testing or certification processes required by the agreement before deployment

The client is also responsible for active participation in User Acceptance Testing (UAT), including the timely execution of agreed test cases, logging of defects, and issuance of formal UAT sign-off upon successful completion. Delays or incomplete UAT participation can directly delay Go-Live and may trigger contractual consequences such as the extension of timelines or the shifting of costs.

Data preparation and migration is another critical area. Where the contract requires the client to extract, cleanse, validate, and deliver legacy data for migration into the new system, failure to do so can result in corrupted or incomplete datasets in production. The client must ensure that all data mapping is confirmed, source data is accurate, and migration rehearsals are supported with the necessary resources.

Furthermore, the client is typically responsible for operational readiness, which includes training internal support teams; preparing runbooks and escalation protocols (if not delivered by the developer); and ensuring that business processes are adapted to the new system's workflows. This may involve updating internal SOPs, preparing user training schedules, and ensuring that super-users or key operators are available during the stabilization period.

From a contractual perspective, these duties are not merely "best practice," they are often express obligations, breach of which can entitle the developer to extensions of time, cost recovery for delays, or, in some cases, a deemed acceptance of the software.

Legal risks for the client

Failure to meet these pre-Go-Live obligations can expose the client to:

- Liability for delay if the client's failure to provide infrastructure, approvals, or data prevents Go-Live on the agreed date
- Deemed acceptance clauses, where failure to complete UAT or sign-off within the contractually specified period results in the software being automatically deemed accepted, limiting the client's ability to claim defects later
- Shift of risk for defects or operational failures caused by environmental issues or bad data supplied by the client
- Termination by the developer if the client's repeated non-performance constitutes a material breach
- Payment obligations being triggered despite the client's unpreparedness if the contract ties payment to the developer's readiness rather than the actual Go-Live date

Evidence in litigation

In a dispute, evidence demonstrating whether the client met its Go-Live preparation obligations is essential. Relevant evidence may include:

- UAT test execution logs, defect reports, and formal sign-off (or correspondence showing refusal or delay)
- Infrastructure readiness checklists and environment configuration logs
- Data migration mapping documents, validation reports, and error logs from rehearsals
- Emails or project meeting minutes showing delays in providing access, approvals, or resources
- Training attendance logs and operational readiness documentation

Well-maintained records can help the client prove that delays or defects were caused by the developer, not by client-side failures.

7.2.2.1 Frequent Litigation Issues in the Preparing for Go-Live Stage (Client-Side)

1. **Failure to Provide a Ready Production Environment**

Typical dispute. Go-Live is delayed because the client's servers, networks, or hosting environment are not ready, configured incorrectly, or lack required capacity.

Example. The contract specifies deployment to a cloud environment with a specific region and capacity, but the client fails to provision the environment until two weeks after the scheduled date.

Legal theories raised by the developer. Client breach of readiness obligations; entitlement to extension of time; recovery of idle resource costs.

Evidence. Cloud provisioning logs, access request records, deployment attempt reports.

Preventive drafting. Include an environment readiness checklist with fixed dates for completion and a clause allowing the developer to claim costs for delays.

2. **Delayed or Incomplete UAT Execution**

Typical dispute. The client fails to execute agreed UAT test cases on time, delaying Go-Live.

Example. Out of 200 planned test cases, the client completes only 60% due to resource unavailability.

Legal theories raised by the developer. Breach of cooperation obligations; deemed acceptance if delay exceeds contractual period; cost recovery for extended project team.

Evidence. UAT schedules, test execution reports, meeting minutes noting delays.

Preventive drafting. Tie UAT execution to fixed deadlines and allow the developer to proceed to Go-Live if tests are not executed within a defined grace period.

3. **Failure to Provide Clean and Valid Data for Migration**

Typical dispute. The new system cannot be launched because the client gives the developer old business data that is wrong, incomplete, or in the wrong format. When the developer tries to move (migrate) this data into the new system, the errors cause the process to fail.

Example. In the old system, customer addresses are stored in one long text box where people typed anything they wanted, sometimes leaving out postal codes or writing them incorrectly. The new system requires the postal code to be in a separate field and follow a strict format (for example, five digits). Because the data from the old system doesn't follow this rule, the migration stops and the software cannot go live until the data is fixed.

Legal theories raised by the developer. Breach of data preparation obligations; liability for rework costs; shifting of defect risk to client.

Evidence. Data extracts; cleansing reports; error logs from migration rehearsals; preventive drafting; require the client to certify data readiness before migration; allow cost recovery for additional cleansing work.

4. **Non-Provision of Required Licenses or Third-Party Components**

Typical dispute. The software cannot be deployed because the client has not procured necessary third-party licenses.

Example. A required analytics tool is licensed under the client's name, but procurement is delayed beyond Go-Live.

Legal theories raised by the developer. Breach of preparatory obligations; no entitlement to liquidated damages from developer.

Evidence. License procurement records, vendor correspondence.

Preventive drafting. Include a license procurement responsibility matrix.

5. **Late or Conditional Sign-Off of UAT**

Typical dispute. The client refuses to sign UAT completion despite defects being classified as minor or cosmetic under the contract.

Example. UAT is passed except for a logo color discrepancy, yet client withholds sign-off to delay Go-Live.

Legal theories raised by the developer. Breach of duty to act reasonably; wrongful delay of acceptance; trigger of deemed acceptance clause.

Evidence. UAT defect logs, contract defect classification tables, correspondence.

Preventive drafting. Define acceptance criteria strictly and limit sign-off refusal to material defects.

6. **Inadequate Resource Allocation for Go-Live Support**

Typical dispute. The system launch is delayed because the client did not assign the right people to work during the Go-Live weekend. Without these key staff members, problems that arise cannot be fixed quickly.

Example. During the data migration, unexpected errors appear in the database. A database administrator (DBA) is needed to fix these issues, but none was scheduled to work. As a result, the migration stops and the Go-Live is postponed until the following week.

Legal theories raised by the developer. Breach of cooperation; delay liability.

Evidence. Go-Live staffing rosters, incident logs showing lack of client-side support.

Preventive drafting. Mandate resourcing commitments in the deployment plan.

7. **Unauthorised Last-Minute Scope Change Requests**

Typical dispute. Client requests significant changes just before Go-Live, halting deployment.

Example. Adding a new payment gateway integration the day before scheduled cutover.

Legal theories raised by the developer. Change control breach; entitlement to cost and time extension for developer.

Evidence. Change request forms, meeting minutes, revised schedules.

Preventive drafting. Enforce a change freeze period before Go-Live.

8. **Lack of Operational Readiness**

Typical dispute. After Go-Live, the client's business operations break down because their internal processes, standard operating procedures (SOPs), or staff were not ready to work with the new system.

Example. The client's call center switches to the new CRM, but the call scripts were never updated to match the new workflow. As a result, agents do not know how to handle customer calls properly, leading to long delays, confused responses, and customer complaints.

Legal theories raised by the developer. Client-contributed failure; limits on developer liability for operational losses.

Evidence. SOP drafts, training attendance logs.

Preventive drafting. Include operational readiness certification as a condition to Go-Live.

9. **Failure to Maintain Compliance Requirements**

Typical dispute. Go-Live is blocked because client has not implemented required compliance measures in its environment.

Example. Client's hosting fails GDPR-required encryption-at-rest settings.

Legal theories. Breach of compliance obligations; shifting of liability for regulatory fines to client.

Evidence. Security audit reports, compliance checklists.

Preventive drafting. Allocate compliance responsibility clearly and require pre-Go-Live certification.

7.2.3 Project Manager's Role and Obligations

The project manager (PM) is the central coordinator for all activities leading up to Go-Live. In the preparing-for-deployment phase, the PM's role extends beyond general scheduling and reporting. They are responsible for ensuring that all readiness tasks are completed in sequence, dependencies are managed, and both the client and developer teams are aligned on scope, timelines, and acceptance criteria.

The PM acts as the bridge between technical teams, business stakeholders, and contractual commitments, making their role critical in avoiding last-minute surprises that could derail Go-Live.

From a contractual standpoint, the PM is not merely an "overseer" but is often explicitly tasked (either by a project charter or contractual annex) with delivering the project on schedule, within scope, and in compliance with acceptance criteria. This includes coordinating User Acceptance Testing (UAT) sign-off, confirming that readiness checklists are completed, and validating that all contractual prerequisites to deployment have been met.

A competent PM in this phase will:

- Ensure all pre-Go-Live tasks from the project plan are completed on time, including UAT remediation, final configuration, data migration rehearsals, and operational readiness checks
- Coordinate cross-team dependencies so that technical, operational, and business readiness activities converge at the agreed deployment window
- Maintain and distribute updated project timelines, highlighting critical paths and potential slippage
- Facilitate risk assessment sessions specifically focused on Go-Live readiness, ensuring that identified risks have mitigation plans
- Verify with the developer and client leads that readiness documentation, SLAs, and change controls are up to date and approved
- Ensure that escalation paths for Go-Live weekend are defined, with key contacts available for rapid decision-making

Legal risks for the project manager's organization

Failure of the PM to adequately coordinate the Go-Live preparation can create exposure under the main contract if delays, cost overruns, or failed deployments are traced to poor project management. This may lead to:

- *Breach of contract* claims if the PM's organization is contractually responsible for delivery oversight

- *Delay damages* if missed deadlines trigger liquidated damages clauses
- *Scope disputes* if poor change control processes lead to unauthorized scope adjustments
- *Negligence claims* if failure to plan or coordinate causes foreseeable and avoidable deployment issues

Evidence in litigation

To protect their position, a PM's organization should maintain:

- Dated Go-Live readiness checklists signed by responsible leads
- Updated Gantt charts and status reports showing timely identification of risks
- UAT issue logs with resolution status before Go-Live
- Change control forms and approval records for any late scope changes
- Communication records (emails, meeting minutes) confirming stakeholder agreement on Go-Live readiness

7.2.3.1 Frequent Litigation Issues in the Preparing for Go-Live Stage (Project Manager)

1. **Ineffective Coordination of UAT Remediation**

Typical dispute. Critical defects remain unresolved at Go-Live because the PM failed to enforce defect resolution deadlines.

Example. UAT identified errors in the payment gateway integration, but these were not tracked to closure before deployment.

Legal theories raised by the client. Breach of coordination duties; contributory cause to missed acceptance criteria.

2. **Poor Risk Management**

Typical dispute. Known risks (e.g., dependency on a pending third-party API update) are not escalated or mitigated, causing Go-Live failure.

Example. The PM knew a required vendor API would not be ready, but the issue was not escalated in time to adjust the plan.

Legal theories raised by the client. Failure to exercise reasonable skill and care; negligent project administration.

3. **Inadequate Resource Planning for Cutover**

Typical dispute. Go-Live stalls because key personnel are not scheduled or available.

Example. No network engineer is assigned for the cutover weekend, delaying environment switchover.

Legal theories raised by the client. Failure to coordinate resources; breach of implied duty to avoid preventable delays.

4. **Weak Change Control Enforcement**

Typical dispute. The PM allows unapproved changes to enter scope late in the project, derailing testing and readiness.

Example. A last-minute feature is added without approval, causing regression failures.

Legal theories raised by the client. Breach of scope control obligations; negligent scope management.

5. **Failure to Align Stakeholders on Go-Live Criteria**

Typical dispute. The client and developer disagree post-Go-Live on whether readiness criteria were met, because the PM failed to secure formal alignment pre-deployment.

Example. The developer assumes UAT sign-off means full readiness; the client insists additional security checks were required.

Legal theories raised by the client. Breach of documentation duties; failure to follow contract-mandated acceptance procedures.

7.2.4 Technology Lawyer's Role and Obligations

As the Go-Live date approaches, the technology lawyer's involvement moves from general contractual oversight into intensive pre-deployment verification. This phase represents a legal checkpoint where operational readiness must align fully with contractual, regulatory, and risk management frameworks. The lawyer acts as the safeguard ensuring that the transition into live operations does not trigger legal exposure, breach of contract claims, or regulatory non-compliance.

The technology lawyer is responsible for verifying that every contractual prerequisite to deployment has been satisfied. This includes ensuring that User Acceptance Testing (UAT) results are properly documented; that acceptance criteria defined in the agreement have been met or formally waived; and that any deviations from the original scope, delivery timeline, or payment schedule have been processed through valid, signed change control procedures.

A critical aspect of the lawyer's role in this phase is confirming compliance with all applicable legal and regulatory requirements before the system processes live data. This may involve reviewing data protection measures for GDPR compliance; verifying that sector-specific data retention and processing obligations (e.g., HIPAA in healthcare, PCI DSS in payments) are implemented; and ensuring that cybersecurity measures meet contractual and statutory standards.

A technology lawyer's duties in the Preparing for Go-Live phase include:

- Reviewing UAT reports, acceptance test results, and formal sign-off documentation to confirm contractual compliance
- Verifying that all readiness criteria stated in the contract—including performance, security, and migration obligations—have been satisfied or lawfully amended
- Checking that change control logs are complete, with all variations approved by authorized representatives
- Assessing the adequacy of security policies, encryption standards, and access controls in light of contractual commitments and regulatory requirements
- Ensuring that the Go-Live date is correctly defined and tied to the agreed contractual triggers (e.g., payment release, start of warranty period)
- Reviewing any third-party licences, API agreements, or hosting contracts to confirm that rights to use the required components in production are valid and in force

Legal risks for the client or developer if the lawyer's duties are neglected

Failure to involve the technology lawyer effectively at this stage can result in:

- *Breach of contract claims* if Go-Live occurs without meeting agreed acceptance criteria
- *Regulatory sanctions* (e.g., GDPR fines) if non-compliant systems are deployed
- *Loss of indemnity protection* if unapproved scope changes or missing compliance measures invalidate warranty clauses
- *Infringement disputes* if third-party IP licences required for production use are missing or expired
- *Increased litigation exposure* from unclear or undocumented acceptance

Evidence in litigation

In the event of a dispute, the technology lawyer's documented work can be decisive. Key evidence may include:

- Signed UAT acceptance forms and readiness checklists
- Change control logs with authorized signatures
- Regulatory compliance audit reports
- Security test results and remediation records
- Confirmations of active third-party licence rights

7.2.4.1 Frequent Litigation Issues in the Preparing for Go-Live Stage (Technology Lawyer)

1. **Go-Live Before Acceptance Criteria Are Met**

Typical dispute. Deployment proceeds despite failed performance or security tests, with the lawyer failing to halt the process.

Example. A financial trading platform launches despite load test failures that breach contractual throughput guarantees.

Legal theories. Breach of condition precedent; negligent professional advice; breach of implied duty to act in client's best interests.

2. **Unapproved Scope and Contract Variations**

Typical dispute. Key features are altered without proper change control, but the lawyer does not detect the lack of signed approvals.

Example. A promised audit logging feature is removed "temporarily," but no change order exists.

Legal theories. Breach of specification; waiver disputes; repudiatory breach claims.

3. **Regulatory Non-Compliance at Go-Live**

Typical dispute. System launches without meeting statutory data protection standards, triggering regulatory action.

Example. A healthcare SaaS goes live without encryption at rest for patient data, breaching HIPAA and contract terms.

Legal theories. Breach of statutory duty; breach of warranty; indemnity claims.

4. **Expired or Missing Third-Party Licences**

Typical dispute. Production deployment includes unlicensed libraries or expired API agreements.

Example. A mapping API used in the production release has no current licence, resulting in suspension of service.

Legal theories. IP infringement; breach of third-party contract; indemnity enforcement.

5. **Ambiguous Acceptance Documentation**

Typical dispute. Parties disagree on whether Go-Live sign-off occurred because the acceptance record is unclear or unsigned.

Example. An email chain contains informal "looks good" messages, but no formal acceptance form exists.

Legal theories. Disputes over condition precedent; interpretation of implied acceptance; evidentiary uncertainty.

7.2.5 Third-Party Vendors and Subcontractors' Role and Obligations

In the Preparing for Go-Live phase, third-party vendors and subcontractors play a pivotal role in ensuring that their respective deliverables are fully integrated, operational, and aligned with the main system's readiness requirements.

These parties may include cloud hosting providers, API service suppliers, security module vendors, payment gateway providers, database administrators, or subcontracted development teams. Their contributions are often mission-critical; any underperformance, delay, or incompatibility can directly jeopardize the primary developer's ability to meet contractual Go-Live obligations.

From a contractual perspective, the obligations of third-party vendors and subcontractors are most effectively managed through **back-to-back provisions** (clauses in their agreements that replicate the service, quality, and delivery requirements imposed on the primary developer in the main client contract). This alignment ensures that if the client contract requires, for example, specific uptime guarantees, security compliance standards, or performance benchmarks, the subcontractor is contractually bound to meet them as well.

These providers are responsible for confirming that their components or services are "production-ready," which involves final testing in the client's staging environment, verifying compatibility with the main system, and delivering complete operational documentation.

They must also coordinate closely with the primary developer to ensure seamless integration; participate in User Acceptance Testing (UAT) where relevant; and promptly communicate any risks, delays, or issues that could affect the Go-Live schedule.

Core responsibilities

- Ensuring that all deliverables (software modules, infrastructure, APIs, or integrations) meet the functional and performance specifications agreed with the primary developer
- Completing end-to-end integration testing with the main system before UAT begins, to avoid incompatibility issues
- Providing installation, configuration, and operational documentation as agreed, along with troubleshooting and escalation procedures
- Meeting all compliance obligations relevant to their deliverables, such as GDPR data handling rules, PCI DSS for payment data, or ISO 27001 for security practices
- Timely notification to the primary developer of any delivery risks, performance issues, or dependency delays that could impact Go-Live

Legal risks if obligations are not met

- ***Breach of subcontract*** if readiness obligations are not satisfied, leading to liability for losses incurred by the primary developer
- ***Flow-down liability***, where the primary developer becomes liable to the client due to the subcontractor's failure, and the subcontractor is in turn liable to the developer
- ***Regulatory penalties*** if the subcontractor's deliverables fail to meet statutory compliance requirements (e.g., hosting provider's failure to secure data in accordance with GDPR)
- ***Termination of the subcontract*** and possible claims for damages if delays or defects materially impact the primary contract

Evidence in litigation

If disputes arise, the following evidence is typically crucial:

- Signed subcontract agreements with back-to-back provisions
- Integration and readiness test reports for third-party components
- UAT participation records and acceptance sign-off for subcontracted deliverables
- Incident logs and communications showing issue reporting timelines
- Compliance certifications or audit reports for the subcontractor's services

7.2.5.1 Frequent Litigation Issues in the Preparing for Go-Live Stage (Third-Party Vendors & Subcontractors)

1. **Failure to Meet Performance Benchmarks**

Typical dispute. A payment gateway vendor fails to meet the agreed transactions-per-second threshold during testing.

Example. Contract required ≥5,000 TPS; actual performance in staging is ~3,200 TPS, blocking Go-Live.

Legal theories. Breach of subcontract; breach of express warranty; liability for delay damages.

2. **Late Delivery of Critical Components**

Typical dispute. Hosting provider delays provisioning production servers, pushing back deployment.

Example. Infrastructure promised for staging by October 1 arrives two weeks late, derailing the test schedule.

Legal theories. Breach of delivery deadlines; liquidated damages under subcontract.

3. **Integration Failures**

Typical dispute. A subcontracted analytics module causes errors when integrated with the main platform.

Example. Reports fail to generate due to mismatched database schema versions.

Legal theories. Breach of integration obligations; negligent services.

4. **Regulatory Non-Compliance**

Typical dispute. Cloud provider's data center is outside agreed jurisdiction, violating contractual data residency requirements.

Example. Client contract mandates EU-only hosting; provider uses U.S.-based failover servers.

Legal theories. Breach of compliance clause; indemnity triggers; potential regulatory fines.

5. **Inadequate Documentation or Handover**

Typical dispute. API vendor delivers a functional service but no operational documentation, causing delays in deployment.

Example. Without endpoint specifications, developer cannot complete final integration.

Legal theories. Breach of deliverables; failure to meet acceptance criteria.

7.2.6 End-Users' Role and Obligations

Although end-users are not typically signatories to the primary software development contract, they play an indispensable role in ensuring operational readiness for Go-Live. Their direct interaction with the system on a day-to-day basis makes them the ultimate test of whether the deployed solution meets functional, usability, and performance expectations under real operating conditions. In the Preparing for Go-Live phase, their participation bridges the gap between technical readiness and practical, real-world usability.

End-users' involvement begins with structured training, designed to equip them with the skills needed to operate the software effectively from the first day of production use. Training programs, which may be contractually stipulated, often include classroom sessions, interactive workshops, e-learning modules, and access to test environments for hands-on practice. In addition to formal training, end-users are expected to review and familiarise themselves with user manuals, quick reference guides, and troubleshooting resources provided by the developer or client's internal training team.

Where applicable, end-users also participate in **final pilot runs or operational simulations**, sometimes referred to as "dress rehearsals" for Go-Live. These simulations validate that workflows, business processes, and user interactions function as intended in a production-like environment. End-user feedback during these pilots is critical; it often identifies usability issues, workflow inefficiencies, or missing functionality that may not have been detected during technical testing or User Acceptance Testing (UAT).

Core responsibilities

- Attending all scheduled training sessions and completing any required assessments
- Reviewing operational documentation, including user guides and process maps, to ensure familiarity with system functions
- Participating in pilot runs, simulations, or soft launches to validate readiness
- Reporting usability concerns, process bottlenecks, or technical issues promptly through the agreed feedback channels
- Adhering to security and access protocols, including password policies and role-based permissions, from the outset

Legal risks related to end-user readiness

While end-users themselves are not generally liable under the primary development contract, their readiness (or lack thereof) can have indirect contractual consequences for the client.

- If end-user training is not completed, and operational failures occur post-Go-Live, the developer may argue that issues stem from user error rather than software defects, limiting the client's ability to claim warranty remedies
- Failure to follow documented usage procedures could void certain support or warranty provisions, particularly where the contract requires adherence to specified operational protocols
- In regulated industries, improper end-user handling of data (e.g., failure to follow security protocols) can expose the client to compliance violations, even if the software itself meets technical compliance standards

Evidence in litigation or dispute resolution

If disputes arise over post-Go-Live performance, relevant evidence concerning end-user readiness may include:

- Training attendance logs and completion certificates
- Pilot run reports documenting end-user participation and feedback
- Email or ticketing system records showing reported issues before and after Go-Live
- Security access logs showing adherence (or non-adherence) to prescribed procedures

7.2.6.1 Frequent Litigation Issues in the Preparing for Go-Live Stage (End-Users)

1. **Incomplete Training Compliance**

Typical dispute. Post-Go-Live errors occur because a significant portion of the user base did not complete training.

Example. In a new warehouse management system, incorrect barcode scanning by untrained staff leads to inventory mismatches.

Legal impact. Developer disputes defect claims, asserting operational error; client struggles to prove the issue is software-related.

2. **Ignored Procedural Guidance**

Typical dispute. End-users bypass mandatory steps, causing failures.

Example. Customer service agents bypass the identity verification workflow in a CRM system, leading to data protection breaches.

Legal impact. Breach of operational protocols undermines the client's warranty claims and triggers compliance risks.

3. **Feedback Suppression Before Go-Live**

Typical dispute. End-users report usability or process issues during pilot runs, but management does not escalate them to the developer.

Example. Cashiers report slow transaction speeds in a new POS system during simulation week, but no action is taken; after launch, queues cause operational disruption.

Legal impact. Client may be seen as having waived objections by not raising concerns before Go-Live.

4. **Security Protocol Breaches**

Typical dispute. End-users fail to follow agreed security measures at launch, causing an incident.

Example. Staff share login credentials contrary to role-based access rules, resulting in an unauthorised transaction.

Legal impact. Client bears liability for regulatory breaches and may lose contractual indemnity protections.

In essence, preparing for Go-Live is a multi-party coordinated process where technical readiness, contractual compliance, and operational preparedness must align. Each party's responsibilities, clearly defined in the contract, must be discharged in full to ensure that Go-Live is not only technically successful but also legally valid, reducing the risk of disputes and ensuring a smooth transition to live operation.

7.3 Training as a Critical Component of Go-Live Readiness

Training is a pivotal element in the Preparing for Go-Live phase, serving as the bridge between technical delivery and operational success.

Regardless of how technically sound a software system may be, its value is only realised when end-users and system administrators can operate it effectively and in compliance with defined processes.

From a contractual perspective, training may be expressly included as part of the core deliverables or specified as a separately billable service, with clear provisions on scope, format, duration, and participant numbers.

Purpose and timing of training

Training is typically delivered either in the immediate lead-up to Go-Live (**Pre-Go-Live training**) or shortly after deployment (**Post-Go-Live training**), depending on the system's complexity and the client's operational priorities.

- **Pre-Go-Live training** ensures that end-users and administrators can perform their tasks productively from the first day the system goes live. It is often aligned with pilot runs, operational rehearsals, or User Acceptance Testing (UAT), enabling participants to work within a realistic environment before full-scale deployment
- **Post-Go-Live training** allows the training content to be tailored to real-world issues that arise once the system is live, providing opportunities to refine workflows, address user questions, and introduce advanced functionalities after initial stabilisation

In both cases, training programs typically combine hands-on demonstrations, guided practice in staging or sandbox environments, and structured materials such as quick reference cards, detailed user manuals, and video tutorials. System administrators may also receive advanced technical training on maintenance, troubleshooting, monitoring, and performance optimisation.

Core training deliverables

Where specified in the contract, training deliverables may include:

- A *detailed training plan*, including learning objectives, agendas, and schedules
- *Session delivery* in the agreed format (in-person, remote, or hybrid) and language(s)
- Distribution of *training materials*, including manuals, process maps, and "cheat sheets"
- *Recording of sessions* for future reference or onboarding of new staff
- *Evaluation and feedback* forms to assess training effectiveness and identify gaps

Legal Risks Associated with Training

Training carries significant legal and operational implications, particularly in environments with regulated processes, high transaction volumes, or critical service delivery.

Breach of Contract. If training is specified as a contractual deliverable and is not provided in full (e.g., fewer sessions than agreed, inadequate materials, or failure to train all designated staff), the client may claim non-performance, potentially delaying Final Acceptance or triggering penalties.

Operational Failures Misattributed as Defects. If end-users are insufficiently trained, operational errors post-Go-Live may be mistaken for software defects. This can lead to disputes over whether the issue is covered under warranty or is attributable to client-side failures.

Regulatory Non-Compliance. In sectors such as finance, healthcare, or aviation, inadequate training on compliance-related workflows (e.g., GDPR consent handling, HIPAA privacy protocols) can lead to breaches with substantial fines, for which the client may seek indemnification if the training shortfall is the developer's fault.

Loss of Warranty Protections. Many contracts condition warranty support on the system being used in accordance with the provided documentation and training. Failure to train staff adequately may allow the developer to deny warranty claims on the basis of improper use.

Evidence in litigation or dispute resolution

In disputes concerning post-Go-Live performance, training records can be decisive. Useful evidence includes:

- Training attendance sheets or participant logs
- Certificates of completion for users and administrators
- Copies of all training materials, agendas, and session recordings
- Feedback forms or post-training assessments demonstrating participant readiness
- Correspondence between the client and developer confirming training dates, scope, and participant lists

7.3.1 Frequent Litigation Issues Involving Training

1. **Incomplete Coverage of Designated Staff**

Typical dispute. The developer trains only a subset of intended users, leaving others unprepared.

Example. Only front-office staff in a retail chain are trained before Go-Live, leaving warehouse personnel unable to process stock in the new system.

Legal impact. Breach of contractual training obligations; potential delay in Final Acceptance.

2. **Outdated or Incorrect Training Materials**

Typical dispute. Training content does not match the final deployed system.

Example. The training manual still references navigation menus from an earlier version of the UI, causing confusion during operations.

Legal impact. Breach of implied duty of reasonable skill and care; risk of operational disruption claims.

3. **Failure to Train on Compliance-Critical Functions**

Typical dispute. End-users are not instructed on legally mandated workflows.

Example. Healthcare staff are not shown how to log patient consent in a manner compliant with GDPR, resulting in unlawful data processing.

Legal impact. Potential indemnity claims for regulatory fines; breach of statutory compliance warranties.

4. **Training Delivered Too Early**

Typical dispute. Training occurs months before Go-Live, and staff forget procedures by launch.

Example. A new CRM is launched six months after training, and sales staff cannot recall how to log deals or run reports.

Legal impact. Client may argue that training timing breached the obligation to ensure operational readiness at Go-Live.

7.4 Deployment Strategies (Phased, Parallel, Big Bang)

Deployment Strategies refer to the methods used to transition software from a development or testing environment to a live, operational environment. The chosen deployment strategy affects the risk, timeline, and contractual obligations associated with the software's implementation, as each approach has unique implications for both the client and developer. The three primary deployment strategies are **Phased Deployment**, **Parallel Deployment**, and **Big Bang Deployment**.

7.4.1 Phased Deployment

In this approach, the software is deployed incrementally, often by module or by specific functional areas, over an extended period. Phased

Deployment is commonly used for complex systems, allowing the client to gradually implement the software and resolve issues within each phase before moving on to the next.

From a legal perspective, Phased Deployment may require detailed contractual specifications for each deployment phase, including acceptance criteria, timelines, and payment milestones.

The contract should define each phase's deliverables and include clauses to address the handling of issues that arise in early phases, as these may impact subsequent stages. Phased Deployment often includes **interim acceptance testing** and **provisional acceptance** at each stage, allowing both parties to review progress before continuing with the next phase.

A key **legal risk** in Phased Deployment is that unresolved defects or scope ambiguities in early phases can cascade into later stages, causing compounded delays, cost overruns, and disputes over whether subsequent performance failures stem from the current phase or from deficiencies left unremedied in prior phases.

7.4.2 Parallel Deployment

Parallel Deployment involves running the new software alongside the existing system for a period of time. This approach allows the client to compare both systems' performance, verify that the new software meets requirements, and ensure that critical functions are maintained before fully switching to the new solution. It reduces the risk of operational disruptions, as users can continue to rely on the original system if issues arise with the new deployment.

Contractually, Parallel Deployment may require provisions for extended support from the developer, as running two systems simultaneously can increase complexity and support needs. The contract should include **dual-system performance criteria** and stipulate a timeline for when the old system can be decommissioned. Clauses may also specify which system takes precedence in the event of conflicting outputs or data inconsistencies, as well as any **additional costs** related to supporting parallel systems.

A significant **legal risk** in Parallel Deployment is the potential for disputes over data discrepancies or conflicting outputs between the old and new systems, particularly if the contract does not clearly define which system's results are authoritative during the overlap period, leading to liability questions in cases of operational or regulatory breaches.

7.4.3 Big Bang Deployment

In a Big Bang Deployment, the entire software system is launched at once, replacing the existing system in a single, comprehensive transition.

This strategy is often faster and may reduce long-term costs, but it carries significant risks due to the complete shift to the new system. Big Bang Deployment is typically best suited for less complex systems or when a phased or parallel approach is not feasible.

Legally, Big Bang Deployment may require extensive **acceptance testing** before the deployment date to ensure the software meets all contractual standards, as there is no fallback system in place. The contract should outline **contingency plans** and **remediation measures** if the software fails to perform after deployment. Furthermore, warranty and post-deployment support clauses become critical under this strategy, as any issues post-launch could significantly impact the client's operations.

Each deployment strategy has distinct legal and operational implications, and the contract should clearly specify the chosen method, including detailed testing requirements, acceptance criteria, support obligations, and timelines. This ensures that both parties are aligned on expectations, reducing potential risks and misunderstandings as the software transitions to live use.

The principal **legal risk** in Big Bang Deployment is that any post-launch failure can immediately halt critical business operations, exposing the developer to breach of contract claims and potentially high consequential damages, especially if the agreement lacks clear limitation-of-liability provisions and emergency remediation obligations.

7.5 Role of Deployment in Contract Fulfilment

The deployment phase holds a fundamental role within the contract, as it represents the realization of the developer's primary contractual obligations. Deployment is the point where the developer's work is officially "delivered" and, as such, can trigger several contractual provisions related to acceptance, payment, warranty, and ongoing support.

Deployment typically initiates the **Acceptance Testing** phase, in which the client evaluates the software in a live environment to confirm it meets all the agreed specifications and performance criteria. For example, if the contract specifies that the software must handle a certain volume of users or transactions, these criteria are formally tested during deployment. Successful testing and acceptance of the software are essential, as they usually constitute the final approval of the deliverable.

If the software passes these tests, the client typically issues a **Final Acceptance Certificate**, which signals that the software meets the contractual standards and that the developer has satisfied their delivery obligations.

Additionally, deployment often **activates payment obligations**. Many contracts specify that a significant portion of the total payment is due upon successful deployment and acceptance of the software. This payment structure incentivizes the developer to complete deployment thoroughly, as any failure to meet the contractual specifications can lead to withheld payments or penalties.

Deployment also frequently marks the beginning of the **warranty period**. During this period, the developer may be obligated to correct any defects or issues identified in the software, often at no additional cost to the client. For example, if the software encounters unexpected functionality issues post-deployment, the contract may require the developer to resolve these issues within a specified timeframe. This warranty period provides the client with additional security, ensuring that they receive a fully functional product and have recourse for resolving issues after the software goes live.

Furthermore, deployment is directly linked to **post-deployment support and maintenance obligations**. The contract may outline a support period during which the developer is responsible for providing updates, technical support, or assistance with any operational issues that arise as users begin to work with the software. For instance, in cases where user training or integration support is necessary, the contract may require the developer to provide this assistance post-deployment.

The contractual clarity around deployment is crucial to ensure both parties understand their respective rights and obligations, providing a structured path to complete the project and transition to operational use.

7.6 Managing Deployment Risks and Most Common Disputes

In the deployment phase several common risks and potential disputes can arise, primarily due to the complexity of moving software into a live environment and the contractual implications involved.

7.6.1 Legal Risks and Common Disputes

Failure to Meet Performance Criteria

If the software does not meet the performance requirements specified in the contract, this can lead to disputes. The client may claim breach of contract and seek remedies, including rework at the developer's expense or, in severe cases, contract termination.

Inadequate Testing or Defects Post-Deployment

Issues with insufficient testing or defects that become apparent after deployment can lead to significant disputes. If the software malfunctions or has bugs that impact operations, the client may argue that the developer did not fulfill their contractual obligations to deliver a functional product.

For example, if the software is designed to calculate taxes or generate financial reports required for submission to tax authorities, any errors in these processes can have legal and financial implications. In such a situation, the client might incur fines or other regulatory penalties due to incorrect filings or miscalculations. From a contractual perspective, this scenario highlights the importance of clearly defined **warranty** and **liability clauses**. A well-drafted contract would specify that the developer is responsible for ensuring the accuracy of the software's core functionalities, including critical features like tax calculations or regulatory reporting. If the software fails to meet these standards and causes financial harm to the client, the client may have grounds to claim damages.

Delayed Deployment

Delays in deployment can be costly for clients, especially if the software is essential for business operations. If the deployment timeline is exceeded, clients may pursue claims for damages or enforce penalty clauses if the contract includes delay provisions.

Data Security and Compliance Issues

If the software fails to meet regulatory or data security requirements, such as GDPR compliance, the client may face legal risks, and disputes can arise over the developer's responsibility for compliance failures.

Post-Deployment Support Conflicts

Disagreements can arise over the scope of post-deployment support. If the client encounters issues post-deployment, they may expect the developer to provide support, whereas the developer may argue that certain issues are outside the support scope or require additional fees.

7.6.2 Management of Deployment Risks

Effective management of deployment risks involves proactive measures, clear contractual provisions, and structured communication between the client and developer. A well-defined risk management strategy helps both parties address potential issues and minimizes the risk of disputes during deployment. Here are key aspects of managing deployment risks and issues:

Pre-Deployment Testing and Quality Assurance

Extensive testing is crucial to ensure that the software meets all contractual criteria before deployment. This includes performance, load, and security testing, verifying that the software can handle live conditions. Contracts should clearly specify testing requirements and acceptance criteria, providing benchmarks for evaluating deployment readiness. For example, the contract may require the developer to conduct both in-house and user acceptance testing (UAT) to confirm functionality and performance.

Contingency Planning and Rollback Options

The contract should outline contingency plans in case deployment does not proceed smoothly. For instance, the agreement may specify a rollback option, where the system can revert to the previous version if severe issues arise, ensuring minimal disruption to business operations. This approach is particularly useful in parallel or phased deployment strategies, where parts of the software can be gradually tested in a live environment without risking the entire system.

Defining Post-Deployment Support Obligations

Clear contractual language regarding post-deployment support is essential to avoid disputes. The contract should specify the length and scope of support, including what constitutes "warranty" support versus billable maintenance. For instance, a common provision may require the developer to resolve defects at no charge during a 90-day warranty period, while other support needs fall under a separate maintenance contract.

Documenting and Addressing Client Feedback

During and after deployment, client feedback is essential for identifying potential issues that may need adjustment. The contract can include provisions for documenting feedback and setting a timeline for the developer to address any legitimate issues. This ensures accountability and a structured approach to resolving minor issues that may arise.

Ensuring Regulatory Compliance

If the software must comply with specific regulations (such as GDPR or the EU AI Act), the deployment phase should involve compliance verification steps. These may include final security audits, user access controls, and data encryption checks. The contract should specify who is responsible for ensuring compliance and how issues will be handled if the software fails to meet regulatory requirements.

Clear Communication Channels

Establishing clear communication protocols for deployment can help prevent misunderstandings and streamline issue resolution. This includes identifying key contacts on both sides, defining reporting channels for issues, and setting a schedule for regular updates throughout the deployment process.

In conclusion, managing deployment risks and issues requires a proactive approach, where both parties are aligned on expectations and prepared to address challenges that may arise. Well-drafted contractual provisions for testing, contingency planning, support, and compliance create a framework for successful deployment, minimizing the likelihood of disputes and ensuring a smoother transition to live use.

7.7 Warranty Period

Following the Go-Live phase, the Warranty period commences, entailing a series of specific obligations that the developer must fulfil. The warranty period is a crucial component of the software contract that protects the client by ensuring that any post-deployment issues are resolved by the developer, free of additional charges.

By defining the scope, duration, and conditions of the warranty, both parties are aligned on post-deployment expectations, minimizing the potential for disputes. Properly structured, the warranty period provides the client with confidence in the software's quality and reliability, while giving the developer a clear and manageable set of obligations. These obligations should be clearly delineated within the contract to ensure compliance and address potential issues post-deployment.

7.7.1 Main Obligations during Warranty Period

Corrective Action on Defects

The primary obligation of the developer during the warranty period is to identify and fix any bugs, errors, or defects in the software. This includes issues that prevent the software from operating according to the requirements laid out in the contract or issues that significantly impact the user experience. For example, if a critical feature fails to work as specified, the developer is responsible for rectifying this promptly, ensuring that the software meets the client's operational needs.

Timely Response and Resolution

The developer is typically required to respond to defect reports within a certain timeframe and resolve issues promptly. The contract may define specific response times based on the severity of the issue. For instance, critical errors that halt core functions may require immediate attention, whereas minor bugs may have a longer response time. This ensures that the client can rely on the software to perform essential tasks without prolonged interruptions.

Performance Standard

During the warranty period, the developer is also expected to maintain the software's performance levels. This includes addressing performance issues that may arise due to overlooked factors during development or deployment. For instance, if the software fails to support the number of concurrent users specified in the contract, the developer must optimize the software to meet this performance standard.

Security

Depending on the contract, the developer may be required to implement necessary security patches if vulnerabilities emerge during the warranty period. As security threats are constantly evolving, this obligation helps protect the client's system and data from potential breaches or cyber-attacks.

Documentation of Changes

When issues are identified and resolved, the developer is often required to document these changes and provide the client with updated records. This documentation ensures transparency and helps the client keep an accurate log of modifications to the software during the warranty period.

7.7.2 Key Provisions to Include in the Warranty Clause

Duration of the Warranty Period

The contract should clearly specify the length of the warranty period, which often ranges from 30 to 180 days, but can extend to a year or more for complex systems. The duration should reflect the project's complexity and the client's need for assurance that the software will perform as expected.

Scope of Covered Issues

The contract should outline the specific types of issues that the developer is obligated to address during the warranty period. Typically, the warranty covers functionality issues, critical bugs, and security vulnerabilities, but may exclude enhancements, feature additions, or adjustments to meet new client needs.

Response and Resolution Timeframes

The warranty clause should specify response and resolution times for different types of issues. For instance, a critical issue might require a response within four hours and resolution within 24 hours, while minor issues could have longer response times. Clearly defined timeframes help manage expectations and ensure prompt action on critical issues.

Exclusions and Limitations

It's essential to clarify any exclusions to the warranty. For example, issues resulting from unauthorized modifications, third-party integrations not covered by the contract, or improper use of the software by the client may fall outside the warranty scope. These limitations protect the developer from responsibility for issues that arise due to factors beyond their control.

Process for Reporting and Tracking Issues

The contract should outline a process for the client to report issues during the warranty period. This often includes setting up a communication channel for reporting defects, assigning responsibility for tracking issue resolution, and defining the necessary documentation to support each reported issue.

Remedies for Non-Compliance

To hold the developer accountable, the contract may specify remedies if they fail to meet their warranty obligations. This can include service credits, extension of the warranty period, or other compensation if issues are not resolved within the agreed-upon timeframe.

Transition to Maintenance

The warranty clause should also specify how support will transition to a formal maintenance agreement once the warranty period expires. This is important for the client's long-term support needs, as it clarifies when the developer's no-cost obligations end and when ongoing support costs will apply.

7.8 Checklist: Key Considerations for Deployment Phase (Client Perspective)

This checklist serves as a practical and legal safeguard for the client, ensuring that all critical elements of deployment are addressed before Go-Live. By systematically verifying each area, the client can minimise operational risk, avoid contractual disputes, and establish a solid foundation for the system's long-term success.

1. **Review of Pre-Deployment Testing Results**
   - Have all contractual acceptance tests (functional, performance, security) been reviewed and formally approved?
   - Does the system meet all Acceptance Criteria as defined in the Statement of Work or Schedule of Specifications?
   - Are any unresolved defects documented, categorised by severity, and backed by a mutually agreed remediation plan?
   - **Legal risk**: Skipping this verification may result in Final Acceptance being implied by conduct, reducing leverage to demand corrections later
2. **Deployment Strategy and Plan**
   - Is there a mutually agreed Deployment Plan specifying the method (Phased, Parallel, Big Bang)?

- Are timelines, milestones, rollback procedures, and contingency triggers documented?
- Has the developer provided a tested rollback option in case of critical failure?
- **Legal risk**: Absence of a documented rollback plan may expose the client to extended downtime and potential breach of SLA without recourse

3. **Data Migration and Integrity Checks**
   - Is there a contractual Data Migration Plan detailing mapping, validation, and reconciliation steps?
   - Have accuracy and integrity checks been executed on migrated data in a staging environment?
   - Are encryption and security measures in place to protect data during transfer?
   - **Legal risk**: Inaccurate migration can breach data protection laws (e.g., GDPR) and result in business process failures, making the client liable to regulators and customers
4. **User Training and Documentation**
   - Has the developer delivered all agreed pre-Go-Live training sessions for end-users and administrators?
   - Are comprehensive user manuals, operational guides, and troubleshooting documentation accessible?
   - Is there a defined post-Go-Live support plan for user queries?
   - **Legal risk**: Inadequate training can impair adoption and trigger disputes over whether the system is "fit for purpose"
5. **Compliance and Regulatory Requirements**
   - Has the developer confirmed, in writing, that the system meets applicable laws (e.g., GDPR, sector-specific regulations)?
   - Have final compliance audits and penetration tests been completed and signed off?
   - Is there documentary proof of compliance (e.g., audit certificates, test reports)?
   - **Legal risk**: Non-compliance can trigger regulatory fines, reputational damage, and indemnity claims against the client
6. **Post-Deployment Support and Warranty Provisions**
   - Is the scope, duration, and response time of warranty support clearly defined?
   - Has the warranty start date been tied explicitly to Go-Live in the contract?
   - Are issue logging, escalation, and resolution procedures documented?
   - **Legal risk**: Ambiguity here may allow the developer to reject defect claims as "out of scope" once the warranty starts

7. **Performance and Scalability Verification**
   - Has the system been tested for contractual load and transaction thresholds in a production-like environment?
   - Does it meet agreed performance benchmarks (e.g., Transactions Per Second, response times)?
   - Are monitoring tools and alerting mechanisms live and configured?
   - **Legal risk**: Performance shortfalls post-Go-Live can lead to SLA breaches and business disruption claims
8. **Communication and Issue Resolution Channels**
   - Have points of contact and escalation levels been designated on both sides?
   - Is there a documented protocol for reporting, triaging, and resolving issues within SLA timeframes?
   - Are escalation steps and timelines contractually binding?
   - **Legal risk**: Weak escalation processes can delay critical fixes and increase exposure to consequential loss claims
9. **Final Acceptance and Sign-Off**
   - Has Final Acceptance Testing been completed in the live environment, within the agreed stabilisation period?
   - Is there a signed Final Acceptance Certificate documenting full contractual delivery?
   - Are any outstanding conditions for the developer's accountability recorded?
   - **Legal risk**: Signing Final Acceptance without conditions can release the developer from obligations, even if latent defects later emerge

7.9 Checklist: Key Considerations for Deployment Phase (Developer Perspective)

This checklist is designed to help the developer ensure that all contractual, technical, and operational requirements for deployment are satisfied before Go-Live. By systematically confirming each item, the developer reduces the risk of post-launch disputes, avoids withholding of payments, and strengthens their position in case of litigation.

1. **Verification of Contractual Readiness Criteria**
   - Have all deliverables been completed in line with the Statement of Work and Acceptance Criteria?

- Are all preconditions to Go-Live (e.g., successful UAT, client sign-off) formally documented?
- Is there written evidence confirming compliance with any performance, security, or migration obligations?
- **Legal risk**: Proceeding without documented proof can lead to disputes over whether Go-Live was valid, risking non-payment or termination

2. **Technical Readiness and Integration Validation**
   - Has final integration testing confirmed that all modules and third-party components work together in the target environment?
   - Have performance and load tests met contractual benchmarks under production-like conditions?
   - Has security testing confirmed compliance with contractual and statutory standards (e.g., GDPR encryption, access control)?
   - **Legal risk**: Failure to meet these standards can trigger breach of contract claims and regulatory liability
3. **Data Migration and Integrity Assurance**
   - Has data migration been rehearsed, validated, and reconciled against agreed mapping and quality standards?
   - Are any exceptions or discrepancies documented and agreed upon with the client?
   - Is there a signed migration acceptance record?
   - **Legal risk**: Unresolved migration defects can lead to claims for operational losses or breach of warranty
4. **Documentation Delivery**
   - Have installation, configuration, and operational manuals been completed and delivered?
   - Is there a troubleshooting guide for common errors and known limitations?
   - Have runbooks and operational handover materials been provided to the client's operations team?
   - **Legal risk**: Missing documentation may delay Final Acceptance and be treated as an incomplete deliverable
5. **Training Completion**
   - Have all contracted training sessions for end-users and administrators been delivered?
   - Is attendance documented, and have training materials been handed over?

- Have follow-up Q&A or refresher sessions been scheduled if agreed?
- **Legal risk**: Inadequate training can be framed as a failure to deliver a "fit-for-purpose" system, leading to warranty disputes

6. **Third-Party Component Readiness**
    - Have all subcontractors or vendors confirmed readiness and compliance with their contractual deliverables?
    - Are third-party licences and SLAs in effect for Go-Live?
    - Has integration with third-party services been re-tested after final configuration?
    - **Legal risk**: Failure of a third-party component may still be attributed to the developer under back-to-back obligations
7. **Environment Compatibility Verification**
    - Has the software been tested in the client's production environment (or exact replica) for configuration alignment?
    - Are all dependencies, libraries, and system versions in sync with the agreed target environment?
    - Have capacity and sizing checks been validated for expected user loads?
    - **Legal risk**: "It works in our lab" is not a defence—mismatch with the client environment can be seen as a failure to deliver a compatible system
8. **Compliance and Regulatory Confirmation**
    - Has the system been reviewed for compliance with applicable legal and regulatory requirements (e.g., GDPR, HIPAA, PCI-DSS)?
    - Are compliance audit results documented and shared with the client?
    - Have any required certifications or sign-offs been obtained?
    - **Legal risk**: Non-compliance discovered post-Go-Live can lead to indemnity claims and regulatory penalties
9. **Issue Logging and Handover**
    - Have all known defects been documented, categorized, and agreed upon with the client for post-Go-Live resolution if necessary?
    - Is there a clear escalation and support process in place for the stabilization period?
    - Has the operational handover been formally signed off by the client's project or operations manager?
    - **Legal risk**: Disputes may arise if issues are found post-Go-Live that the client claims were undisclosed; contemporaneous records protect the developer

7.10 Final Acceptance

7.10.1 Definition and Role in the Contractual Lifecycle

Final Acceptance marks the **formal and definitive confirmation** by the client that the delivered system meets **all contractual requirements in full** and can be deemed *fully delivered* from the standpoint of the developer's implementation obligations. It is the **point of contractual closure** for delivery, after which no further obligations relating to build or deployment remain, except for those expressly continuing under warranty or maintenance agreements.

While **Go-Live** represents the operational transition, moving the system from development or staging into the live production environment, **Final Acceptance** represents the *legal and contractual closure* of the delivery phase. In other words, Go-Live is a **technical milestone**, whereas Final Acceptance is a **legal milestone**.

From a **project management perspective**, Final Acceptance is typically the **last sub-phase of Deployment**, following the stabilization or "hypercare" period. Project teams view it as the point at which the system is considered fully bedded-in, all identified post-Go-Live defects have been resolved or formally waived, and operational performance has been proven in real-world conditions.

From a **contractual perspective**, Final Acceptance is treated as a **separate legal stage** with its own prerequisites, triggers, and consequences. It is often tied to:

- The release of final retention payments or performance bonds
- The start (or continuation) of the warranty period, if the warranty is linked to Final Acceptance rather than Go-Live
- The transfer of intellectual property rights or licensing rights to the client
- The expiry of the client's right to reject the deliverable for non-compliance with contractual specifications

The distinction is therefore critical: **project managers** may see Final Acceptance as the administrative "end" of deployment, while **lawyers** see it as the moment when contractual risks shift, payment obligations crystallize, and residual rights or liabilities are formally locked in.

A well-drafted contract will clearly separate these two milestones, Go-Live and Final Acceptance, defining the precise conditions for each, specifying the evidence required (e.g., defect closure reports, compliance certificates, operational performance logs), and outlining the consequences of granting or withholding Final Acceptance.

This clarity helps prevent disputes over whether delivery obligations have been fully discharged and ensures that both technical and legal closure occur in a structured and verifiable manner.

Distinction Between Go-Live and Final Acceptance

Although frequently conflated, the two milestones serve different purposes:

Go-Live is both a technical and contractual event in which the system is released into the live production environment and becomes available to end-users, typically followed by a stabilization period.

Final Acceptance is a contractual act granted after this stabilization period, once the system has been proven to operate reliably in real-world conditions and all agreed defects, particularly critical (P1) and major (P2) issues, have been resolved.

7.10.2 Typical Preconditions for Final Acceptance

Well-drafted contracts stipulate that Final Acceptance should only be issued after:

A. **Completion of Stabilization/Hypercare Period**

A prerequisite for **Final Acceptance** in many software contracts is the successful completion of the **stabilization** or **hypercare** period, a defined post-Go-Live timeframe, typically ranging from **14 to 45 calendar days**, during which the system operates in the client's live environment under full production conditions while receiving enhanced monitoring and support.

Purpose of the Stabilization Period

The stabilization phase functions as a real-world proving ground for the system. While User Acceptance Testing (UAT) and pre-Go-Live simulations aim to replicate production conditions, only live operation can fully validate the software's performance, integration stability, and user adoption. This period allows:

- Detection and remediation of residual defects not identified before Go-Live
- Fine-tuning of configurations, workflows, and performance parameters based on actual usage patterns
- Verification that all integrations, third-party services, and data flows remain stable under full operational loads
- Validation that trained users can execute their roles effectively and in accordance with documented procedures

Contractual Definition and Scope

In well-drafted contracts, the **hypercare/stabilization period** is expressly defined in the acceptance provisions, specifying:

a) **Start trigger**—almost always the Go-Live date (T0);
b) **Duration**—usually 14–45 days, but may extend for high-complexity or regulated systems;
c) **Developer obligations**—enhanced support availability (often 24/7), accelerated defect resolution SLAs, daily or weekly status reporting, and dedicated on-call resources;
d) **Client obligations**—timely reporting of issues, provision of logs and diagnostics, and refraining from unauthorized system changes during this phase.

Criteria for Successful Completion

For the stabilization period to be deemed complete, the following conditions are typically required:

a) No **material failures** (e.g., Severity 1 or Severity 2 defects) remain unresolved at the end of the period;
b) Agreed performance benchmarks (e.g., transaction throughput, response times, uptime percentages) have been consistently met during the period;
c) All integrations and data exchanges have functioned without critical interruption;
d) Operational monitoring and alerting tools have been validated in live conditions;
e) The client confirms that the system has been fit for intended use without unplanned downtime exceeding the contractual thresholds.

Evidence and Verification

Completion must be **documented** to withstand any future dispute. Common forms of evidence include:

a) Defect logs showing closure of all critical and major issues reported during hypercare;
b) System performance reports from monitoring tools demonstrating compliance with contractual SLAs;
c) Incident reports with root cause analyses and implemented fixes;
d) Formal sign-off from both technical and business stakeholders confirming that stabilization objectives have been met.

Legal Significance

The stabilization period has a **dual legal function**:

Operational assurance—It acts as a safeguard for the client, ensuring that the system is genuinely stable before final contractual closure.

Acceptance trigger—Completion without material issues often serves as a condition precedent to Final Acceptance, meaning the contract prohibits issuing the Final Acceptance Certificate until this stage is complete.

If the system experiences a **material failure** during stabilization, the contractual clock for the stabilization period may reset, effectively extending the hypercare phase until the system operates continuously for the agreed period without such failures.

Legal Risks if Skipped or Shortened

For the client—Accepting the system without a full stabilization period can weaken the ability to claim defects later as delivery-phase issues, potentially relegating them to narrower warranty remedies.

For the developer—Failing to provide the agreed hypercare level of support or to resolve critical issues within the period can be treated as a breach of acceptance obligations, delaying payment milestones or exposing them to liquidated damages.

Example: A logistics management platform goes live on 1 June, with a contractually agreed 30-day stabilization period. On 10 June, a critical integration with a third-party carrier API fails intermittently, causing shipment delays. The developer resolves the issue on 15 June, and the stabilization clock is reset—meaning the system must now operate for 30 consecutive days without material failures before the client can issue Final Acceptance.

B. **Closure of all critical and major defects identified before or immediately after Go-Live.**

A core prerequisite for granting **Final Acceptance** is the resolution of all defects classified as **critical** or **major** under the contractual defect severity classification. These are issues that materially impact the system's ability to function as intended, compromise key business processes, or create non-compliance with contractual, regulatory, or security requirements.

Understanding Defect Severity Levels

Contracts typically define defect severity levels (often in a service level annex) to distinguish between issues that must be resolved before Final Acceptance and those that can be deferred. A common classification is:

Critical Defects (Severity 1)—Issues that prevent the system, or a substantial part of it, from operating at all, or that cause complete failure of a core business process. Examples include system crashes, inability to process transactions, or complete loss of data integrity.

Major Defects (Severity 2)—Issues that significantly impair functionality but may have workarounds. While the system may still operate, performance, accuracy, or compliance is materially compromised. Examples include calculation errors in financial modules, non-functioning integration with essential third-party systems, or failure to enforce mandatory security protocols.

Timing of Defect Identification

These defects can be identified:

Before Go-Live—typically during **User Acceptance Testing (UAT)** or final pre-deployment checks, where they must be documented, tracked, and resolved before the system goes live, unless the client expressly agrees to defer them.

Immediately After Go-Live—during the stabilization (hypercare) period, where real-world usage exposes defects that were not detected during testing. Such defects, if classified as critical or major, must still be addressed before Final Acceptance.

Why Closure Is Contractually Essential

Leaving such defects unresolved undermines the legal and operational basis for Final Acceptance because:

a) The system may fail to meet contractual acceptance criteria;
b) The client's operational continuity and regulatory compliance could be at risk;
c) The developer's liability exposure increases if defects cause quantifiable business losses.

Evidence and Verification:

The closure of these defects must be **objectively verifiable** and **formally documented**. Best practice is to require:

a) **Defect resolution logs** showing the defect ID, severity level, fix applied, and retest results;
b) **Client sign-off** confirming that the defect is resolved to their satisfaction;
c) **Regression test results** to confirm that the fix has not caused new issues.

Exceptions and Deferrals

In some cases, non-critical defects (Severity 3 or 4) may remain open at Final Acceptance, provided they do not impact contractual compliance and are formally agreed to be addressed under warranty or maintenance. However, **critical and major defects cannot be contractually "deferred" without a signed waiver or variation order**, as doing so effectively alters the acceptance criteria.

Legal Risks if This Prerequisite Is Skipped

If Final Acceptance is granted without closure of all critical and major defects:

a) The client may lose the ability to compel fixes under delivery obligations, leaving only warranty remedies, which may have narrower scope;
b) The developer may argue that acceptance waived any claim that the system was non-conforming at delivery;
c) Disputes may arise over whether subsequent failures were "new" issues or unresolved pre-acceptance defects.

Example: During UAT for a payroll system, a **critical defect** is discovered: the system fails to calculate statutory pension contributions correctly, resulting in underpayment. The developer applies a fix, but post-Go-Live, payroll reports still show discrepancies (a **major defect)** due to rounding errors. Until both defects are corrected, tested, and signed off by the client, **Final Acceptance cannot be validly granted** under the contract's acceptance criteria.

C. **Validation of the system's performance against contractual Service Level Agreements (SLAs) under real operating conditions.**

Validation of the system's performance against contractual Service Level Agreements (SLAs) under real operating conditions means confirming that, once the system is live, it consistently delivers the level of service promised in the contract. This involves monitoring the system during the stabilization period to ensure it meets agreed targets such as uptime, response times, transaction speeds, and error rates, using the measurement methods specified in the agreement. The results are compared with the contractual thresholds, and any breaches must be fixed and re-tested before the client grants Final Acceptance. If these performance standards are not met, the client may be entitled to remedies such as service credits, extended stabilization, or, in serious cases, refusal of Final Acceptance. This step is essential because it proves that the system works as promised not just in tests, but in real business conditions.

D. **Confirmation of data integrity, accuracy, and consistency across critical business processes.**

Confirmation of data integrity, accuracy, and consistency across critical business processes means verifying that all data handled by the system after Go-Live is complete, correct, and aligned across every module or integration point.

This involves checking that migrated data matches the source records; that new transactions are recorded without loss or corruption; and that related processes, such as reporting, invoicing, or inventory updates, produce consistent results in every part of the system.

Any discrepancies must be investigated, corrected, and revalidated before the client grants Final Acceptance. This step ensures that the system can be trusted to process and store business information reliably, safeguarding both operational continuity and compliance with contractual or regulatory obligations.

E. **Delivery of complete "as-built" technical and operational documentation, including updates made post-Go-Live.**

Delivery of complete "as-built" technical and operational documentation, including updates made post-Go-Live, means providing the client with a final, accurate record of the system exactly as it exists in the production environment.

This includes detailed architecture diagrams, configuration settings, integration mappings, database schemas, and operational procedures, all reflecting any changes or fixes applied during the stabilization period.

It also covers updated user manuals, administrator guides, and troubleshooting instructions so that the client's team can operate, maintain, and support the system without relying on the developer's day-to-day involvement. Having this documentation is a contractual safeguard, ensuring knowledge transfer is complete and that the client retains full operational control and continuity beyond project closure.

F. **Transfer of all contractual intellectual property rights and, where applicable, delivery of source code or escrow release.**

Transfer of all contractual intellectual property rights, and where applicable, delivery of source code or escrow release, refers to the final legal handover of ownership and usage rights from the developer to the client as stipulated in the contract.

This means the client gains the agreed rights to use, modify, and, if permitted, further develop the software without further approval from the developer.

In cases where the contract provides for the delivery of source code, either directly or through an escrow arrangement, the release occurs at this stage, ensuring the client has full access to the underlying code in situations such as the developer's insolvency or termination of support. This step is critical for securing the client's long-term operational independence and protecting their investment in the system.

G. **Written confirmation of compliance with all legal, regulatory, and security requirements applicable to the system.**

Written confirmation of compliance with all legal, regulatory, and security requirements applicable to the system involves the developer providing a formal statement (often supported by audit reports or test results) affirming that the deployed software fully meets the applicable laws, industry regulations, and contractual security standards.

This may include data protection laws such as GDPR, sector-specific compliance obligations, and any cybersecurity measures agreed in the contract, such as encryption, access controls, and logging requirements.

This confirmation serves both as a legal safeguard for the client, demonstrating due diligence before full acceptance, and as an evidentiary record in case of future disputes or regulatory inquiries.

7.10.3 Obligations of the Parties During the Final Acceptance Phase

Developer: The developer must remedy all validated defects reported during the stabilization period; provide objective evidence of SLA compliance; finalize and deliver all outstanding contractual documentation; and ensure that operational and technical handover to the client's teams is complete.

Client: The client must carry out Final Acceptance testing in the live environment; raise any objections or defect notices within the contractually agreed timeframe; and sign the Final Acceptance Certificate once all preconditions have been met.

Project Manager: The project manager coordinates the execution of the final acceptance test plan; ensures all open items are closed; verifies delivery of documentation; and prepares the final project closure report.

Technology Lawyer: The lawyer reviews whether all contractual prerequisites for Final Acceptance have been satisfied; verifies compliance with applicable laws and regulations; confirms that all change requests have been formally approved; and ensures that intellectual property rights and licensing are correctly transferred.

7.10.4 Legal Risks Associated with Final Acceptance

Premature Issuance

Granting Final Acceptance too early can extinguish the client's rights to pursue remedies for certain defects discovered later, especially if the contract includes a waiver of claims upon acceptance.

Premature issuance of Final Acceptance occurs when the client formally signs off on the system before all contractual requirements have been fully met, which can significantly limit their ability to claim remedies for defects discovered later.

In many contracts, the act of issuing Final Acceptance is tied to a waiver of claims, meaning that once the acceptance certificate is signed, the client may be deemed to have released the developer from liability for any unreported issues, except for those explicitly covered under warranty.

For example, if a client signs Final Acceptance after a short operational period without fully testing critical functions (e.g. financial reporting in an ERP system) they may later discover that quarterly tax calculations are incorrect.

If the acceptance certificate includes a waiver of claims, the client might be unable to compel the developer to fix the defect without paying additional fees, even though the error existed before acceptance. Similarly, in a healthcare application, if reporting modules for regulatory compliance are not fully verified before acceptance, and deficiencies are only uncovered during an audit months later, the client could face regulatory penalties without recourse against the developer.

To prevent premature acceptance, contracts and project governance should include safeguards such as clearly defined acceptance criteria tied to measurable performance indicators, completion of the stabilization or hypercare period without material failures, and closure of all critical and high-severity defects.

Conditional acceptance provisions can also be used, allowing the client to accept the system subject to a documented list of outstanding issues, which must be resolved within a specified timeframe.

Additionally, the acceptance process should require formal sign-off from both technical and operational stakeholders, ensuring that the decision reflects not just project management timelines but also operational readiness and compliance assurance. These measures protect the client's rights, reduce the risk of waiving legitimate claims, and ensure that Final Acceptance is issued only when the system is demonstrably complete and compliant.

Unjustified Refusal

A client's refusal to grant Final Acceptance without valid, contractually recognized grounds may constitute a breach of contract and trigger the developer's right to payment and potential damages.

Unjustified refusal to grant Final Acceptance occurs when a client withholds formal acceptance of the system despite the developer having met all contractual requirements, passed the agreed acceptance criteria, and completed the stabilization period.

In such cases, if the refusal is not based on valid, contractually recognized grounds (such as the presence of unresolved critical defects, documented performance failures, or non-compliance with regulatory obligations) it can amount to a breach of contract by the client. This breach may entitle the developer to claim payment of any outstanding contractual amounts, recover damages for delays, and, in some cases, terminate the agreement for cause.

For example, if a software platform for an e-commerce retailer has successfully completed all contractual performance tests, achieved the agreed transaction-per-second rate, and passed data migration validation, yet the client refuses to sign Final Acceptance citing cosmetic UI preferences not covered in the specifications, this refusal would likely be considered unjustified. Similarly, in a financial services deployment, if all service-level targets have been met and compliance audits passed, but the client delays acceptance to postpone triggering the final payment milestone, this may be interpreted as an intentional breach designed to avoid contractual obligations.

To prevent disputes over unjustified refusal, the contract should define Final Acceptance criteria in precise, measurable terms and limit the grounds for withholding acceptance to specific, material nonconformities.

Including deemed acceptance clauses, whereby acceptance is automatically granted if the client fails to respond within a set timeframe after successful testing, can also reduce the risk of tactical delays.

Furthermore, requiring the client to provide written, detailed reasons for any refusal, along with objective evidence of non-compliance, ensures that the acceptance process remains fact-based and defensible. These safeguards protect the developer's right to timely payment while maintaining the client's legitimate ability to reject delivery when genuine contractual breaches exist.

Ambiguity in Acceptance Criteria

Poorly defined acceptance standards can lead to disputes about whether the system meets contractual requirements.

Ambiguity in acceptance criteria arises when the contract fails to clearly define the measurable standards, performance thresholds, and functional requirements that must be met for Final Acceptance to be granted. Without precise and objective benchmarks, both the client and the developer may interpret "acceptance" differently, creating fertile ground for disputes. This lack of clarity can lead to situations where the developer believes all obligations have been met, while the client insists that certain expectations, often unstated or implied, remain unfulfilled.

For example, in a logistics management system deployment, if the contract simply states that the system must "handle high transaction volumes efficiently" without specifying exact performance metrics (e.g., 2,000 shipments processed per hour with less than a 1% error rate), the client may argue post-Go-Live that the system's speed or accuracy is insufficient, even though no objective threshold was ever agreed. Similarly, in a customer relationship management (CRM) project, vague requirements such as "user-friendly interface" can lead to prolonged disputes if users find the system cumbersome, despite the developer having met all documented functionality points.

To prevent such disputes, contracts should replace subjective language with quantifiable acceptance criteria tied directly to the Statement of Work or Specifications Schedule. This includes setting clear performance benchmarks, defect severity classifications, compliance checklists, and completion of specific business process tests.

Acceptance procedures should also outline the exact steps for validation, such as which test scripts will be run, what constitutes a "pass" or "fail," and how defects will be logged and classified.

Where possible, both parties should sign off on a detailed Acceptance Test Plan before UAT begins, ensuring mutual understanding of the final yardstick for performance. By eliminating ambiguity at the drafting stage, the acceptance process becomes more predictable, legally defensible, and resistant to opportunistic challenges.

Regulatory Non-Compliance

If compliance obligations are unmet at Final Acceptance, both parties may face liability, with risk allocation dependent on the contract's indemnity clauses.

Regulatory non-compliance represents a critical legal risk in software development contracts, particularly at the stage of Final Acceptance. This risk arises when the delivered system fails to meet applicable statutory or regulatory obligations, such as data protection, financial reporting, healthcare confidentiality, or sector-specific cybersecurity requirements. In such cases, liability may extend not only to the developer, who failed to ensure compliance by design, but also to the client, who deploys and operates a non-compliant system. The apportionment of this liability typically depends on the scope of the warranties, representations, and indemnity clauses negotiated in the contract.

For example, in the development of a health-tech platform, non-compliance with data protection frameworks such as the EU's General Data Protection Regulation (GDPR) or the U.S. Health Insurance Portability and Accountability Act (HIPAA) may result in significant administrative fines, civil liability, or reputational harm. Even where the developer has delivered a system that is technically functional, the absence of features such as consent mechanisms, audit trails, or encryption protocols may expose both parties to enforcement action. Similarly, in the financial services sector, a trading system that fails to align with regulatory reporting obligations can trigger supervisory sanctions against both the service provider and the regulated entity.

To prevent such outcomes, contracts should incorporate explicit compliance obligations tied to the relevant legal framework and allocate responsibility for ensuring adherence. Best practice includes:

- **Compliance warranties**, whereby the developer affirms that the delivered system complies with specified laws and standards
- **Indemnity provisions**, allocating liability where non-compliance results in third-party claims, fines, or enforcement actions
- **Audit and monitoring rights**, permitting the client to verify that compliance requirements have been implemented throughout the development lifecycle
- **Regulatory updates clauses**, ensuring that adaptive modifications are undertaken if legal frameworks evolve prior to or shortly after deployment

Furthermore, the acceptance process should integrate **regulatory compliance testing** into User Acceptance Testing (UAT) or a parallel validation process. This may include simulated data processing scenarios, penetration tests, or third-party audits confirming conformity with relevant statutes. By embedding compliance verification into the acceptance procedure, parties significantly reduce the likelihood of deploying a system that inadvertently exposes them to legal and financial sanctions.

Ultimately, clarity in drafting, through well-defined compliance obligations and indemnity structures, renders liability allocation predictable, enhances legal defensibility, and strengthens the overall resilience of the contractual framework.

*7.10.5 Evidence and **Frequent Litigation Issues***

Evidence

In disputes, documentary evidence surrounding Final Acceptance is crucial. Key items include:

a) Signed Final Acceptance Certificates or formal rejection notices with detailed defect lists;

b) Final acceptance test results, including performance and security benchmarks;
c) Correspondence confirming the resolution of all outstanding issues;
d) Compliance certificates and audit reports;
e) Updated as-built documentation and intellectual property transfer records.

Frequent Litigation Issues in the Final Acceptance Stage

Premature Acceptance Under Pressure: Client signs Final Acceptance to release withheld payments under commercial pressure, then discovers defects shortly after.

Legal impact: Waiver of claims; disputes over whether defects were latent or discoverable during testing.

Refusal Without Contractual Basis: Client refuses to sign despite all contractual criteria being met, using acceptance as leverage for unrelated concessions.

Legal impact: Breach of contract; developer may claim payment plus delay damages.

Failure to Complete Acceptance Testing: Client does not perform required final testing, then disputes system performance months later.

Legal impact: Risk of deemed acceptance clauses triggering automatically.

Outstanding Defects Not Properly Documented: Parties disagree on whether certain minor defects were to be resolved post-acceptance or pre-acceptance.

Legal impact: Conflicting interpretations of defect classification tables in the contract.

Preventive Drafting Recommendations

To prevent disputes and ensure legal clarity, the contract should define Final Acceptance criteria in clear, measurable, and objective terms; require written confirmation that explicitly references the fulfilled criteria; include provisions for conditional acceptance of minor defects with defined remediation timelines; clearly articulate the relationship between Final Acceptance and the commencement of the warranty period; and allocate specific responsibility for verifying regulatory and legal compliance prior to acceptance.

CHAPTER 8

Maintenance and Support

8.1 Importance of Ongoing Maintenance in Software Development

Ongoing maintenance in software development is crucial for ensuring that a deployed software application remains functional, secure, and aligned with evolving business needs. Unlike physical products, software requires continuous updates and modifications to stay relevant and efficient over time.

Table 8.1 Legal Risk Matrix for Maintenance and Support Clauses

Risk Category	*Description*	*Potential Consequences*	*Mitigation Measures*
Ambiguity in Scope	Vague definitions of "maintenance," "enhancements," or "support."	Contract disputes, refusal to act, project delays.	Use precise definitions; separate warranty from paid support.
Unclear SLAs	Absence of concrete response/ resolution times or uptime guarantees.	Operational downtime, inability to enforce performance.	Include detailed SLA terms; tie to remedies or penalties.
Security Update Failures	No obligation to apply critical patches post-deployment.	Breach of data protection laws; liability exposure.	Require patch protocols and indemnity clauses.
Dependency Risks	Developer liable for third-party APIs or hosting failures.	Claims for outages or failures beyond developer's control.	Exclude third-party dependencies or limit liability.

(*Continued*)

DOI: 10.4324/9781003669609-8

Table 8.1 (Continued)

Risk Category	*Description*	*Potential Consequences*	*Mitigation Measures*
Unlimited Support Expectations	Broad or implied support commitments without scope limits.	Developer resource overload, scope creep, financial loss.	Bound obligations by ticket types, time, and fees.
Non-Compliance with Regulations	No contractual obligation to implement compliance updates.	Regulatory fines (e.g., GDPR, HIPAA), client liability.	Assign responsibility and timelines for regulatory updates.
Weak Termination Clauses	Lack of termination clarity or unfairly biased conditions.	Inability to exit or recover costs in case of breach.	Use balanced termination triggers and transition terms.

This phase often includes fixing bugs, improving performance, adapting the software to new operating environments, and implementing updates to keep the system aligned with technological advancements or regulatory changes.

From a contractual standpoint, the importance of maintenance lies in protecting the client's investment. Maintenance ensures that the software continues to deliver value, supporting smooth business operations and preventing disruptions. Additionally, as new security vulnerabilities emerge and technologies advance, regular maintenance mitigates the risk of potential security breaches or incompatibilities that could compromise the software's effectiveness.

Ongoing maintenance also allows for incremental enhancements and feature updates, enabling the software to adapt to the client's changing needs. Without maintenance, software can quickly become outdated or inefficient, resulting in reduced productivity or even failure to meet critical business objectives.

In summary, maintenance ensures:

- System stability and uptime
- Responsiveness to user feedback
- Long-term business continuity
- Adaptability to shifting operational demands

8.1.1 Technical Scope of Maintenance

Software maintenance encompasses several **key activities**:

Corrective Maintenance: Fixing bugs or malfunctions that arise in real-world use.

Corrective maintenance refers to the ongoing process of identifying and fixing errors, bugs, or malfunctions that are discovered after the software has been deployed and is in active use. These issues may not have been detected during testing or may only become apparent under real-world operating conditions, such as specific user behaviors, data inputs, or system interactions that were not replicated in the development or staging environment.

The primary goal of corrective maintenance is to restore the software to its expected performance and functionality, as originally specified in the contract. This includes resolving defects that hinder normal operations, impair user experience, or cause system instability. For example, if an invoicing module generates incorrect totals due to a calculation error, the developer is typically obligated to fix this under the corrective maintenance clause.

From a legal perspective, corrective maintenance is particularly significant when the defect affects critical business functions or regulatory compliance. If the contract includes a warranty period, the developer may be required to remedy such issues at no additional cost. After the warranty expires, the right to corrective maintenance depends on the terms of the ongoing support agreement. Failure to perform timely corrective maintenance may constitute a breach of contract, especially if it leads to operational losses, data integrity issues, or violations of applicable laws.

In short, corrective maintenance safeguards the client's ability to rely on the software for its intended purposes and forms the foundation of a developer's post-deployment support obligations.

Adaptive Maintenance: Updating the software to remain compatible with changes in hardware, operating systems, or third-party services.

Adaptive maintenance involves modifying the software to ensure it remains compatible with changes in the client's technical environment, such as updates to hardware, operating systems, network infrastructure, browsers, or third-party services and APIs. These changes are often beyond the control of either party but can render software partially or entirely non-functional if not addressed in a timely manner.

For example, if a cloud-based CRM solution stops functioning properly because the client upgrades its server operating system, the developer must adjust the software's configuration or code to restore compatibility. Similarly, if a payment gateway changes its API specifications, adaptive maintenance requires the software to be updated so it can continue processing transactions.

From a legal standpoint, adaptive maintenance protects the client's long-term ability to use the software in a dynamic and evolving IT landscape. Contracts should clearly specify whether and to what extent the developer is responsible for maintaining compatibility with third-party updates. If adaptive maintenance obligations are vaguely defined or omitted, the client risks being left with unusable software or facing additional fees for changes not covered under the support agreement. Conversely, developers may face liability if compatibility issues disrupt business operations and the contract requires ongoing adaptability.

Thus, adaptive maintenance is essential to preserving the operational continuity of software and should be governed by well-defined contractual terms that allocate responsibility and cost for supporting changes in the surrounding environment.

Perfective Maintenance: Enhancing features or improving performance based on client feedback or business needs

Perfective maintenance refers to improvements made to the software after deployment in order to enhance functionality, optimize performance, or respond to evolving user expectations and business objectives. Unlike corrective maintenance, which addresses defects, perfective maintenance is driven by a desire to refine and expand the software's capabilities, often based on client feedback, analytics, or strategic developments within the organization.

Typical examples include improving the user interface for better usability, accelerating system response times, or adding filters and automation features that streamline workflows. These changes do not fix errors but instead make the software more effective, user-friendly, or aligned with new business priorities.

From a legal perspective, perfective maintenance must be carefully delineated in the contract. It is often excluded from standard support obligations and may be treated as a separate, billable service. If the scope of perfective maintenance is not clearly defined, disputes may arise over whether a client's request is a reasonable enhancement or a new development effort requiring additional fees. Developers must also manage the risk that continuous feature requests, if not contractually limited, could lead to scope creep or unanticipated resource burdens.

Well-structured agreements should outline the process for requesting enhancements, approval workflows, cost implications, and implementation timelines. This ensures transparency, budget control, and alignment with the client's strategic goals while protecting the developer from unreasonable or ambiguous obligations.

Preventive Maintenance: Implementing proactive measures to prevent future defects or performance degradation, including regular security updates and refactoring.

Preventive maintenance involves taking proactive actions to reduce the likelihood of software failures, security breaches, or performance issues before they occur. Unlike corrective or adaptive maintenance, which responds to issues after they arise, preventive maintenance focuses on anticipation and early intervention. This includes activities such as applying regular security patches, monitoring system performance to detect degradation trends, updating outdated libraries or dependencies, and refactoring sections of code that pose long-term risks due to poor design or technical debt.

For example, a developer may routinely update encryption protocols to protect against emerging cyber threats or rewrite inefficient code modules that, while functional, could cause scalability issues as usage grows. These actions help maintain the software's long-term stability, reliability, and compliance with evolving industry standards.

From a legal standpoint, preventive maintenance plays a key role in risk mitigation and contractual diligence. If neglected, it may expose both parties to operational disruptions or legal liability, particularly in regulated environments where data protection and system availability are mandated by law (e.g., GDPR, HIPAA, or financial services regulations).

Contracts should clearly address whether preventive maintenance is included in the base support package, define its scope, and establish obligations for scheduling, testing, and documenting preventive actions. Failing to include such provisions may result in disputes over responsibility for avoidable system failures or escalating support costs.

These services extend the lifecycle of the application by preserving its functional integrity, security, and usability over time. They ensure that the software continues to meet contractual and business performance expectations even as technological environments, user demands, or regulatory requirements evolve. Without ongoing maintenance, even well-designed systems risk becoming obsolete, non-compliant, or vulnerable to failures, potentially exposing the client to operational downtime, financial loss, or legal liability.

8.2 Legal and Contractual Significance

From a legal and contractual perspective, post-deployment maintenance plays a critical role in safeguarding the client's long-term investment. Unlike physical goods, software is not static, it must be actively maintained to preserve its functionality, ensure data security, and remain compatible with evolving technologies and legal frameworks.

A well-drafted maintenance clause ensures that the application continues to operate as intended and protects against costly business disruptions, reputational harm, or legal exposure.

In this context, maintenance obligations are not merely technical details but essential contractual commitments that influence the software's reliability, security posture, and regulatory compliance. Failing to define these obligations with precision may lead to litigation, service degradation, or liability transfers that were not anticipated at contract signature.

8.2.1 Legal Risks Arising from Poorly Defined Maintenance Obligations

Ambiguity Over Scope

Unclear delineation between warranty services (typically included in the original development fee) and paid maintenance can create major disputes. For instance, the client may assert that a bug fix is covered by the warranty, while the developer classifies it as a new enhancement subject to additional fees. Such ambiguity can delay essential repairs and strain the client-developer relationship, potentially escalating into a payment or breach-of-contract conflict.

To avoid the legal and operational pitfalls associated with unclear boundaries between **warranty** and **maintenance services**, the contract must explicitly define the scope, duration, and nature of each obligation.

Define Terms Separately

The contract should include distinct definitions for:

Warranty Services: Typically limited to correcting defects that prevent the software from functioning as promised, during a fixed period (e.g., 90 days post-acceptance).

Maintenance Services: Cover updates, upgrades, performance improvements, and adaptations after the warranty period expires.

Clarify Timing and Triggers

State the exact duration of the warranty and indicate when maintenance obligations begin (e.g., after warranty expiration or upon signing of a separate SLA).

Differentiate Bug vs. Enhancement

Include criteria for classifying an issue as a "bug" (i.e., deviation from agreed specs) or an "enhancement" (i.e., functional expansion or optimization).

Sample contract clause: warranty vs. maintenance clarification clause

> The Developer shall provide warranty services for a period of ninety (90) calendar days from the date of Final Acceptance. During this period, the Developer shall, at no additional cost, correct any material defects that cause the Software to deviate from the functional specifications outlined in Annex [X].
>
> Following expiration of the warranty period, any further services—including but not limited to software updates, feature enhancements, performance tuning, or compatibility adaptations—shall be provided under a separate Maintenance Agreement.
>
> For the purposes of this Agreement:
>
> a) A *defect* is defined as a reproducible error or malfunction that prevents the Software from performing in accordance with the specifications;
> b) An *enhancement* refers to any change that introduces new functionality or modifies existing functionality beyond the agreed specifications.

8.2.2 Security Liability

A failure to deploy critical security patches in a timely manner exposes the system to cyber threats. If a data breach occurs due to outdated code or unpatched vulnerabilities, the consequences may include regulatory fines, civil litigation by affected users or business partners, operational disruptions, and reputational damage to the client.

The allocation of liability in such cases depends heavily on whether the contract clearly defines the developer's post-deployment obligations to provide ongoing security updates, as well as on the applicability of indemnity clauses or limitations of liability.

A developer's refusal or delay in patching known vulnerabilities, especially when those vulnerabilities were publicly disclosed or known in industry databases, may constitute negligence or even gross negligence, weakening contractual liability caps. Conversely, if the contract is silent or vague about security updates, the client may struggle to claim damages unless statutory duties (such as GDPR security obligations) fill the gap.

To prevent Legal and Operational Exposure:

a) Write Explicit Security Maintenance Obligations (the contract should state that the developer is responsible for providing critical security updates for a defined period, even if broader maintenance is not included. This obligation should cover both internally discovered vulnerabilities and those identified by third-party libraries or frameworks used in the software).
b) Define Update Timeframes (The agreement should require deployment of high-severity security patches within a defined timeframe (e.g., 48–72 hours), and include classification guidelines).

c) Ask for Compliance with Standards (Reference applicable cybersecurity standards to define "reasonable security," especially for regulated sectors).
d) Include Indemnity Clauses (include specific indemnification language for losses arising from the developer's failure to implement agreed security measures or patches).

Sample contract clause: security maintenance and indemnity clause

> The Developer shall monitor the Software for security vulnerabilities on an ongoing basis and shall deploy critical security patches within seventy-two (72) hours of discovery or notification.
>
> Security vulnerabilities are defined as software weaknesses rated 'High' or 'Critical' under the Common Vulnerability Scoring System (CVSS). The Developer shall ensure compatibility of patches with the Client's production environment and shall provide reasonable notice before deployment.
>
> The Developer shall indemnify and hold harmless the Client from any damages, regulatory penalties, or third-party claims resulting from a security breach attributable to the Developer's failure to timely implement required security patches, unless such failure was caused by the Client's own negligence or unauthorized modifications to the Software.

As regulations such as the GDPR, HIPAA, or national cybersecurity laws evolve, failure to update the software accordingly can result in serious compliance violations. If maintenance clauses do not expressly allocate responsibility for implementing legal or technical updates, the client may face enforcement actions, fines, or forced shutdowns, while the developer denies responsibility. This is particularly relevant in sectors where compliance is a condition for operating licenses or government contracts.

8.2.3 Operational and Financial Risks

In addition to legal exposure, vague or poorly defined maintenance obligations can lead to serious operational and financial consequences for the client. When the contract fails to specify performance standards, update responsibilities, or service response times, the result is often degraded software functionality, prolonged downtime, or unresolved defects.

This lack of clarity may allow the developer to delay addressing performance bottlenecks or compatibility issues, claiming they fall outside of scope. Over time, this can erode productivity, interrupt critical workflows, and force the client to absorb unexpected remediation or third-party consulting costs to maintain business continuity. Moreover, inconsistent support damages user confidence, undermines internal adoption, and increases the risk of business process failures tied to the software system.

Without clear timelines, prioritization schemes, or escalation paths, the client may also lack the means to enforce corrective action—leaving critical incidents unresolved during business hours or peak operating periods.

How to Mitigate Operational and Financial Exposure

Service Level Definitions (SLAs): Clearly specify acceptable service standards—such as uptime percentages (e.g., 99.9%), response/resolution times by severity level, and escalation protocols.

Scope and Boundaries: Distinguish routine maintenance (e.g., patching, optimization) from out-of-scope requests (e.g., major feature changes), and outline fee structures accordingly to avoid billing surprises.

Remedy and Credit Clauses: Include financial remedies (e.g., service credits, fee reductions) for failure to meet minimum service standards.

Monitoring and Reporting: Require periodic performance reports, uptime logs, and incident tracking dashboards to ensure real-time accountability.

8.3 Service Level Agreements (SLAs) and Their Role

8.3.1 Definition and Overview

A Service Level Agreement (SLA) is a key contractual provision that defines the post-deployment standards of performance the client can expect from the developer or service provider. It serves as a governance framework for maintenance and support services, establishing measurable commitments, such as uptime percentages, incident response times, and issue resolution deadlines.

SLAs are particularly important in software development contracts because they transform vague service expectations into concrete, enforceable obligations. They provide clarity by detailing what constitutes acceptable service, how issues will be prioritized, and what remedies apply in case of non-performance. This alignment reduces ambiguity, ensures operational continuity, and offers legal safeguards in the event of service failure.

From a risk management perspective, the absence of well-structured SLAs may expose the client to prolonged downtime, unresolved defects, or inadequate support, all of which can result in financial losses, business disruption, and reputational harm. Without defined escalation procedures or penalties for breach, the client may have no practical recourse when critical incidents are mishandled or ignored.

By contrast, a well-drafted SLA not only holds the developer accountable through escalation paths and penalties but also incentivizes service consistency. This is especially crucial for business-critical systems, where any deviation from performance standards can have cascading effects across operations. For this reason, SLAs often include service credits, structured reporting obligations, and review mechanisms, ensuring transparency and fostering a responsive client-developer relationship.

SLAs play a critical role in software development contracts by creating a structured and legally enforceable standard for service quality after deployment. Here's how they contribute to a successful client-developer relationship. SLAs set explicit expectations for both parties, detailing what the client can expect regarding response times, availability, and support levels.

This clarity helps prevent misunderstandings and aligns the developer's obligations with the client's operational needs.

8.3.2 Key Components of an SLA

Performance Metrics and Standards

SLAs typically include detailed metrics for service performance, such as system uptime, response time, and resolution time. For example, an SLA may guarantee a minimum of 99.9% uptime per month, meaning that the software should be operational and available for use 99.9% of the time. Performance metrics are often tailored to the software's importance to the client's operations; for instance, critical systems may require higher uptime guarantees and faster response times than non-critical applications.

Incident Classification and Response Times

SLAs categorize incidents by severity, defining different response and resolution times for each category. For instance:

Critical Incidents are issues that halt core functionalities or disrupt operations entirely. The SLA might require immediate acknowledgment (within 15 minutes) and resolution within four hours.

High-Priority Incidents impact essential features but do not completely halt operations. The SLA might set a response time of one hour and a resolution within 24 hours.

Medium or Low-Priority Incidents are minor issues that don't significantly impact operations. The response time may be set to within 24 hours, with resolution within three to five business days.

By defining these categories, the SLA ensures that the developer addresses critical issues promptly, while minor issues are handled in a reasonable timeframe.

Uptime and Availability Guarantees

For software that is essential to business operations, SLAs often include uptime guarantees, specifying the percentage of time the software must be available. Uptime is usually measured monthly, and clauses may include penalties for downtime beyond the agreed limits. For example, if a client's business relies on a real-time inventory management system, the SLA might require 99.9% uptime, allowing for only a limited amount of downtime.

Maintenance Windows and Scheduled Downtime

SLAs also account for **planned maintenance**, during which the software may be temporarily unavailable. Maintenance windows are pre-scheduled times when updates, patches, or improvements are made to the system. The SLA should specify the notice period required for scheduled maintenance (e.g., 48 hours' notice) and define acceptable hours for maintenance (such as non-peak hours to minimize disruption). By including this provision, both parties can plan for these occurrences without unexpected downtime affecting the client's operations.

Remedies and Penalties for Non-Compliance

To ensure accountability, SLAs often include **penalties or remedies** if the developer fails to meet the agreed service levels. These can take the form of financial compensation, such as service credits, which reduce the client's future service fees based on the downtime or performance failure. For instance, if the software's uptime drops below the agreed 99.9%, the client may receive a service credit for each hour of unplanned downtime. Such penalties create a financial incentive for the developer to maintain the specified service levels and protect the client from the costs associated with inadequate service.

Escalation Procedures

SLAs usually outline **escalation procedures** for situations where issues cannot be resolved within the agreed timelines. Escalation involves moving the problem to a higher level of technical support or management to expedite resolution. The SLA may specify the levels of escalation, providing the client with a structured path to follow if the developer fails to address an issue within the standard resolution time. This process helps ensure that critical issues receive immediate attention, reducing the risk of prolonged service disruptions.

Review and Reporting Requirements

Regular reporting and reviews are often required as part of the SLA to verify compliance and assess ongoing service quality. The SLA may require the developer to provide monthly or quarterly reports documenting system performance, incident response, and resolution times. These reports enable the client to track whether the service levels are being met consistently and give both parties an opportunity to address any patterns of non-compliance.

8.3.3 Checklist: Effective Maintenance and Support Clauses (Client Perspective)

This checklist helps ensure that the maintenance and support clauses in a software contract comprehensively cover the client's needs, protect their investment, and set clear expectations for post-deployment support.

1. **Scope of Maintenance and Support Services**
   - Does the contract specify the types of maintenance included, such as corrective, adaptive, perfective, and preventive maintenance?
   - Are clear definitions provided for each type of maintenance to avoid ambiguity?
   - Are enhancements or feature upgrades included in the support, or are they billed separately?
2. **Response and Resolution Timeframes**
   - Does the contract include specific response and resolution times for different levels of issues (e.g., critical, high, medium, low)?
   - Are timeframes for addressing critical issues (e.g., 24 hours for critical errors) clearly stated to ensure timely support?
   - Is there an escalation process for unresolved or recurring issues?
3. **Warranty Period and Transition to Maintenance**
   - Is there a clear distinction between the warranty period and the ongoing maintenance period?
   - Does the contract specify the length of the warranty period and what issues are covered without additional fees?
   - Are provisions for transitioning from warranty to paid maintenance services clearly outlined?
4. **Availability and Uptime Guarantees**
   - Does the contract define acceptable uptime percentages (e.g., 99.9%) to ensure reliable software performance?
   - Are any penalties or remedies specified if the agreed uptime is not met?
   - Are scheduled maintenance windows defined to minimize disruption to the client's operations?
5. **Fee Structure for Maintenance Services**
   - Are the fees for maintenance and support services clearly defined (e.g., monthly, annually, or hourly rates)?
   - Are there clear terms on what is included in the base fee and what may incur additional costs?
   - Are fees for out-of-scope work, such as custom modifications or additional feature requests, addressed?
6. **Process for Reporting and Tracking Issues**
   - Is there a clear, accessible method for the client to report issues (e.g., a dedicated support portal or email)?
   - Does the contract specify tracking and documentation requirements for reported issues, ensuring accountability?
   - Are provisions included for regular updates on issue status and resolution progress?

7. **Regular Updates and Patches**
   - o Are the developer's obligations to provide software updates, patches, and security fixes during the maintenance period specified?
   - o Is there a schedule for updates or a commitment to notify the client of new releases?
   - o Are there requirements for testing and documenting updates before deployment to avoid compatibility issues?
8. **Data Security and Compliance**
   - o Does the contract include security measures for maintenance services to protect client data (e.g., data encryption, access controls)?
   - o Are compliance requirements addressed, especially if regulatory updates are needed (e.g., GDPR, HIPAA)?
   - o Are protocols for incident response and data breach reporting included?
9. **Termination and Renewal Options**
   - o Are conditions for terminating maintenance and support services clearly outlined (e.g., breach of contract, non-performance)?
   - o Does the contract specify automatic renewal terms or the process for renewing support services?
   - o Are any fees or penalties for early termination or non-renewal stated?
10. **Service Level Agreement (SLA) Compliance**
   - o Is there an SLA that defines service levels for response times, resolution times, and uptime?
   - o Are remedies or penalties for non-compliance with SLA terms included, such as service credits or fee reductions?
   - o Does the SLA include reporting requirements to track compliance and document performance?

8.3.4 Checklist: Effective Maintenance and Support Clauses (Developer Perspective)

This checklist helps ensure that the maintenance and support provisions in a software contract are precise, balanced, and protect the developer from unanticipated obligations, commercial losses, or legal exposure.

1. **Scope of Maintenance and Support Services**
   - Is the scope of maintenance clearly limited to defined types (e.g., corrective, adaptive, perfective, preventive)?

- Are optional enhancements and change requests explicitly excluded from base support?
- Are deliverables and service boundaries specified to avoid "unlimited support" assumptions?

2. **Response and Resolution Timeframes**
   - Are response and resolution times realistic based on team size, workload, and issue complexity?
   - Are timeframes tiered by severity and clearly subject to business hours (unless otherwise agreed)?
   - Are force majeure and dependency-based delays (e.g., client response) carved out?
3. **Warranty vs. Maintenance Delineation**
   - Is the warranty period and scope (e.g., defect correction only) explicitly defined and time-limited?
   - Does the contract state that maintenance begins only after warranty expiry or upon separate SLA activation?
   - Are defects caused by client misuse, third-party tools, or environment changes excluded?
4. **Uptime and Availability Guarantees**
   - Are uptime guarantees limited to components directly under developer control?
   - Are exclusions for hosting providers, infrastructure, or third-party APIs clearly stated?
   - Are penalties for breach capped or limited to service credits?
5. **Fee Structure and Compensation Terms**
   - Are maintenance fees fixed or variable, and tied to scope and hours?
   - Is out-of-scope work (e.g., major upgrades or integrations) billable separately under a change order?
   - Are rate increases, renewal terms, or minimum commitment periods included?
6. **Issue Reporting and Communication Channels**
   - Is a structured issue reporting process defined (ticketing system, email, SLA clock triggers)?
   - Are channels and hours for support clearly stated (e.g., Mon–Fri, 9–5)?
   - Is an audit trail of communications or client inaction maintained to prevent future disputes?
7. **Update and Deployment Protocols**
   - Is the developer's discretion over timing and method of updates preserved (e.g., security patches grouped into periodic releases)?

- Are test environments, rollback plans, and client cooperation requirements detailed?
- Does the client bear responsibility for post-deployment testing or rollback if changes conflict with internal systems?

8. **Security and Compliance Limitations**
   - Is the developer's role in compliance updates (e.g., GDPR, HIPAA) clearly limited to technical implementation, not legal interpretation?
   - Are disclaimers for client configuration errors or third-party integrations that compromise security included?
   - Are indemnity and liability limitations in place for breaches not directly caused by the developer?
9. **Termination and Liability Protections**
   - Are termination conditions balanced (e.g., material breach, failure to pay)?
   - Are there provisions for transition assistance, paid exit services, or return of deliverables?
   - Are limitations of liability and caps on damages reinforced, especially in the post-warranty phase?
10. **Service Level Monitoring and Dispute Resolution**
    - Are SLAs monitored using objective and auditable metrics (e.g., ticket timestamps)?
    - Are dispute resolution mechanisms outlined (e.g., mediation before litigation)?
    - Is the client required to notify the developer of dissatisfaction and give time to cure before withholding payment?

This section highlights key legal risks that arise when maintenance and support obligations are poorly drafted, omitted, or misaligned with the realities of post-deployment software operation. The matrix provides a practical framework for identifying, evaluating, and mitigating risks that impact both clients and developers.

CHAPTER 9

Software Development Contracts

9.1 Fixed-Price Contracts

9.1.1 Definition and Overview

A **Fixed-Price Contract** in software development is an agreement where the client and developer set a predetermined, fixed price for the entire project before work begins. This contract type is often used when project requirements are well-defined and unlikely to change, allowing both parties to agree on the scope, deliverables, and price upfront.

In a Fixed-Price Contract, the total cost is established at the beginning, covering all work needed to complete the project to the client's specifications. The developer agrees to deliver the software within the specified timeline, and the client agrees to pay the agreed amount upon completion (or, in some cases, in instalments tied to project milestones). The developer assumes the risk of any cost overruns or delays, as they are committed to delivering the project at the agreed price regardless of the resources or time it may require.

Sample scope of work clause:

> The Developer hereby agrees to design, develop, and deliver a [specific software solution, e.g., "custom enterprise resource planning (ERP) system" or "client relationship management (CRM) software"] for the Client in strict accordance with the specifications, features, functionalities, and performance standards outlined in **Appendix A: Project Specifications** (hereinafter, the "Scope of Work"). This Scope of Work comprehensively encompasses all technical, functional, and aesthetic requirements necessary to meet the Client's operational objectives, and shall be completed on a fixed-price basis of [insert fixed price]. The fixed price includes all resources, tools, and labor required for full development, quality assurance, testing, and initial deployment of the software. The Developer shall bear the risk of any unforeseen cost fluctuations or additional resource demands necessary to meet the obligations herein. Any deviation from or addition to the Scope of Work, including but not limited to modifications of features, functionalities, or performance criteria, shall constitute a Change Request, subject to a formal written amendment approved by both parties. Such changes may impact the project timeline and fixed-price terms as stipulated in the **Change Management** section of this Agreement. The Developer shall ensure that all deliverables, as specified in the Scope of Work, are met in a timely and efficient manner

 DOI: 10.4324/9781003669609-9

and in full compliance with applicable industry standards and best practices. Failure to deliver in accordance with this Scope of Work may constitute a material breach of this Agreement, entitling the Client to pursue remedies as outlined herein.

Real-World Examples of Fixed-Price Contracts Use

Fixed-price contracts are commonly used in projects where requirements are stable, and there is limited risk of scope changes. For example:

Website Redesign for a Corporation: A corporation might engage a development team for a fixed-price contract to redesign its website. In this scenario, the developer is provided with a list of specific functionalities and design preferences, such as mobile responsiveness, e-commerce integration, and enhanced SEO features. Because the project scope is clearly outlined, the developer can quote a fixed price, delivering the final product as specified within the set budget.

Custom CRM Software for a Mid-Sized Company: A mid-sized business might request a customized Customer Relationship Management (CRM) tool with specific features for tracking leads, managing customer data, and generating reports. If these requirements are detailed and unlikely to change, a fixed-price contract allows the company to manage costs and ensures that the developer is incentivized to deliver efficiently.

Mobile App Development for an Event: Fixed-price contracts are often chosen for mobile apps developed for one-time events, such as conferences or festivals. With a defined end date (the event date) and specific features needed (like a schedule, speaker information, and ticketing), both client and developer can agree on the budget and scope at the outset, ensuring that the app is ready in time without budget fluctuations.

9.1.2 Advantages and Disadvantages

Advantages of Fixed-Price Contracts

Cost Predictability. Fixed-price contracts offer budget certainty, which is beneficial for clients who need to plan financially. Clients can rely on a known cost, with less risk of budget overruns due to scope creep or resource changes.

Efficient Development Incentives. Developers are incentivized to work efficiently to protect their profit margins. Since payment is fixed, developers benefit from completing work within the allocated time and resources, encouraging streamlined project management.

Clear Scope and Expectations. With a detailed scope established at the outset, both parties have clear expectations. This reduces misunderstandings about deliverables and project boundaries, simplifying the development process.

Disadvantages of Fixed-Price Contracts

Limited Flexibility. Fixed-price contracts can become challenging if requirements change during development. Adjusting the scope after the project begins may require renegotiation, potentially delaying the project or incurring additional costs.

Higher Initial Planning Requirements. Fixed-price contracts require a well-defined scope from the beginning. This demands thorough planning and documentation, which may require significant time and effort from both client and developer before any actual development begins.

Increased Risk for Developers. Developers assume the risk of any unforeseen challenges or cost increases. If project complexity or required resources exceed initial estimates, developers may face reduced profitability, leading to potential tensions if issues arise.

9.1.3 Key Clauses and Considerations

To protect both parties, a well-drafted Fixed-Price Contract should include key clauses and considerations that address the following:

Scope of Work (SoW)

This clause should define the project's exact requirements, deliverables, and functionality in detail, as any ambiguity may lead to disputes. The contract should clarify what is and is not included to avoid misunderstandings.

Sample contract clause:

> The Scope of Work is intended to comprehensively define the Developer's obligations under this Agreement, and all deliverables, including but not limited to [insert general categories, e.g., "front-end user interface, back-end architecture, integration with third-party services, and security features"], must adhere strictly to the specifications contained in Exhibit A. To ensure clarity, this Agreement expressly limits the Developer's obligations to those items expressly enumerated within the Scope of Work. Any tasks, features, or services not explicitly listed in Exhibit A shall be deemed outside the scope of this Agreement and shall require a formal amendment to be incorporated, subject to additional costs and mutually agreed upon terms as set forth in the Change Management provision. Ambiguity or omissions in the Scope of Work shall not relieve the Developer of their obligation to deliver a complete and functional solution as defined by the agreed-upon

requirements. In case of any conflict between the Scope of Work and subsequent project clarifications or communications, the provisions contained in Exhibit A shall govern.

Milestone Payments

For larger projects, consider milestone-based payments tied to specific deliverables or project phases. This structure allows the client to assess progress and provides the developer with ongoing compensation.

Sample contract clause:

> The Client agrees to pay the Developer for services rendered under this Agreement on milestone basis, with each payment contingent upon the satisfactory completion of specific deliverables, as outlined in **Exhibit B: Milestone Schedule**. Each milestone includes clearly defined deliverables, acceptance criteria, and associated payment amounts. Payment for each milestone shall be due only upon the Client's written approval, confirming that the milestone deliverables meet all specified requirements and standards outlined in the **Scope of Work (Exhibit A)** and any applicable specifications detailed in this Agreement. Upon delivery of each milestone, the Developer shall provide all necessary documentation, reports, or other materials requested by the Client to facilitate the review and acceptance process.
>
> The milestone payment structure is as follows:
>
> 1. **Milestone 1**: [Brief description of deliverables, e.g., "Initial design mockups and project plan"], payment of [X% of total project cost].
> 2. **Milestone 2**: [Brief description of deliverables, e.g., "Completion of front-end development"], payment of [X% of total project cost].
> 3. **Milestone 3**: [Brief description of deliverables, e.g., "Backend integration and system testing"], payment of [X% of total project cost].
> 4. **Final Milestone**: [Description of final deliverables, e.g., "Project deployment and client training"], payment of [remaining balance].
>
> Should the Client determine that a milestone does not meet the agreed-upon criteria or requirements, the Developer shall be notified in writing of any deficiencies. The Developer will then be given an opportunity to make corrections within [a mutually agreed period, e.g., 10 business days] at no additional cost, after which the Client will re-evaluate the deliverable. Only upon acceptance will the associated payment be released. The Client reserves the right to withhold payment if the milestone deliverables fail to meet the agreed standards, specifications, or timelines, as outlined in the **Scope of Work**. Any disputes regarding milestone acceptance shall be resolved in accordance with the **Dispute Resolution** section of this Agreement.

Change Management Process

Since scope changes can significantly impact fixed-price projects, a change management clause is essential. This clause should outline a process for documenting, assessing, and approving any scope changes, including associated costs and time impacts.

Sample contract clause:

> Both parties recognize that the scope of work as defined in **Exhibit A: Scope of Work** is intended to be comprehensive; however, modifications or additions

may be required during the project's course. To manage such changes effectively, the following **Change Management Process** shall be adhered to:

Request for Change: Any party requesting a change to the original scope of work, timeline, or deliverables must submit a written Change Request specifying the nature and details of the proposed alteration. This includes any adjustments to features, functionalities, performance requirements, or other aspects of the project.

Documentation and Assessment: Upon receipt of a Change Request, the Developer shall conduct a thorough assessment of the requested change, providing a written response to the Client within [5 business days]. The response will outline: i) the feasibility of implementing the requested change; ii) any anticipated impact on the project timeline, including adjustments to milestone deadlines; iii) an estimate of additional costs associated with implementing the change.

Approval and Authorization: If the Client agrees to the proposed adjustments in timeline and costs, the parties shall execute a formal Change Order Amendment to this Agreement, reflecting the approved modification. The Change Order Amendment must be signed by authorized representatives of both parties before the Developer proceeds with any work outside the original scope. The Change Order Amendment will specify any changes to project milestones and associated payment amounts, as applicable. Adjustments to the payment schedule shall be made to reflect the additional work, ensuring that milestone payments correspond with the revised deliverables. Unless otherwise agreed in the Change Order Amendment, all additional work associated with a Change Request shall be billed at a rate of [insert rate] per hour or in accordance with a separate fixed price agreed upon in the Amendment. Any delay caused by assessing or implementing a Change Request shall extend the overall project timeline accordingly.

If the parties cannot reach an agreement regarding the terms of a Change Request, the original scope, timeline, and payment terms of this Agreement shall remain in effect. Disputes regarding Change Requests shall be managed in accordance with the **Dispute Resolution** section of this Agreement.

All Change Requests, assessments, and Change Order Amendments shall be documented in writing and form part of this Agreement as appendices. Failure to comply with this Change Management Process shall render any unapproved changes null and void, and the Developer shall not be obligated to incorporate unapproved changes into the project deliverables.

9.1.4 Legal Risks in Fixed-Price Contracts

While Fixed-Price Contracts provide budget certainty and clear expectations, they also concentrate specific legal risks that both clients and developers must anticipate and mitigate. These risks often arise from the rigidity of the fixed-price structure, the dependency on an accurately defined scope of work, and the potential for disputes over performance and acceptance.

Scope Creep and Ambiguity in Requirements: If the Scope of Work is not drafted with absolute precision, disagreements can emerge over whether certain features, integrations, or enhancements are included in the original price.

Example: A contract for a custom CRM system specifies "integration with the company's ERP," but does not define which ERP or the depth of integration. The developer may claim a basic data export satisfies the clause, while the client expects full two-way synchronization.

***Legal Risk*:** Ambiguity may be interpreted against the drafter under contra proferentem rules, potentially obligating the developer to deliver more than originally intended without additional payment.

Change Requests and Delay Claims: Fixed-Price models are vulnerable to disputes over additional time and cost arising from mid-project changes. If the change management clause is vague or unenforced, parties may disagree over whether a request is a legitimate scope change or simply part of the original deliverable.

***Legal Risk*:** A developer refusing to implement a requested change without additional payment risks being found in breach if a court deems the change within the original scope. Conversely, a client insisting on changes without formal amendment may be liable for payment disputes or delay-related claims.

Performance and Acceptance Disputes: Since payment is often linked to final acceptance or milestone sign-off, disagreements about whether deliverables meet contractual specifications are common.

Example: The client withholds final payment claiming that the delivered e-commerce site "loads too slowly" and "is not mobile-optimized," but the acceptance criteria in the contract lack specific, measurable benchmarks.

***Legal Risk*:** The absence of objective acceptance criteria increases the likelihood of litigation or arbitration, with each party presenting conflicting technical evidence.

Delay and Liquidated Damages Exposure: Fixed-Price Contracts frequently include strict delivery dates backed by liquidated damages clauses. If unforeseen complexities arise, the developer bears the cost of delays.

***Legal Risk*:** In jurisdictions where liquidated damages must represent a genuine pre-estimate of loss, excessive penalties may be unenforceable. However, if valid, such clauses can lead to significant financial liability for the developer.

Quality Standards and "Fitness for Purpose" Claims: Even if the developer meets the explicit scope, the client may assert implied obligations, such as delivering software "fit for purpose" or meeting industry standards.

Legal Risk: In some jurisdictions, statutory or implied warranties can impose additional obligations regardless of the written contract, creating exposure for defects discovered post-delivery.

Evidence Challenges in Disputes: Without robust documentation, such as version-controlled code repositories, meeting minutes, and signed change orders, either party may struggle to prove whether a feature was in scope, when delays occurred, or whether acceptance criteria were met.

Legal Risk: The absence of contemporaneous records can shift the evidentiary balance in litigation or arbitration.

Practical Safeguards:

- Draft an **exhaustive Scope of Work** with measurable deliverables and clear exclusions
- Enforce a **formal Change Management process** for all deviations
- Define **objective acceptance criteria** and measurable performance benchmarks
- Maintain **detailed project records** for evidentiary purposes
- Use **realistic delivery schedules** with mutually agreed buffer periods

9.2 Time and Materials (T&M) Contracts

9.2.1 Definition and Overview

A **Time and Materials (T&M) Contract** in software development is an agreement where the client pays the developer based on the actual time spent (resources) and materials used in the project, rather than a fixed total price. This contract type is commonly used when project requirements are flexible or not fully defined at the start, allowing both parties to adapt the scope and scale of the work as development progresses.

In a T&M Contract, the developer provides services at an agreed hourly or daily rate, and the client covers any additional costs for materials, tools, or software licenses required to complete the project. This arrangement allows for flexibility, as the scope can evolve without requiring a formal renegotiation of the contract. However, it places the financial risk of extended timelines or changing requirements on the client, as the developer is compensated for each hour worked.

Sample of scope of work clause:

> The Developer agrees to perform software development services for the Client on a Time and Materials basis, with all work performed in accordance with **Appendix A: Project Scope** (hereinafter, the "Scope of Work" or "SoW"). The Scope of Work provides an initial outline of the project's objectives,

deliverables, and requirements; however, it is understood by both parties that the scope may evolve as the project progresses. The Developer shall provide weekly timesheets detailing the hours worked and the tasks completed, as well as any materials used in the project. The Client shall compensate the Developer at the agreed hourly rate of [insert rate], plus reimbursement for approved materials and expenses incurred in connection with the project. The Client reserves the right to review timesheets and invoices to confirm that work is in alignment with project requirements.

Real-World Examples of Time and Materials Projects

Time and Materials contracts are commonly used for projects where flexibility is needed, and requirements may evolve over time. For example:

Prototype Development for a Start-Up: A start-up may engage a developer to build an initial prototype of a new software application. Since the requirements are likely to change based on user feedback and testing, a T&M contract allows the start-up to adapt the project scope as necessary without a fixed price constraint.

Feature Enhancements to an Existing System: A company with an existing CRM system may hire a development team on a T&M basis to add new features based on evolving business needs. This type of contract provides flexibility, as the company can direct the developer to prioritize different features as requirements shift.

Long-Term Maintenance and Support Services: For projects where ongoing maintenance, support, and iterative improvements are expected, a T&M contract enables the client to access development services as needed. This allows for continuous updates, bug fixes, and enhancements based on operational demands.

9.2.2 Advantages and Disadvantages

Advantages of Time and Materials Contracts

Flexibility in Scope. T&M contracts allow for adjustments to the project's scope and requirements without needing to renegotiate the contract, making them ideal for projects where requirements are expected to evolve.

Transparency in Costs. Since the client is billed based on actual time and resources, they can monitor the budget closely and manage spending according to priorities.

Focus on Quality and Iteration. Developers can dedicate time to improving the software iteratively, without constraints imposed by a fixed budget, resulting in potentially higher-quality deliverables.

Disadvantages of Time and Materials Contracts

Potential for Budget Overruns. T&M contracts place the financial risk on the client, as there is no fixed cap on the total project cost. If the project's timeline extends, the client may face higher costs than initially anticipated.

Less Cost Predictability. With payments based on hours worked, it can be challenging for the client to forecast the exact cost of the project, particularly if the project scope is unclear.

Risk of Inefficiency. The developer may have less incentive to work efficiently under a T&M model, as they are compensated based on hours rather than deliverables. This requires the client to actively manage and monitor the project.

In T&M Contracts, a significant risk lies in the possibility that the developer may provide labour (resources) without guaranteeing the end results or committing to any specific project outcomes. In such cases, the developer's responsibility may be limited to allocating resources and hours toward the project, rather than delivering a fully functional product. This structure can be particularly dangerous for the client, as it effectively places the entirety of the development risk on the client's shoulders.

9.2.3 Client's Risk

Risk of Lack of Result Commitment: In T&M contracts, developers are typically paid based on time and resources, with payment linked to hours worked rather than deliverables. When the contract does not include a clear commitment to achieving specific outcomes, there is a risk that the developer's team may be engaged in activities that do not contribute directly to the project's success or may not even result in a usable end product. This lack of commitment to deliverables often leaves the client in a vulnerable position, as the client could incur significant costs without any assurance that the software will meet their operational needs.

No Guarantee of Functionality or Performance: When developers do not offer guarantees regarding functionality or performance, the client has no recourse if the end product fails to perform as expected. In such cases, the contract may explicitly state that the developer's obligation is limited to providing a set number of hours or team members, with no warranty regarding the functionality, quality, or usability of the final deliverables. This creates an imbalanced scenario where the client is responsible for all development risks, including the risk of incomplete or non-functional software, without the ability to hold the developer accountable for results.

In this arrangement, the client assumes full responsibility for the outcome of the project, including risks such as: i) *Incomplete or Unsatisfactory Deliverables*, where the client may be left with a partially finished product that fails to meet business needs, with no mechanism to enforce completion or quality standards; ii) *Extended Timelines and Escalating Costs*, without a guarantee of completion (the project could drag on indefinitely, accruing higher costs without clear milestones or deliverables); iii) *Future Maintenance and Issue Resolution*, since the developer is not bound to provide warranty and the client will bear the additional burden of resolving issues or maintaining the software independently, leading to further costs and operational disruptions.

To protect against these risks, clients can include certain clauses in T&M contracts that require the developer to take on a more result-oriented approach. Here are some strategies:

Define Clear Deliverables and Acceptance Criteria. Even in a T&M contract, clients should insist on defining key deliverables and acceptance criteria to ensure that work completed meets minimum quality and functional standards.

Milestone and Progress Reporting. Regular milestones tied to progress reviews can help the client track the developer's output. This way, the client can assess whether the work aligns with the project's goals and stop further work if it appears the project is not meeting expectations.

Include Warranty or Guarantee Clauses for Core Functionality. The client can negotiate limited warranties for core functionalities, requiring the developer to ensure specific aspects of the software function as intended. This can help safeguard against the risk of receiving an incomplete or ineffective product.

Shift Some Risk to the Developer through Penalty Clauses. Including clauses that impose penalties for unreasonable delays or failure to achieve specific goals can incentivize the developer to work efficiently and meet agreed-upon standards, even within a T&M framework.

Hold Regular Steering Meetings for Ongoing Assessment. Regular steering committee meetings or project reviews can allow the client to stay closely involved in the project's direction, ensuring that resources are focused on valuable, outcome-driven work rather than hours for hours' sake.

Sample contract clause for performance expectations

> Notwithstanding that this is a Time and Materials Contract, the Developer agrees to use all reasonable efforts to ensure that the services provided meet the Client's objectives as outlined in Exhibit A: Project Scope. The Developer shall ensure that work performed meets functional and performance standards

> acceptable to the Client, and agrees to undertake corrective actions for any work deemed non-compliant with mutually agreed specifications, at no additional cost to the Client.

By adding clauses that set expectations for functional standards and incorporating oversight mechanisms, the client can reduce the risk of paying for work that does not deliver value. Taking these steps can help shift some responsibility back to the developer and provide the client with greater control and protection in a T&M contract structure.

9.2.4 Key Clauses and Considerations

To protect both parties, a well-drafted Time and Materials Contract should include the following key clauses and considerations.

Scope of Work (SoW)

This clause should provide an outline of the initial project objectives, deliverables, and functionality but allow flexibility for modifications as the project progresses.

Sample contract clause:

> The Scope of Work provides a preliminary framework for the project's goals and intended functionalities. It is understood by both parties that, due to the nature of a Time and Materials Contract, the Scope of Work may evolve. The Developer will undertake tasks as directed by the Client and will document any adjustments in scope as they arise, ensuring transparency and alignment with project goals. Any substantial changes or new functionalities shall be discussed with the Client to confirm budget and timeline implications.

Rates and Fee Structure

This clause defines the hourly or daily rates for all development work, as well as any materials or additional costs to be billed to the client.

Sample contract clause:

> The Client hereby agrees to compensate the Developer at the rate of [insert hourly or daily rate] for all hours worked by the Developer's personnel in connection with the services provided under this Agreement. Payment shall be due on a monthly basis, contingent upon submission and approval of detailed, itemized timesheets that accurately reflect the time expended on the project and the specific tasks performed. The Developer shall submit such timesheets to the Client for review and written approval no later than [insert time period, e.g., 'five business days'] following the end of each billing period.
>
> In addition to labour fees, the Client shall reimburse the Developer for any pre-approved materials, equipment, software licenses, or third-party services required to perform the services herein, provided such expenses are substantiated by supporting documentation. Any individual expense or cumulative monthly expense exceeding [specified threshold] shall require prior written authorization from the Client, which authorization must be obtained in advance of the Developer incurring the expense. The Developer's

failure to secure prior written approval for expenses exceeding the specified threshold shall result in the Client's right to deny reimbursement for such expenses.

The Developer agrees to maintain detailed records of all hours worked, materials used, and third-party services obtained under this Agreement. Such records shall be made available to the Client upon request and shall be retained for a period of no less than [insert period, e.g., 'two years'] from the date of invoice submission, in accordance with applicable record-keeping and audit standards. Failure to comply with these requirements may result in the withholding of payment until all relevant documentation is provided to the Client's satisfaction.

Budget Cap and Client Approval

A budget cap or regular client approval checkpoints can help control spending and provide a safety net for the client.

Sample contract clause:

> The total project budget under this Agreement shall not exceed [insert maximum amount] (the "Budget Cap") unless expressly authorized in writing by the Client. This Budget Cap includes all fees for hours worked, reimbursable expenses, and any other costs incurred in relation to the project. The Developer is responsible for managing resources effectively to complete the project within this budgetary limit. Upon reaching [e.g., 75%] of the Budget Cap, the Developer shall immediately notify the Client in writing and provide a detailed, updated forecast of the hours and associated costs required to complete the remaining project tasks. This forecast shall include an assessment of the anticipated time and resources needed for each remaining deliverable, identifying any potential budgetary or resource constraints that may impact project completion. In response to the Developer's notice, the Client reserves the following rights: i) Approval of Additional Funding: The Client may, at its sole discretion, authorize additional funding beyond the Budget Cap to cover any projected budget overages necessary to complete the project as originally scoped; ii) Reprioritization of Project Tasks: Should additional funding not be granted, the Client may reprioritize or adjust project tasks and deliverables to remain within the established Budget Cap. This may involve deferring or modifying non-essential features, functionalities, or other aspects of the project to accommodate the remaining budget.
>
> The Developer acknowledges that failure to provide timely notice upon reaching the specified budget threshold may result in the Client's refusal to authorize additional funding or adjustments, and the Developer shall bear the risk and responsibility for any unapproved costs incurred beyond the Budget Cap. No additional funds or adjustments to the Budget Cap shall be deemed approved without a formal written amendment to this Agreement, signed by authorized representatives of both parties. The Client's decision to authorize additional funding or modify the project scope shall not be construed as a waiver of the Budget Cap, except as explicitly provided in such written amendment.

9.2.5 Legal Risks in Time and Materials Contracts

While Time and Materials (T&M) Contracts provide flexibility and adaptability, they introduce distinct legal vulnerabilities that can significantly impact both clients and developers. The core issue is the misalignment between resource-based billing and deliverable-based expectations, which often fuels disputes over efficiency, value for money, and accountability.

Absence of Result Commitment: Because T&M contracts compensate based on hours worked rather than deliverables produced, developers may be legally shielded from claims related to incomplete or underperforming software if no specific outcomes are guaranteed in the contract.

Example: A start-up hires a developer for 400 billable hours to build a prototype, but the delivered product is non-functional. Without contractual performance commitments, the client has limited recourse.

Legal Risk: In many jurisdictions, unless there is a breach of express obligations (e.g., using "reasonable skill and care"), the developer may have no legal duty to deliver a usable product.

Escalating Costs Without Budgetary Control: Without a budget cap or client approval checkpoints, costs can spiral far beyond initial expectations, even when progress is slow or misaligned with business goals.

Legal Risk: The client remains liable for all invoiced hours unless it can prove overbilling, fraud, or a breach of contractually agreed work management processes—often a high evidentiary burden.

Inefficiency and Misallocation of Resources

A T&M framework can lead to inefficient use of resources, particularly if the developer reallocates personnel to non-priority tasks or repeatedly refactors code unnecessarily.

Legal Risk: Inefficiency alone is not usually grounds for breach unless specific productivity or progress obligations are set out in the agreement.

Disputes Over Scope and Prioritization

Without clear deliverables or prioritization protocols, clients and developers may disagree on whether work done aligns with the intended business objectives.

Legal Risk: This often results in "value disputes," where the client argues the billed work does not advance the project as expected, while the developer maintains that all tasks were within scope.

Quality Deficiencies and No Warranty Coverage

In the absence of warranty clauses, T&M developers are rarely obligated to correct defects free of charge.

***Legal Risk*:** Clients may face additional cost exposure to fix defects, even if the work was performed under the same contract, unless they can establish negligence or breach of agreed functional standards.

Evidentiary Weakness in Cost and Output Tracking

Disputes over hours billed or the value of work delivered are difficult to win without granular, contemporaneous documentation.

***Legal Risk*:** If timesheets, task logs, and code commit histories are incomplete or vague, a court or arbitral tribunal may side with the developer's invoices as prima facie evidence of work performed.

9.3 Agile Contracts

9.3.1 Overview of Agile Methodology

An **Agile Contract** in software development is designed to accommodate the iterative, flexible nature of Agile methodology, which emphasizes adaptability, client collaboration, and incremental development. Unlike traditional fixed-price or time and materials contracts, Agile Contracts are structured to allow frequent adjustments to the project's scope, requirements, and priorities throughout the development process. This type of contract often includes provisions for iterative delivery, enabling the client to review and approve features at the end of each sprint or iteration.

In an Agile Contract, deliverables are broken down into smaller, manageable units, typically called sprints. Each sprint delivers a usable version or increment of the product that the client can review and provide feedback on. The Agile approach works well in projects with evolving requirements or where client feedback plays a critical role in shaping the final product. While Agile Contracts offer greater flexibility, they require close collaboration between the client and developer, as well as a structure that supports continuous feedback and adaptation.

Sample Agile development scope of work clause:

> The Developer shall render software development services in strict adherence to the Agile methodology, under which project deliverables are created and refined through a series of iterative sprints, as outlined in **Exhibit A: Project Scope and Sprint Schedule** (hereinafter referred to as the "Scope of Work"). The Scope of Work shall comprise multiple defined sprints, each of which will include specific objectives, tasks, and deliverables. Each sprint will result in a functional increment of the software, which will be made available to the Client for review, feedback, and potential acceptance at the conclusion of each sprint cycle.

The Developer and Client agree to collaborate actively on the prioritization and organization of the project backlog, including individual features, enhancements, and functionalities to be addressed in each sprint. Such prioritization will be conducted with due consideration of the Client's evolving operational needs and strategic objectives. The Scope of Work shall remain dynamic and shall be subject to modification and refinement at the close of each sprint, based on the Client's feedback, Developer recommendations, and any adjusted priorities mutually agreed upon.

The Client reserves the right, at the end of each sprint, to request reasonable modifications to the feature backlog, task priorities, or sprint objectives to better align with their requirements. Any such modifications shall be documented in writing, reviewed, and mutually agreed upon by authorized representatives of both parties prior to the initiation of the subsequent sprint. Unless otherwise agreed in writing, no modifications shall take effect that materially alter the project timeline, budget, or development resources allocated under this Agreement.

In case any requested modifications to the backlog or sprint priorities have an impact on the overall project timeline, estimated costs, or resource allocation, the Developer shall provide a written assessment of these impacts, including an estimate of any additional time, costs, or resources required to implement the requested changes. The Client shall then have the option to either approve the modifications along with the associated adjustments to the project scope or retain the existing backlog and sprint priorities as previously outlined.

The Developer's obligation to deliver services in alignment with the Agile methodology is conditional upon the Client's active participation in sprint reviews, timely provision of feedback, and collaboration in prioritization discussions. Failure by the Client to engage in these collaborative processes may impact the progress and delivery schedule, and the Developer shall bear no liability for delays arising from such circumstances.

Real-World Examples of Agile Projects

Agile Contracts are often used in projects where requirements are expected to evolve or where frequent client feedback is essential. For example:

a) **Custom Software for a Start-Up**, where a start-up may need a custom application but cannot define all features at the outset. Using an Agile Contract, the development team can build the application incrementally, allowing the client to adjust priorities based on user feedback and evolving business needs.
b) **Large Enterprise Application Development**, where a large company may engage a developer to build a complex enterprise application with multiple modules. Agile methodology allows the project to be developed in increments, enabling the client to test and provide feedback on each module individually.
c) **Ongoing Product Enhancement for Software as a Service (SaaS)**, where a SaaS provider may enter into an Agile Contract for

ongoing product development, adding new features and improving existing ones through regular sprints, ensuring that the product continuously adapts to market demands and user feedback.

9.3.2 Advantages and Disadvantages

Advantages of Agile Contracts

Flexibility in Scope and Requirements. Agile Contracts allow for real-time adjustments, making it easier to accommodate changes in project scope based on feedback or evolving business requirements.

Enhanced Client Collaboration. Frequent check-ins and sprint reviews allow the client to be actively involved in the development process, providing ongoing feedback and ensuring the product aligns with their needs.

Incremental Delivery and Early Testing. By breaking the project into sprints, Agile Contracts enable the client to test and use parts of the software as they are developed, reducing the risk of unexpected issues at the end of the project.

Disadvantages of Agile Contracts

Less Cost Predictability. Since the scope is flexible, it can be challenging to predict the total project cost accurately, particularly for larger or long-term projects where the requirements may expand.

Dependency on Client Engagement. Agile Contracts require active participation from the client to provide feedback and make priority decisions, which may not always be feasible for clients with limited availability.

Potential for Scope Creep. Without proper controls, Agile projects are susceptible to scope creep as new features or changes are continuously introduced, potentially leading to higher costs and extended timelines.

9.3.3 Key Clauses and Considerations

To protect both parties, a well-drafted Agile Contract should include the following key clauses and considerations:

Scope of Work and Sprint Structure

This clause should establish the initial project goals and define the process for prioritizing and scheduling sprints, acknowledging that the Scope of Work will evolve.

Sample contract clause:

The Scope of Work under this Agreement comprises a structured backlog of prioritized items, each representing specific tasks, features, or functionalities essential to the project's objectives. These backlog items shall be addressed through a series of iterative development cycles, hereinafter referred to as "Sprints," in accordance with the Agile methodology. Each Sprint shall be of a duration agreed upon by the parties in **Exhibit A: Sprint Schedule** [e.g., two (2) weeks], during which the Developer shall design, code, and deliver a functional increment of the software, aligned with the Client's requirements for that Sprint cycle. At the conclusion of each Sprint, the Developer shall present the completed increment to the Client for review, feedback, and, where applicable, formal acceptance. The Client shall conduct its review within [insert specified time, e.g., five (5) business days] following Sprint completion, during which time the Client may request modifications or provide feedback to refine the deliverable further. Any such requests for modifications shall be documented in writing and, if applicable, incorporated into the backlog for prioritization in subsequent Sprints, without additional costs.

The Developer and Client shall collaborate continuously to review and reprioritize backlog items at the end of each Sprint. This prioritization process will be based on the Client's evolving business needs, strategic goals, and any feedback generated from prior Sprint deliverables. The parties agree that any changes to Sprint priorities or backlog content that materially impact project scope, budget, or timeline shall require mutual agreement and documented authorization prior to the commencement of the following Sprint.

The Developer shall not undertake any work outside the scope of the Sprint as agreed for that cycle without the Client's prior written consent. Should the Client request work outside the current Sprint scope or backlog, the Developer shall assess the impact of such work on project costs, timelines, and resource allocations. The Developer shall provide a written proposal for the additional work, detailing any adjustments to time, cost, or resource requirements. The Client shall have the right to approve, reject, or defer such additional work requests, with any approved work documented as an amendment to the Scope of Work.

This clause does not relieve the Developer of its obligation to exercise reasonable diligence, skill, and care in fulfilling each Sprint, and the Developer shall utilize industry-standard Agile practices to ensure efficient Sprint management. The Client's active participation in Sprint reviews, timely provision of feedback, and collaboration in prioritization efforts are essential to the Agile process, and any failure by the Client to engage in these processes may impact the delivery schedule. In such cases, the Developer shall not be held liable for any resulting delays.

The parties acknowledge that the iterative and adaptive nature of Agile development requires flexibility, and both agree to engage in good faith collaboration to address any adjustments to the Scope of Work, Sprint schedule, or priorities as the project evolves. Any disputes regarding Sprint scope or prioritization shall be resolved according to the Dispute Resolution provisions set forth in this Agreement.

Rates and Fee Structure

This clause should define the rates for development work and any other costs involved in each sprint.

Sample contract clause:

> The Client agrees to compensate the Developer at a rate of [insert hourly or daily rate] for all hours worked within each sprint. Payment for each sprint shall be due upon completion, contingent upon the Client's approval of sprint deliverables. In addition, the Client shall reimburse the Developer for any approved third-party materials or services, subject to prior written authorization.

Sprint Review and Acceptance Criteria

This clause should outline the review and acceptance process for each sprint, allowing the client to confirm that the deliverables meet requirements before moving to the next sprint.

Sample contract clause:

> At the conclusion of each sprint, the Developer shall present the increment to the Client for review. The Client shall have [insert timeframe, e.g., 'five business days'] to evaluate the deliverables and provide written feedback or acceptance. Should the Client identify issues that do not align with the agreed sprint objectives, the Developer shall rectify these issues within the following sprint cycle at no additional cost.

Change Management for Backlog Adjustments

In Agile, it is crucial to manage adjustments to the backlog and priorities. This clause establishes the process for such changes.

Sample contract clause:

> The Client may request adjustments to the sprint backlog at the start of each sprint, subject to mutual agreement. Any significant additions that affect the overall timeline or cost shall require a Change Request, outlining the revised priorities and budget implications. The Developer shall assess the impact of any backlog changes and provide a written estimate of additional hours or resources required. No changes shall take effect without prior written approval from both parties.

Budget Cap

To maintain budget control, Agile Contracts may include a cap on total project costs or require periodic client approval for additional work.

Sample contract clause:

> The total budget for this project shall be capped at [insert amount] unless explicitly authorized by the Client. Upon reaching [e.g., 75%] of the budget cap, the Developer shall provide a detailed budget review, including an estimate for remaining sprints. The Client reserves the right to authorize additional funding or reprioritize backlog items to ensure adherence to the budget cap.

9.3.4 Checklist: Drafting an Agile Contract

This checklist ensures that essential elements are addressed in an Agile Contract:

1. **Clearly Defined Initial Goals and Sprint Structure**: Outline the initial objectives and the structure of sprints to set expectations for iterative delivery.
2. **Flexible Scope of Work**: Acknowledge that the scope will evolve and establish a process for prioritizing tasks within each sprint.
3. **Sprint Review and Acceptance Criteria**: Set a structured review and approval process for deliverables at the end of each sprint.
4. **Change Management for Backlog Adjustments**: Define a process for managing changes to sprint backlogs, including approvals and budget implications.
5. **Budget Cap and Periodic Approval Checkpoints**: Set a budget cap with provisions for client review and approval of additional costs as the project progresses.
6. **Termination and Payment Terms**: Specify conditions for termination, payment obligations for completed sprints, and notice requirements.

9.3.5 Types of Agile Contracts (Timebox, Fixed-Scope with Flexibility)

Agile contracts are designed to accommodate the flexibility and iterative nature of Agile methodology, enabling both developers and clients to adapt to evolving requirements throughout a project. Unlike traditional contracts, which often lock in specific deliverables, timelines, and costs, Agile contracts allow for dynamic prioritization and adjustments in response to feedback, shifting priorities, or unforeseen technical challenges. The most common types of Agile contracts include **Timebox** and **Fixed-Scope with Flexibility**, each catering to different project needs and risk preferences.

Timebox

In a **Timebox** contract, the focus is on a set duration rather than a fixed list of deliverables. The client and developer agree on a maximum time frame, such as a certain number of sprints or a fixed period (e.g., six months), within which the development team works on prioritized backlog items. The client plays an active role by continuously reviewing and adjusting these priorities based on the project's progress and emerging requirements.

Since the scope remains flexible, the project's final deliverables are not defined upfront. Instead, the development team aims to complete as many high-priority items as possible within the allotted time. This approach benefits clients who value responsiveness and adaptability over a specific set of features, as it allows for frequent reassessment and prioritization while controlling time and budget. However, the client assumes some risk, as the final output may vary depending on project complexity and evolving requirements.

Fixed-Scope with Flexibility

The **Fixed-Scope with Flexibility** contract model, by contrast, involves a more defined set of deliverables but allows room for adjustments within the overall scope. Under this model, the client and developer agree upon an initial list of core features or functionalities to be delivered. These features are flexible to an extent, allowing for re-prioritization, refinement, or minor changes as development progresses.

However, significant deviations from the core deliverables or major new feature requests typically require formal approval through a structured change management process. This approach is useful for clients who need specific features but also require some flexibility to refine and adapt these features based on user feedback or testing. The Fixed-Scope with Flexibility model balances a certain degree of structure with the adaptability of Agile, providing both parties with clarity on essential requirements while enabling iterative refinement to enhance the final product.

Each type of Agile contract offers unique advantages, but both emphasize collaboration, responsiveness, and ongoing communication between client and developer. The choice between Timebox and Fixed-Scope with Flexibility depends on the project's priorities, with Timebox favouring adaptability within a set timeframe and Fixed-Scope with Flexibility favouring specific deliverables with controlled flexibility. Both models are particularly suited to projects where client engagement and evolving requirements play a critical role in defining success, offering structured yet flexible frameworks that cater to the inherent uncertainties of software development.

9.3.6 Aligning Agile Practices with Contract Terms

Aligning Agile practices with contract terms requires a careful balance between the flexibility inherent in Agile methodology and the legal precision expected in contract agreements. Agile development emphasizes adaptability, collaboration, and iterative progress, while traditional contracts typically focus on clearly defined deliverables, fixed timelines, and set costs. To bridge this gap, Agile contracts must be crafted to accommodate iterative adjustments, without sacrificing the necessary legal safeguards and clarity for both parties.

A key aspect of aligning Agile practices with contract terms is the structuring of **Scope of Work (SoW)**. In Agile, the project scope is usually broken down into prioritized backlog items, each representing tasks or features to be completed in iterative sprints. Unlike traditional contracts, which often define a static scope, Agile contracts must allow for scope flexibility, enabling adjustments to backlog priorities based on ongoing client feedback and evolving requirements.

To support this approach, Agile contracts typically include provisions for periodic sprint planning sessions, where the client and developer collaboratively define the specific deliverables for each sprint. This process ensures that the contract terms can evolve along with the project while keeping both parties aligned on current priorities.

Sprint-based deliverables and milestone payments are another way to integrate Agile practices into contract terms. Instead of tying payment to a single end deliverable, Agile contracts can establish a payment structure based on completed sprints or milestones. At the end of each sprint, the client reviews the deliverable and provides feedback, allowing both parties to assess progress and agree on further adjustments if needed. By linking payments to the completion of sprints, the contract aligns with Agile's incremental delivery model and ensures that the client maintains control over quality and progress throughout the project lifecycle.

Change management clauses are essential in Agile contracts to handle adjustments to scope, priorities, or requirements as the project progresses. Agile contracts should clearly define a process for documenting and approving changes, especially if they significantly impact the timeline or budget. This might involve a structured change request procedure, where any major modifications are discussed and mutually agreed upon, with written documentation of any cost or time implications. This approach protects both parties by maintaining flexibility within a controlled framework, ensuring that Agile's iterative nature is supported without risking budget overruns or unmanageable delays.

Finally, **client involvement and responsibilities** must be explicitly outlined in Agile contracts to ensure successful alignment. Agile development relies heavily on client engagement, with regular sprint reviews, feedback sessions, and backlog prioritization. Agile contracts should detail the client's responsibilities in terms of feedback timeliness, decision-making participation, and availability for sprint planning. Setting clear expectations for client involvement ensures that both parties are fully engaged, supporting Agile's collaborative approach and reducing the risk of miscommunication or delays.

In conclusion, aligning Agile practices with contract terms involves creating a flexible, iterative framework that respects the collaborative and adaptive nature of Agile while maintaining the legal protections of a structured contract. By carefully addressing scope management, milestone-based payments, change procedures, and client involvement, Agile contracts provide a structured path for adaptive development, allowing both parties to benefit from Agile's responsiveness without compromising on clarity or accountability.

9.3.7 Risk Management in Agile Contracts

Risk management in Agile contracts requires an approach that acknowledges and addresses the uncertainties and dynamic nature of Agile development. Traditional contracts often allocate risk through strict definitions of scope, timelines, and deliverables. However, Agile contracts must accommodate evolving project requirements, iterative feedback, and client collaboration, creating unique risk factors that require thoughtful management strategies.

One primary risk in Agile contracts is **scope creep**, where ongoing adjustments or new feature requests can lead to an expansion of project requirements without a corresponding adjustment to budget or timeline. To manage this risk, Agile contracts benefit from incorporating structured change management processes. This includes establishing clear procedures for documenting and assessing any changes to the project scope. When the client requests additional features or significant modifications, the contract should specify that these changes will be evaluated for their potential impact on costs and timelines. Mutual agreement on each change, ideally documented through a change request form, helps keep scope manageable while allowing flexibility.

Another key risk is **timeline uncertainty**. Agile projects do not always have a rigid completion date due to the iterative nature of the methodology. To manage this, Agile contracts can include milestone-based checkpoints at the end of each sprint. These milestones provide opportunities for the client to review progress, reassess priorities, and decide whether additional sprints or modifications are necessary. Setting these checkpoints in the contract offers a structured way to evaluate timelines incrementally, reducing the risk of unexpected delays at the end of the project and providing transparency throughout the development process.

Budgetary control is also a critical consideration in Agile contracts, as iterative development can lead to extended timelines and increased costs if not carefully managed. To prevent budget overruns, Agile contracts can establish a budget cap or ceiling that cannot be exceeded without written authorization from the client. Additionally, tracking and reporting requirements can be incorporated, where the developer provides regular budget updates based on hours worked and resources used. If the project approaches a certain percentage of the budget cap (e.g., 80%), the developer should alert the client with an updated estimate for remaining work. This allows the client to decide whether to allocate additional funds, adjust project priorities, or conclude the project.

Dependency on client involvement is another risk factor in Agile projects. Agile development relies heavily on regular client feedback and engagement, especially during sprint reviews and backlog prioritization. If the client is unavailable or does not provide timely feedback, it can lead to delays or misalignment in project objectives. Agile contracts should address this risk by clearly defining the client's responsibilities, including expectations for attendance at sprint planning sessions, prompt feedback on deliverables, and timely decision-making. This clarity helps ensure that the client understands their role in the project's success and reduces the risk of delays attributable to client-side obstacles.

Finally, **quality assurance and acceptance criteria** in Agile projects are essential for managing risk. Unlike fixed-scope projects where acceptance is often linked to a final deliverable, Agile projects require ongoing acceptance of each sprint's output. The contract should specify that the client will review and formally accept or provide feedback on each sprint increment within a defined timeframe. This incremental acceptance process minimizes the risk of unexpected quality issues at the end of the project and allows for continuous improvement based on client input.

In sum, risk management in Agile contracts involves creating a framework that balances flexibility with control. By incorporating change management processes, budget and timeline checkpoints, clear client responsibilities, and incremental acceptance criteria, Agile contracts address the specific risks associated with iterative development while maintaining the adaptability that defines Agile methodology. This balanced approach allows both parties to navigate uncertainties effectively, fostering a successful project outcome.

9.3.8 Checklist: Ensuring Agile Contract Success

1. **Clear Scope of Work (SoW) Definition**
   - Define the initial project goals and objectives
   - Outline backlog items with a clear understanding that they may evolve
   - Set expectations for iterative sprint-based development
2. **Establish Sprint Structure and Milestone Payments**
   - Outline sprint durations and deliverables for each cycle
   - Link payments to sprint completions and deliverable acceptance to incentivize progress

   - Include provisions for incremental review and approval at each sprint's end
3. **Detailed Change Management Process**
   - Define procedures for submitting, reviewing, and approving changes
   - Specify impacts of scope changes on costs, timeline, and priorities
   - Require written approval for all significant modifications to backlog items or priorities
4. **Budget Cap and Financial Controls**
   - Set a maximum project budget (cap) with client approval for additional costs
   - Require periodic budget updates and forecasts from the developer
   - Include a notification threshold (e.g., 75–80% of budget cap) for reassessing funding
5. **Regular Communication and Reporting Requirements**
   - Schedule routine sprint planning and review sessions with both parties
   - Outline frequency and format for progress and budget reports
   - Set expectations for transparency regarding hours worked and resource allocation
6. **Defined Client Responsibilities and Involvement**
   - Clarify the client's role in backlog prioritization and sprint reviews
   - Specify requirements for timely feedback and decision-making
   - Address potential impacts of client delays on timelines and costs
7. **Acceptance Criteria for Each Sprint**
   - Establish clear criteria for sprint deliverable reviews and acceptance
   - Require client approval or feedback within a set period after each sprint
   - Outline the process for addressing issues or revisions identified during reviews
8. **Risk Management Provisions**
   - Identify key risks (e.g., scope creep, budget overruns, client availability) and mitigation measures
   - Include provisions to control scope, manage quality, and handle delays

- Address dispute resolution in cases of disagreement on project direction or deliverables

9. **Warranties and Quality Assurance**
    - Define any warranties regarding the functionality or quality of incremental deliverables
    - Include quality standards or industry best practices the developer must follow
    - Address the developer's responsibility to correct defects or rework deliverables
10. **Termination and Exit Strategy**
    - Define the conditions under which either party may terminate the contract
    - Outline payment obligations for completed sprints up to the termination date
    - Provide an exit plan that protects the client's rights to any work completed

9.3.9 Legal Risks in Agile Contracts

While Agile Contracts provide adaptability and ongoing collaboration, they introduce unique legal risks stemming from the methodology's iterative, evolving nature. These risks often arise from the tension between Agile's flexibility and the legal need for certainty, enforceability, and measurable performance.

Ambiguity in Scope and Deliverables

Agile's evolving backlog can make it difficult to define the final scope of work in legally enforceable terms. Without a fixed list of deliverables, disputes may arise over whether the developer has fulfilled contractual obligations.

Legal Risk: In litigation or arbitration, the absence of a clearly defined end product may make it challenging for the client to prove breach of contract, as the developer can argue that work was performed in accordance with the agreed Agile process.

Scope Creep Without Budget or Time Adjustments

Continuous reprioritization can lead to incremental increases in scope without formal change approvals.

Legal Risk: If the contract lacks a robust change management process, the client may face escalating costs or delays without recourse, or the developer may be pressured to absorb additional work without compensation.

Disputes Over Sprint Acceptance

Each sprint produces an increment for review, but without clear, objective acceptance criteria, disagreements can arise over whether the increment "meets requirements."

***Legal Risk*:** A lack of documented, signed-off acceptance (or rejection) for each sprint may weaken a client's ability to withhold payment or demand rework.

Over-Reliance on Client Involvement

Agile requires active client engagement, yet contracts often understate the legal consequences if the client fails to participate in sprint reviews or backlog prioritization.

***Legal Risk*:** Delays caused by the client's inaction may excuse the developer from meeting timelines, potentially undermining claims for late delivery.

Uncertain Final Delivery Date

Because Agile focuses on iterative delivery rather than a fixed completion date, the "end" of the project may be unclear.

***Legal Risk*:** Without a contractual longstop date, disputes may arise over prolonged development cycles, additional sprints, and unpaid final deliverables.

Intellectual Property (IP) Fragmentation

As Agile produces deliverables incrementally, IP rights may need to be transferred sprint-by-sprint.

***Legal Risk*:** If IP transfer clauses only apply at final acceptance, the client may not have clear ownership of completed increments if the project terminates early.

Budget Overruns Due to Open-Ended Iterations

Without caps or staged budget approvals, Agile projects can exceed the client's financial expectations.

***Legal Risk*:** In the absence of a budget ceiling or formal authorisation process, the client may still be liable for all hours billed, even if the project is abandoned before completion.

Quality Assurance Gaps Between Sprints

If defects are not addressed within the same sprint or lack warranty protection, issues may compound over multiple increments.

***Legal Risk*:** The developer may resist fixing defects discovered later, arguing they were accepted in an earlier sprint and thus outside warranty.

9.3.9.1 Practical Safeguards

- **Define measurable acceptance criteria** for each sprint and require written sign-off or rejection
- **Include a clear change management process** for backlog adjustments that affect budget or schedule
- **Set a final longstop date** for completion, even in a flexible scope framework
- **Allocate IP rights progressively** upon payment for each sprint to protect early deliverables
- **Establish a budget cap** with mandatory client approval for additional expenditure
- **Specify consequences for client non-participation** in sprint activities
- **Provide defect remediation obligations** that extend beyond the sprint in which the defect arose

9.4 Milestone-Based Contracts

9.4.1 Definition and Overview

A **Milestone-Based Contract** in software development is a structured agreement where the developer's compensation is directly linked to the achievement of defined project milestones. Rather than being compensated hourly or for overall project completion, the developer receives payment at various stages, contingent upon meeting specific objectives or deliverables outlined in the contract.

This approach allows the client to monitor progress, ensuring that each milestone is reached before additional funds are released. Milestone-Based Contracts provide a balance between flexibility and control, particularly beneficial for projects with well-defined stages but the need for adaptive adjustments as each stage is completed.

Milestone-Based Contracts are ideal when there is a clear path to completion, divided into distinct phases or functionalities that can be assessed independently. This contract structure mitigates risks for the client by ensuring that payments are only made upon completion of measurable deliverables, while also giving the developer an incentive to meet agreed standards. However, defining milestones precisely is essential to prevent disputes over whether they have been met, and both parties must agree on detailed criteria for each phase.

9.4.2 Structuring Contracts Around Milestones

In Milestone-Based Contracts, a **Scope of Work (SoW)** clause should provide a roadmap that breaks down the project into distinct phases or modules, each representing a milestone. The SoW outlines the expected deliverables, standards, and timelines associated with each milestone. Milestones should be designed with realistic deliverable timelines and clear specifications. For example, an initial milestone might include a project blueprint, system architecture, or proof of concept, with subsequent milestones covering coding phases, testing, and deployment.

Each milestone should include specific **Acceptance Criteria** that define the standards for completion. These criteria allow the client to verify that the milestone deliverables meet the agreed specifications. A failure to meet these criteria may give the client the right to withhold payment until the developer has corrected the deficiencies. This structure protects the client by providing regular assessments and only releasing payment once the agreed standards are met.

9.4.3 Payment Schedules and Milestones

A Milestone-Based Contract should include a detailed **Payment Schedule** outlining when and how payments will be made for each milestone. Payments are typically tied to the completion and acceptance of each milestone, ensuring that the client retains financial control and oversight throughout the project.

Sample contract clause:

> Payments under this Agreement shall be tied to the successful completion of designated milestones, as outlined in **Exhibit B: Milestone Payment Schedule**. Upon completion of each milestone, the Developer shall submit the milestone deliverables for review by the Client. The Client shall have [insert timeframe, e.g., 'five business days'] to assess the deliverables against the specified acceptance criteria. If the Client determines that the milestone requirements are met, the Developer shall be paid the corresponding amount outlined in the Payment Schedule. If the milestone deliverables do not meet the agreed acceptance criteria, the Client reserves the right to withhold payment until the Developer has rectified the issues. The Developer agrees to address all identified deficiencies within [insert timeframe, e.g., 'ten business days'], at no additional cost, after which the Client shall re-evaluate the deliverables. Failure to achieve milestone criteria within the stipulated period may result in penalties, as further detailed in this Agreement.

9.4.4 Ensuring Accountability Through Milestone Deliverables

As mentioned above, Milestone-Based Contracts enhance accountability by setting clear, measurable deliverables for each project phase. Each milestone should be accompanied by specific **Acceptance Criteria**, which serve as the benchmarks for determining whether the developer has met the required standards for that phase. These criteria should be detailed, objective, and agreed upon by both parties before the project begins. For instance, acceptance criteria might specify performance standards, functionality, user interface requirements, or integration capabilities. This clarity ensures that both the client and developer have a mutual understanding of what each milestone entails.

To further enforce accountability, contracts may include a **Correction Period** for any deficiencies identified in milestone deliverables. This allows the developer a specified period to rectify issues at no additional cost to the client, ensuring that quality standards are met without impacting the project timeline or budget. Additionally, some contracts may include **Penalty Clauses** for repeated failure to meet milestone criteria, which can incentivize the developer to maintain high standards and adhere to project timelines.

Sample clause for correction period and penalties

> Should any milestone deliverables fail to meet the agreed-upon acceptance criteria, the Developer shall have a Correction Period of [insert timeframe, e.g., 'ten business days'] to address and resolve any deficiencies identified by the Client. If the Developer fails to meet the milestone criteria after the Correction Period, the Client reserves the right to impose penalties, including but not limited to withholding further payments, reducing the overall project fee, or, in the case of persistent non-compliance, terminating the Agreement. Such penalties shall be calculated as [insert percentage or fixed amount] of the payment associated with the unmet milestone.

9.4.5 Checklist: Creating Milestone-Based Contracts

A well-structured Milestone-Based Contract includes several key elements to ensure clarity, accountability, and a successful outcome for both parties. This checklist provides a foundation for creating a robust contract:

1. **Defined Scope of Work and Project Roadmap**
    - Outline each project phase, including specific deliverables and objectives associated with each milestone
    - Clearly document the functionality, standards, and goals to be achieved in each milestone
2. **Detailed Acceptance Criteria for Each Milestone**
    - Specify measurable criteria for evaluating milestone completion
    - Define performance, functionality, or integration standards that must be met
3. **Payment Schedule Linked to Milestone Completion**
    - Set a payment structure based on successful milestone achievement
    - Include a timeframe for client review and approval of each milestone deliverable

4. **Correction Period and Penalty Clauses**
   - Establish a Correction Period for the developer to address any deficiencies at no extra cost
   - Detail penalties for persistent non-compliance, including potential payment reductions or contract termination
5. **Process for Client Feedback and Milestone Approval**
   - Outline a timeline and method for client feedback and milestone evaluation
   - Specify how feedback will be documented, addressed, and incorporated into future milestones
6. **Change Management Provisions**
   - Include a process for managing changes to milestone deliverables, acceptance criteria, or timelines
   - Require mutual agreement on scope adjustments to avoid unforeseen costs or delays
7. **Dispute Resolution Mechanism**
   - Define a method for resolving disputes related to milestone completion, acceptance criteria, or payment
   - Include options such as mediation, arbitration, or a specific dispute resolution clause to prevent project interruptions
8. **Termination Clause Linked to Milestone Failure**
   - Include terms for contract termination if the developer fails to meet multiple milestones
   - Specify the conditions under which the client can terminate the contract without penalty if performance issues persist

By ensuring that these components are incorporated into a Milestone-Based Contract, both the client and developer can navigate project phases with greater confidence and clarity. This contract structure provides a clear pathway for achieving project goals while managing risks, timelines, and costs, fostering a cooperative environment and reducing the potential for disputes.

9.4.6 Legal Risks in Milestone-Based Contracts

Milestone-Based Contracts can provide a strong framework for accountability, but they also carry specific legal risks tied to how milestones, acceptance criteria, and payment triggers are structured. Poorly defined or inconsistently applied milestone terms can create disputes, delay payments, and increase the likelihood of litigation or arbitration.

Ambiguity in Milestone Definitions

If milestones are described vaguely (e.g., "Module Completed" without technical or performance criteria), each party may interpret completion differently.

***Legal Risk*:** Ambiguity can make it difficult for the client to reject substandard deliverables or for the developer to claim payment, increasing the potential for disputes.

Disputes Over Acceptance Criteria

Acceptance criteria that are too subjective ("satisfactory performance") or not linked to measurable tests can lead to disagreement over whether a milestone is complete.

***Legal Risk*:** Without objective, documented acceptance metrics, a rejecting party may appear to be acting unreasonably, risking breach of contract claims.

Delayed or Withheld Payments

When payments are tied strictly to milestone completion, a single dispute over deliverables can freeze project cash flow.

***Legal Risk*:** Developers may face liquidity issues if a client withholds payment pending minor corrections; conversely, clients may be pressured to release payment prematurely to avoid delays.

Overlapping or Dependent Milestones

If one milestone's deliverables depend on prior incomplete work, disputes can arise about which milestone failed.

***Legal Risk*:** Developers may argue that delays are due to dependencies outside their control; clients may argue that missed dates constitute breach.

Excessive Correction Period Delays

Correction periods intended to allow for fixes can be used to stall payment or extend timelines without resolution.

***Legal Risk*:** Without limits, a party could repeatedly claim minor defects to delay payment indefinitely, effectively altering project economics.

IP Transfer Risks Between Milestones

If intellectual property transfer only occurs at final acceptance, the client may have no legal rights over partially completed work if the project terminates early.

***Legal Risk*:** This can hinder the client's ability to continue development with a new vendor, leading to sunk cost losses.

Milestone Creep

Uncontrolled expansion of what constitutes "completion" for a milestone can create unbudgeted work.

***Legal Risk*:** Developers may be forced to deliver additional features without payment if milestone definitions expand informally, while clients may incur unexpected costs.

Dispute Resolution Bottlenecks

If a disagreement over one milestone must be resolved before progressing to the next, the entire project can stall.

***Legal Risk*:** This can lead to breach claims, termination, or the need for costly interim dispute resolution.

Practical Safeguards

- **Use precise, measurable acceptance criteria** for each milestone, ideally linked to documented tests, demonstrations, or audits
- **Require written acceptance or rejection** within a fixed review period to avoid indefinite delays
- **Include partial payment mechanisms** for partially achieved milestones to protect both parties' cash flow
- **Transfer IP rights progressively** upon payment for each completed milestone
- **Set limits on correction periods** to prevent abuse
- **Define dependencies explicitly** in the contract and clarify how they affect delivery and payment obligations
- **Incorporate a fast-track dispute resolution process** (e.g., expert determination) to prevent project standstill

9.5 Hybrid Contracts

9.5.1 Definition and Overview

A **Hybrid Contract** in software development combines elements from multiple contract types to address the unique requirements and complexities of a project. Rather than relying on a single structure, such as a Fixed-Price, Time and Materials, or Milestone-Based model, a Hybrid Contract allows for a more tailored approach by integrating aspects of each type to maximize the benefits and mitigate the limitations of traditional contracts.

Hybrid Contracts are particularly valuable in complex or large-scale projects, where flexibility, defined milestones, and cost control are essential. This approach enables clients and developers to adapt to evolving requirements while maintaining a clear framework for accountability and performance.

9.5.2 Combining Different Contract Types

Hybrid Contracts can take various forms, each suited to different project needs. Here are some common combinations and their unique characteristics:

Fixed-Price with Time and Materials (T&M) Elements

This combination is often used when the core scope of the project is well-defined and stable, yet additional tasks or enhancements are expected. The **Fixed-Price** component covers the core deliverables, providing the client with budget certainty for the foundational work. Meanwhile, a **T&M** arrangement is used for additional features or iterative improvements that may emerge. This structure allows for adaptability in the project's scope without affecting the main budget or timeline, as any extra tasks can be billed separately based on actual time and materials.

Example: This contract was used for an enterprise resource planning (ERP) system project where a Fixed-Price core contract was covering essential modules, while additional integrations or customizations were handled under a T&M arrangement.

Milestone-Based with Time and Materials (T&M)

Here, the contract is structured around distinct milestones, each with defined deliverables and payment schedules. However, a T&M component is included to address unforeseen changes or adjustments within each milestone. This is particularly useful for projects with multiple phases where initial requirements may evolve as each milestone is completed. The **Milestone-Based** component provides structure and accountability, while the **T&M** aspect enables flexibility for each phase.

Example: This contract was used for a mobile application project, core functionality was delivered through milestone-based payments, while additional feature adjustments and refinements based on user testing were covered under T&M.

Agile with Fixed Milestones

This approach combines the iterative nature of Agile methodology with fixed milestone payments. The contract is structured so that the project follows Agile principles, such as sprints and backlog prioritization, while also defining specific milestones with clear deliverables. Each milestone payment is released upon achieving certain deliverables, while interim work is completed through Agile sprints. This combination is suitable for projects requiring regular client feedback and flexibility but where financial oversight and deliverable tracking are also necessary.

Example: This model was used in a web platform development project, where the basic framework was built in Agile sprints, with fixed milestone payments at key phases on initial launch, feature integration, and final testing.

Agile with Fixed-Price for Core Deliverables, and T&M for Additional Features

In this model, the core deliverables, such as primary system architecture or critical module, are provided at a Fixed Price, ensuring that the client has a defined budget for essential parts of the project. Agile sprints are employed to handle the development process within the core scope, allowing iterative development and client feedback.

Additionally, Time and Materials (T&M) components cover additional features or enhancements that arise as development progresses. This approach keeps the primary project budget predictable while allowing flexibility for new requirements.

Example: This contract was used in the development of a corporate intranet platform, where the client and developer agreed on a Fixed-Price contract for the core system, including user authentication, basic content management, and access controls. As development continues, additional features like real-time chat or data analytics might be added on a T&M basis.

Agile with Milestone Payments for Structured Progress Monitoring

This model combines Agile development with a Milestone-Based payment structure. Each Agile sprint delivers a functional increment of the software, but payments are released at pre-defined milestones (such as the completion of each major functionality). This combination offers iterative feedback and refinement, while the milestone payments ensure that the project is progressing according to the client's priorities and timeline.

Example: A large e-commerce platform used Agile development to build its features, like product description, shopping carts, and payment gateways. Milestone payments were released after completing each key feature, ensuring that the project advanced steadily and aligned with the client's goals.

Fixed-Price Core with Agile for User Experience (UX) and Interface Design

In projects where core functionality is well-defined, but user experience and design need iterative refinement, a Fixed-Price contract can cover back-end infrastructure, while Agile sprints focus on front-end UX and design. This combination provides cost certainty for the foundational technology while allowing flexibility for user-focused aspects that benefit from client feedback.

Example: In developing an educational platform, the Fixed-Price element might cover data management and security, while Agile sprints handle the design and improvement of the user interface based on regular student and instructor feedback.

Milestone-Based with Agile for Iterative Testing and Quality Assurance

This combination uses Milestone-Based payments to track project progress, with Agile sprints dedicated to ongoing testing and quality assurance (QA). As each milestone is completed, Agile sprints focus on testing and refining deliverables based on client feedback or end-user testing results. This model is particularly effective for large, complex projects requiring high standards of reliability and performance.

Example: A banking application development project might have milestone payments for core functionalities (e.g., account management, fund transfers), while Agile sprints are dedicated to ensuring compliance, testing security, and fine-tuning the user interface across devices.

Fixed-Scope Initial Phases with Agile for Customization and Scaling

In some large projects, a Fixed-Scope structure governs the initial project phases, such as developing a basic framework or core functionality, followed by Agile customization to scale or adapt the system based on organizational needs. The client gains a stable foundation, while Agile phases allow for customizations tailored to emerging business needs.

Example: An enterprise resource planning (ERP) system for a manufacturing company begun with a Fixed-Scope setup covering inventory, production, and payroll functionalities. As the company grew, Agile sprints enabled the customization and expansion of the ERP system to include new functionalities, such as advanced analytics or integrations with new equipment.

9.5.3 Flexibility vs. Complexity in Hybrid Contracts

While Hybrid Contracts offer flexibility by combining the strengths of various contract types, they also introduce a degree of complexity in contract management. This structure requires careful planning and coordination, as each component may have unique requirements, timelines, and billing structures.

The parties must clearly outline when each contract type applies, how adjustments to one component affect others, and what documentation and approvals are necessary for each phase. Additionally, managing hybrid contracts often involves more rigorous oversight, as the interplay of fixed costs and variable elements demands close monitoring to prevent scope creep or budget overruns.

Hybrid Contracts require well-defined **roles and responsibilities**, especially regarding client approval, milestone completion, and budget adjustments. Flexibility must be balanced with strict guidelines for project adjustments, ensuring that the client retains control over budget and scope without unnecessary delays or misalignment between project phases.

9.5.4 Managing Risk and Uncertainty in Hybrid Contracts

Risk management in Hybrid Contracts involves addressing the specific risks associated with each component type. For instance, the Fixed-Price portions may limit flexibility, creating risks if the project scope changes, while the T&M elements may expose the client to cost variability.

Effective **change management** processes are critical in Hybrid Contracts to evaluate and approve any changes in scope, budget, or timeline that arise from the flexibility built into the T&M or Agile components.

To mitigate risks, Hybrid Contracts should include a **budget cap** for T&M portions to control spending. Additionally, **milestone acceptance criteria** should be detailed to ensure that each phase meets agreed-upon standards. The contract should also clarify how disputes related to milestone acceptance, Agile deliverables, or unexpected costs will be resolved, providing a clear path for both parties to address issues as they arise.

Furthermore, **regular project reviews** and **client-developer communication** are essential in Hybrid Contracts. Steering committees or project review meetings provide ongoing oversight, allowing both parties to assess progress, adjust priorities, and manage any unforeseen challenges.

By establishing these checkpoints, the client can ensure that the project stays aligned with its original objectives and budget.

9.5.5 Checklist: Creating a Successful Hybrid Contract

1. **Clearly Defined Scope of Work and Project Components**
   - Specify which portions of the project are Fixed-Price, T&M, or Milestone-Based
   - Outline how each contract type applies to different phases or deliverables
2. **Comprehensive Acceptance Criteria for Each Milestone**
   - Detail the standards and metrics for milestone completion
   - Define client review timelines and criteria for payment release
3. **Budget Controls and Cap on T&M Elements**
   - Set a maximum budget or spending limit for T&M portions
   - Implement regular budget reviews and client approval for additional costs
4. **Structured Change Management Process**
   - Outline steps for submitting and approving changes to the project scope or priorities
   - Define the impact of changes on budget, timelines, and deliverables

5. **Payment Schedule and Milestone-Based Compensation**
   - Link payments to milestone completion or key deliverables, with clear conditions for payment release
   - Define the billing process for T&M components and set expectations for timesheet or expense reporting
6. **Defined Roles and Responsibilities**
   - Clarify the client's involvement in Agile sprints, backlog prioritization, and milestone approvals
   - Detail the developer's responsibilities in adhering to deliverables, quality standards, and change processes
7. **Regular Project Reviews and Communication Protocols**
   - Establish periodic check-ins or project review meetings to assess progress and address challenges
   - Define the format and frequency of reporting to maintain transparency
8. **Dispute Resolution Mechanism**
   - Include procedures for handling disagreements over milestone completion or budget adjustments
   - Specify whether mediation, arbitration, or other dispute resolution methods apply
9. **Termination and Exit Strategy**
   - Define conditions for terminating the contract, including requirements for notice and final payments
   - Outline a plan for handling incomplete deliverables or transferring work in progress if the contract ends prematurely

9.5.6 Legal Risks in Hybrid Contracts

Hybrid Contracts offer adaptability by combining multiple contractual models, but they also introduce layered legal risks due to the interplay of different pricing, delivery, and acceptance structures. These risks often arise from **inconsistencies, conflicts, or gaps** between the rules governing each contract type within the hybrid framework.

Conflicting Clauses Across Contract Types

When Fixed-Price, T&M, Milestone-Based, or Agile elements coexist, overlapping clauses can create contradictory obligations. For example, a Fixed-Price section may require all changes to be formally approved, while the Agile component allows backlog reprioritization without formal amendments.

Legal Risk: Ambiguity over which clause prevails in a given situation can lead to disputes over payment, deliverables, or scope management.

Scope Definition Gaps and "Grey Zones"

Hybrid Contracts may leave certain deliverables unassigned to a specific contract type (e.g., a feature not clearly covered under the Fixed-Price or T&M portion).

***Legal Risk*:** This creates opportunities for cost-shifting disputes, clients may argue it is part of the Fixed-Price core, while developers claim it falls under T&M billing.

Misaligned Acceptance Criteria

Milestone-Based components require precise acceptance tests, whereas Agile elements may rely on iterative reviews without formal acceptance.

***Legal Risk*:** A client may reject a milestone on the grounds that features are incomplete, while the developer argues they were not part of that milestone but rather a future sprint, resulting in payment delays and potential breach claims.

Budget Overruns on Variable Components

While Fixed-Price components cap costs, T&M or Agile segments can expand without strict controls.

***Legal Risk*:** Without clear budget caps or approval checkpoints, cost escalation in the flexible portion can erode the client's financial predictability and expose the developer to non-payment if the client refuses to approve overages.

Timeline Disruptions Due to Interdependency

Delays in one contract component (e.g., milestone acceptance) can stall dependent tasks in other components (e.g., Agile sprints or T&M work).

***Legal Risk*:** Parties may dispute who is responsible for the delay, with each side blaming the other's contractual phase, potentially triggering penalties or termination.

Change Management Conflicts

Different parts of the contract may have different change approval processes (formal amendments for Fixed-Price vs. backlog reprioritization for Agile).

***Legal Risk*:** Lack of a unified process can cause procedural disputes—changes may be implemented without formal approval in one component, leading to claims of unauthorized work in another.

Termination and Exit Rights Confusion

Termination clauses tied to failure in one component may not clearly address obligations for ongoing work in other components.

***Legal Risk*:** If a client terminates due to a Fixed-Price breach, unclear terms could lead to disputes over payment for partially completed T&M or Agile work.

Intellectual Property (IP) Transfer Timing Issues

If IP transfer is linked to milestone payments in one part and to sprint acceptance in another, ownership of certain deliverables may be unclear mid-project.

***Legal Risk*:** This can hinder the client's ability to continue development with another vendor or enforce IP rights against third parties.

Practical Safeguards

- **Harmonize clauses** across all contract components to avoid conflicting obligations
- **Allocate every deliverable** to a specific contract type in the SoW to prevent scope disputes
- **Adopt a unified acceptance process** that applies across milestones, sprints, and T&M work
- **Set budget caps and approval thresholds** for all variable-cost portions
- **Define dependency management rules** so delays in one component do not paralyze others
- **Create a single, integrated change management process** that covers all components consistently
- **Clarify termination effects** on each contract portion, including payments for partial work and IP transfer rights
- **Stage IP transfers progressively** upon payment for each component to avoid ownership gaps

Hybrid Contracts, while complex, offer a flexible, structured approach to software development. By integrating multiple contract models, both client and developer gain the benefits of adaptability and accountability, enabling the successful delivery of projects that may otherwise be challenging to manage under a single contract type.

9.6 Licensing and SaaS (Software as a Service) Contract

9.6.1 Definition and Overview

A **Licensing and Software as a Service (SaaS) Contract** is distinct from traditional software development agreements in that it governs the ongoing use, access, and support of a software product rather than a one-time development project.

Licensing contracts typically grant the client the rights to use specific software under predefined conditions, while SaaS contracts provide users with access to a software application hosted by the provider, usually in exchange for recurring subscription fees.

These contracts outline the terms of software access, intellectual property rights, service levels, and ongoing support, and they are particularly common in enterprise solutions and consumer applications where clients need reliable, scalable software solutions without ownership or direct hosting responsibilities.

Licensing and SaaS contracts differ from other contract types in that they focus on **use rights and access to software** rather than the creation of a custom product.

The **ownership of intellectual property (IP)** generally remains with the developer or provider, allowing them to license the software to multiple clients, typically under non-exclusive rights.

SaaS agreements may also include provisions for data security, uptime guarantees, and support, given that the client's ability to access the software depends on the provider's infrastructure and service performance.

9.6.2 Intellectual Property and Ownership

Intellectual property is a core element of Licensing and SaaS agreements. In contrast to Fixed-Price or Time and Materials (T&M) contracts, where the client may gain ownership of the developed software, **Licensing and SaaS contracts rarely transfer IP rights** to the client. Instead, the provider retains ownership, licensing the rights to use the software under specified conditions. This arrangement allows the provider to license the software to multiple clients, spreading development and maintenance costs.

Sample IP clause:

> The Client acknowledges that all intellectual property rights, including copyrights, patents, trade secrets, and other proprietary rights, in and to the software remain exclusively with the Provider. The Client is granted a non-exclusive, non-transferable license to use the software solely for its internal business purposes, subject to the terms and conditions outlined in this Agreement. No ownership rights are transferred to the Client, and the Client shall not reverse engineer, decompile, or otherwise attempt to derive the software's source code, except as permitted by law.

This clause clarifies that the client is a licensed user and prohibits them from engaging in activities that could compromise the provider's intellectual property, such as reverse engineering. This setup protects the provider's IP, a common priority in SaaS and Licensing agreements, where maintaining exclusive control over software is key to ongoing revenue.

9.6.3 Payment Structure

In Licensing and SaaS contracts, payment is typically structured as a recurring **subscription fee** rather than a one-time project fee. The subscription grants the client access to the software and may include provisions for updates, support, and maintenance. The fees may vary based on the number of users, features, data storage requirements, or usage volume.

Sample subscription clause:

> The Client agrees to pay the Provider a monthly subscription fee of [amount], due on the first day of each calendar month. This subscription entitles the Client to use the software in accordance with the licensing terms, including access to all updates and support as outlined in Exhibit B: Support and Maintenance. The Provider reserves the right to adjust the subscription fee upon [insert time, e.g., '60 days'] notice, provided any fee adjustment applies uniformly to all clients of the same service level.

This clause ensures the provider has the flexibility to adjust prices while maintaining transparency with the client. Subscription fees linked to service levels also allow for tiered offerings, where clients can choose different levels of access and support based on their needs.

9.6.4 Service Level Agreements (SLAs) and Performance Guarantees

Since SaaS contracts involve access to software hosted by the provider, **Service Level Agreements (SLAs)** play a critical role. SLAs specify the provider's obligations regarding **uptime**, **data security**, and **response time** for issues, and **backup protocols**.

This is crucial because clients rely on uninterrupted access to the software for their operations. SLAs typically include remedies for service failures, such as fee reductions, penalties, or additional support if service levels are not met.

Sample SLA clause:

> The Provider commits to maintaining an uptime of 99.9% per calendar month. In the event of an uptime rate falling below this threshold, the Client shall be entitled to a service credit as follows: [specify amount or percentage]. The Provider further agrees to implement commercially reasonable security measures to protect Client data and shall notify the Client promptly in the event of any data breach or significant disruption.

This clause protects the client by establishing a baseline for service reliability and gives the client a remedy if the provider fails to meet expectations. SLAs offer legal recourse and incentivize the provider to maintain service quality, making them a cornerstone of SaaS agreements.

9.6.5 Data Ownership and Confidentiality

In SaaS contracts, client data is stored on the provider's servers, making **data ownership and confidentiality** clauses essential. These clauses outline who owns the data, how it can be used, and the provider's obligations for data protection. Typically, the client retains ownership of their data, and the provider commits to safeguarding it according to industry standards.

Sample data ownership and confidentiality clause:

> The Client retains full ownership of all data submitted to and processed within the software. The Provider shall implement security protocols in compliance with [insert relevant standards, e.g., GDPR] to protect Client data. The Provider shall not access or use Client data for any purpose other than providing the contracted services, except as required by law. The Provider agrees to maintain the confidentiality of all Client data and will not disclose it to third parties without the Client's prior written consent.

This clause ensures that the client's data remains private and protected, which is particularly important in sectors with strict regulatory requirements, such as finance or healthcare.

9.6.6 Limitations on Liability and Warranty Disclaimers

Licensing and SaaS contracts often contain **limitations on liability and warranty disclaimers**, reflecting the shared nature of software use among multiple clients. Providers generally limit their liability for damages resulting from software downtime, data breaches, or other issues to avoid excessive financial risk.

Sample limitation of liability clause:

> The Provider's liability for any claim arising out of this Agreement, whether in contract, tort, or otherwise, shall not exceed the total fees paid by the Client in the six (6) months preceding the claim. The Provider makes no warranty, express or implied, as to the functionality, performance, or suitability of the software for any particular purpose. The software is provided 'as-is,' and the Provider disclaims all implied warranties, including but not limited to warranties of merchantability and fitness for a particular purpose.

This clause protects the provider from significant financial exposure while clarifying that the client assumes certain risks associated with using the software as-is. Liability caps and disclaimers are standard in SaaS and Licensing agreements, where the provider cannot tailor the software to each client's unique requirements.

9.6.7 Checklist: Creating a Successful Licensing or SaaS Contract

1. **Clearly Defined License Scope and Usage Rights**
    - Specify whether the license is exclusive or non-exclusive
    - Define acceptable usage, including any limitations on user numbers or geographic scope
2. **Intellectual Property Ownership and Protections**
    - Confirm that IP rights remain with the provider, with appropriate prohibitions on reverse engineering
    - Outline the client's obligations to protect the provider's IP
3. **Subscription Fees and Payment Terms**
    - Structure recurring fees based on usage, user numbers, or service level
    - Include provisions for fee adjustments and any notice requirements for price changes
4. **Service Level Agreement (SLA) Terms**
    - Detail uptime guarantees, support response times, and remedies for SLA breaches
    - Include penalties or credits to incentivize high service standards
5. **Data Ownership and Confidentiality Clauses**
    - Affirm the client's ownership of their data and define data protection standards
    - Specify confidentiality terms to protect client information and restrict third-party access
6. **Limitation of Liability and Warranty Disclaimers**
    - Cap the provider's liability to a reasonable amount relative to contract value
    - Disclaim any implied warranties and clarify that the software is provided 'as-is'
7. **Termination and Exit Strategy**
    - Define conditions for early termination, including data transfer or deletion requirements
    - Outline post-termination access or support if needed for data migration
8. **Compliance with Applicable Laws and Standards**
    - Address regulatory requirements such as GDPR, or industry-specific standards
    - Ensure the provider's data security practices align with the client's compliance obligations

9.6.8 Legal Risks in Licensing and SaaS Contracts

Licensing and SaaS agreements introduce a distinct set of legal risks compared to traditional software development contracts because they govern **ongoing rights of access and use**, not the creation or transfer of ownership of software. The ongoing, service-based nature of SaaS, combined with strict intellectual property protections in licensing, means that risks are heavily tied to **service continuity, data security, and enforceability of usage limitations**.

Intellectual Property (IP) Misuse or Infringement

Since the provider retains ownership of the software, unauthorized copying, modification, or distribution by the client (or conversely, the provider's inadvertent infringement on a third party's IP) can trigger disputes.

***Legal Risk*:** For the **provider**, inadequate monitoring of client compliance (e.g., overuse beyond licensed limits) can result in revenue loss and IP dilution.For the **client**, using the software beyond licensed parameters may constitute a material breach, leading to license revocation and damages claims.

Ambiguity in License Scope

Poorly defined license terms (e.g., unclear limits on number of users, permitted locations, or usage scenarios) can lead to scope creep and disagreements over whether certain uses are allowed.

***Legal Risk*:** For the **client**, ambiguous clauses can allow the provider to retroactively claim overuse and demand additional fees or terminate the agreement.For the **provider**, unclear scope definitions may weaken enforcement and make it difficult to prevent unauthorized usage.

Service Downtime and SLA Breaches

In SaaS models, the client's operational continuity depends entirely on the provider's infrastructure and uptime commitments. Failure to meet SLA guarantees can disrupt client operations and lead to financial loss.

***Legal Risk*:** Clients may be limited to service credits as their sole remedy, which might not cover the actual business losses caused by downtime. Providers face reputational harm, increased churn, and potential litigation if SLA metrics (e.g., 99.9% uptime) are consistently missed.

Data Breach and Privacy Compliance Failures

With client data stored and processed on provider-controlled servers, breaches or non-compliance with data protection laws (e.g., GDPR, CCPA, HIPAA) can result in significant liabilities.

***Legal Risk*:** **Provider liability** if inadequate security controls lead to unauthorized access or loss of client data. **Client liability** if the provider's non-compliance exposes the client to regulatory enforcement, especially in regulated industries such as finance or healthcare.

Unilateral Fee Increases or Service Modifications

Many SaaS agreements allow the provider to adjust fees or change service features with notice. If these rights are too broad, they can be abused.

***Legal Risk*:** For the **client**, sudden price hikes or removal of critical features may force unplanned budget changes or operational disruptions. For the **provider**, poorly structured modification rights may lead to breach of contract claims if changes materially alter agreed service levels.

Vendor Lock-In and Termination Risks

SaaS clients often become dependent on a provider's infrastructure and data formats, making migration costly or technically challenging.

***Legal Risk*:** Clients may face excessive costs or data access issues upon termination if the contract lacks clear data export and transition assistance clauses.Providers risk losing leverage if they fail to define termination rights that protect their business from abrupt or strategic client exits.

Limitation of Liability Gaps

Overly restrictive liability caps or broad warranty disclaimers may leave clients without adequate remedies for serious issues such as extended downtime, security breaches, or data loss.

***Legal Risk*:** For **clients**, limitations may mean absorbing substantial losses without recourse. For **providers**, if liability caps are deemed unenforceable (e.g., under consumer protection laws), exposure can exceed intended contractual limits.

Jurisdiction and Regulatory Exposure

Licensing and SaaS contracts often serve global client bases, raising issues over which jurisdiction's laws apply and whether the provider complies with foreign data protection and trade laws.

***Legal Risk*:** For **providers**, failure to address jurisdiction-specific regulations (e.g., data localization laws) may result in contract unenforceability or regulatory sanctions. For **clients**, unfavorable choice-of-law clauses can force dispute resolution in distant or unfamiliar jurisdictions, increasing costs and complexity.

Practical Safeguards

- Define license scope **with precision**, including user limits, geographic restrictions, and permitted uses
- Implement **IP monitoring mechanisms** and include clear audit rights for the provider

- Draft **robust SLA clauses** with measurable metrics, meaningful remedies, and escalation procedures
- Include **data protection obligations** aligned with applicable laws, with clear breach notification and liability provisions
- Limit fee adjustments to **predefined triggers** and require reasonable notice periods
- Establish **exit strategies** with guaranteed data export formats, timelines, and optional transition assistance
- Ensure **balanced liability caps** that do not exclude remedies for gross negligence or willful misconduct
- Address **jurisdiction and governing law** clearly, with provisions for compliance with applicable regulatory regimes

In summary, Licensing and SaaS contracts establish the terms of access, use, and support for software while safeguarding the provider's intellectual property and limiting liability. These contracts rely on clearly defined SLAs and data protection standards to protect client interests and establish expectations for service quality, making them particularly suited to projects where ongoing support and scalability are critical.

9.6.9 Selecting the Contract

Selecting the appropriate contract type for a software project is not merely an administrative step, it is a strategic decision that defines how risks, responsibilities, and incentives are allocated between the parties. Fixed-Price, Time and Materials, Agile, Milestone-Based, Hybrid, and Licensing/SaaS agreements each distribute financial, technical, and operational risks differently. The choice must be made with careful consideration of factors such as the clarity of requirements, the degree of technical uncertainty, third-party dependencies, and budget constraints.

Equally important is ensuring a **balanced allocation of risks** within the contractual terms. Disproportionate risk allocation, for example, placing the full burden of technical or financial risk on one party, can undermine collaboration, distort performance incentives, and significantly increase the likelihood of project failure. Such imbalance often leads to missed deadlines, substantial additional costs, and protracted, expensive disputes.

A well-structured contract should therefore:

a) Clearly define scope, deliverables, and acceptance criteria.
b) Include mechanisms for managing change, controlling costs, and resolving disputes.
c) Allocate risks in a manner proportionate to each party's ability to manage and influence them.

By approaching contract selection and drafting with this balanced, strategic mindset, parties can greatly improve the likelihood of delivering a successful software project on time, within budget, and without the shadow of long and costly litigation. This volume has mapped the legal risks inherent in each phase of the software development lifecycle, showing how operational decisions and governance failures translate into contractual exposure and disputes. Yet identifying risk is only the first step. Effective risk management requires these insights to be translated into contractual structure, allocation of responsibilities, and enforceable remedies. The companion book Effective Software Development Contracts builds upon this risk-based foundation by demonstrating how software development contracts can be drafted, negotiated, and structured to reflect operational reality and to control the risks identified throughout the SDLC. Read together, the two volumes form an integrated framework for understanding not only where legal risk arises in software projects, but how it can be contractually anticipated, managed, and reduced.

INDEX

acceptance: defining acceptance criteria 84; final acceptance checklist 151; final acceptance 199–207; typical preconditions for final acceptance 200–201; obligations during final acceptance 206; legal risks associated with final acceptance 207; *see also* delivery; milestones
acceptance criteria 74, 84, 127
acceptance testing 128, 130
Agile 22–25
Agile contracts 240–246
AI-generated code 98–101
ambiguity: in deliverables 67; in acceptance 208; over scope 217; in requirements 231; in agile contracts 251; in milestones definitions 256; *see also* scope; specifications
APIs: unauthorized use beyond licence scope 113; API keys and access/ control issues 113; evidence in litigation 114; call logs 132
architecture: software 76; software architecture document 81; documentation expectations 62, 92
audit 89, 100, **12**, 126, 137
authentication 29, 59, 87, 120–121, 153
authorization 101, 145–146, 231, 237, 243, 248

backlog 241–244, 247
budget: cap 238–239, 244–245, 250; certainty 231, 259; control 248; overruns as dispute trigger 43, 53, 228, 235, 247, 252, 261, 264
business needs 33, 46, 53, 61, 88, 243

change management 230–231, 244, 247, 251
change requests 43, 51, 71, 75, 172
client involvement 22–23, 130–145, 247, 249, 252
code 105, 196
confidentiality 108, 119, 122, 268

data protection 17, 60, 73, 83, 89, 108, 124, 206
defect severity levels 202
deliverables 236, 239, 240, 247, 251, 254
dependencies 15, 30, 36, 80, 108, 257
documentation 37, 44, 62, 70, 76, 92, 152, 166, 193, 205
due diligence 99, 130, 206

evidence: design phase 75; management platforms 104; code 110; lawfully build software 112; compliance with vendor licence 114; open-source components 118; leak of confiential information 121; quality 123; regulatory 125; testing 130; integration 132, 135; legal defensability 139; regresion testing 141; performance 143; UAT 148; final acceptance 151–154; documentation 164; Go-Live preparation 169; subcontracting 179; post Go-live 182; completion 201–203
escrow: source code escrow 95; escrow release 205
exclusions: scope exclusions 52; warranty 193

feedback 162, 181, 183, 185, 191, 249
final acceptance: start and obligations 147–149; legal risks and evidence 150; check list 151; final acceptance ccertificates (templates) 154–155

functional requirements 44, 49, 54

go-live 146–147, 159, 162–165, 169, 171–173
governance 33, 89, 104, 111, 207, 220
guarantees 221, 235, 267

handover: documentation 151; checklist 154, 198; risks 167; inadequate 180
hardening 165

incident 124, 167, 179, 201, 220, 221
indemnity 98, 103, 113, 209, 219
intellectual property: warranty clause 102; risks 109, 257; matrix 126; transfer 147, 205, 265; fragmentation 252; ownership 266; infringement 270
interoperability: interoperability requirements 131; disputes 132; checks 153
iterative: development model 23–24; comparison checklist 25; sprints 240, 247; progress 246; feedback 248; delivery 252

jurisdiction 64, 68, 74, 130, 232, 271

knowledge transfer 161, 167, 205

liability 99–101, 122–125, 128, 179, 190, 218, 268
licensing 94, 100, 108, 115, 119, 265
liquidated damages 123, 144, 148, 167, 232

milestones 29, 47–48, 52, 236, 253–255
monitoring 120, 133, 201, 210, 220, 226, 260

non-functional requirements 45, 54, 80, 134
notice 110, 112, 116, 146–149, 157, 238

ownership: deliverables 17, 51; ownership vs licensing 94; unclear 99; AI generated code 101, 109; integration points 133; IP 266, 270; data 268–269; *see also* intellectual property

penalties 52, 179, 222, 236, 255
personal data 63–65, 68, 119, 124
pricing 51, 119, 263
project management 27, 71, 88, 173, 199

quality assurance 16, 49, 52, 80, 87, 89, 131, 190, 249

remedies 28, 91, 128, 134, 194, 220, 222
reporting 55, 138, 147, 194, 201, 220, 222
risk allocation 7, 25, 209, 272

scope creep 36, 54, 64, 70, 231, 242, 248, 251
source code: ownership 95; open 97, 111; file 110; review 137; delivery 205–206
sprint review 242, 244–245, 249, 252
subcontractor 178–179, 198

termination: for cause 128, 138, 144, 148, 158, 189; of access 113; rights 159, 164, 169; of subcontract 179; of support 224; checklist 226, 245, 251, 256; effects 265

unauthorized use 73, 113
updates 29, 67, 93, 140, 205, 210, 213

validation: sesions 60; delayed 63; client 88, 145, 148; independent 89; end-to-end 134; human 140; operational 153; data migration 160, 164, 169, 195; integration 197; system performance 204
vendor lock-in 95, 271

warranties: clause 53, 100; compliance 96, 186, 209, 210; contractual 113; checklist 251, 269; IP 102; implied 233, 268; limited 236, 268